DICKENSIAN FAVOURITES

Created with the help of the characters
in the writings of Charles Dickens

ROCHESTER FROM STROOD

Compiled by
Edith Ingram

With paintings by F. W. Haslehust R.A.
and drawings by "Phiz"
George Cruikshank and John Leech

SALMON

English Country Fare

"Do you see this? said Miss Brass, slicing off about two square inches of cold mutton."
The Old Curiosity Shop

'ENGLISH COUNTRY FARE' SERIES
Published by J Salmon Limited,
100 London Road, Sevenoaks, Kent TN13 1BB

Designed by the Salmon Studio
Cover painting and all colour reproductions copyright © 1996 J Salmon Limited
Text copyright © 1996 Edith Ingram

ISBN 1 898435 48 0

All rights reserved. No part of this publication may be reproduced, stored in a retrieval system, or transmitted, in any form or by any means, electronic, mechanical, photocopying, recording or otherwise, nor may any of the illustrations be framed, mounted or converted in any manner for resale, without the prior permission of the copyright holder.

Neither this book nor any part or any of the illustrations, photographs or reproductions contained in it shall be sold or disposed of otherwise than as a complete book and any unauthorised sale of such part illustration photograph or reproduction shall be deemed to be a breach of the Publisher's Copyright.

Printed in England by J Salmon Limited, Tubs Hill Works, Sevenoaks, Kent

Front Cover: "Mr. Weller began to speak . . ." by George Fox
Back Cover : "God bless you, merry gentlemen!" by Charles T. Howard

Dickensian Favourites

Index

Abernethy Biscuits 26
Apple Pasties 6
Bread and Butter Pudding 25
Christmas Pudding 21
Cuxton Biscuits 29
Dundee Marmalade 31
Kentish Apple Cake 17
Meat and Vegetable Stew 19
Mince Pies 7
Mixed Sweet Pickle , ... 13
Mr. Barley's Breakfast 25
Mulligatawny Soup 20
Oxtail Soup with Rice and Barley 26
Pettitoes or Pigs' Trotters 30
Potted Game 9
Punch 11
Rich Fruit Cake 27
Rich Pound Cake 9
Sausages 17
Savoy Biscuits or Ladies' Fingers . . . . ,. 15
Sherry Cobbler . , ... 11
Smoking Bishop 15
Special Bread Pudding 19
Steak and Kidney Pudding 12
Toasted Cheese 30
Tripe and Onions 12
Twelfth Cake 29
Wassail 23
Whitebait 6
Yorkshire Tea Cakes 20

English Country Fare

Job Trotter encounters Sam in Mr Muggles Kitchen

We have said in walked Mr. Job Trotter, but the statement is not distinguished by our usual scrupulous adherence to fact. The door opened and Mr. Trotter appeared. He *would* have walked in, and was in the very act of doing so, indeed, when catching sight of Mr. Weller, he involuntarily shrank back a pace or two, and stood gazing on the unexpected scene before him, perfectly motionless with amazement and terror.

The Pickwick Papers

CHARLES DICKENS is one of the greatest novelists in the English language, and his descriptive writing is second to none.

There occur in almost all of his novels and writings, wonderfully written passages about food. How we enjoy reading about the Veneering households with their excellent dinners and the comfortable suppers and breakfasts in the home of Mr Wardle! On the other hand, he tells us of the resourcefulness of families such as the Micawbers, with the difficulty of making ends meet in times of great poverty; no one of his day understood the circumstances of England better. We are indebted to him for giving us such an accurate picture of domestic life in Victorian England.

With a little help from the characters in the novels and writings, I have tried to collate a selection of recipes which might have been used by them, together with a relevant quotation.

Only the quotation at the beginning of each recipe is by Charles Dickens, with the exception of Mr Barley's Breakfast, from "Great Expectations", where Dickens himself has given the ingredients.

I would like to thank Catherine Thompson for her invaluable help in testing out the recipes, and for her suggestion that the inclusion of some drinks would be welcome.

Last, but not least, our grateful thanks to Cedric Charles Dickens, great grandson of Charles Dickens, for allowing us to include the family recipes for 'Smoking Bishop' and 'Sherry Cobbler'.

Edith Ingram

"Now, Pa," said Bella, hugging him close, "take this lovely woman out to dinner."
"Where shall we go, my dear?"
"Greenwich!" said Bella valiantly. "And be sure you treat this lovely woman with everything of the best."
The little expedition down the river was delightful, and the little room overlooking the river into which they were shown for dinner was delightful. Everything was delightful. The park was delightful, the punch was delightful, the dishes of fish were delightful.
OUR MUTUAL FRIEND

Whitebait

1 lb. whitebait	½ level teaspoon cayenne
1 tablespoon plain flour	pepper
Lemon	Fat or oil for frying

Wash and dry the whitebait. Toss in a mixture of flour and cayenne pepper so that they are well coated. Place in small quantities in a hot frying basket and fry in hot fat or oil until the whitebait are golden brown. Drain on kitchen paper and serve on hot plates garnished with slices of lemon. Wafer-thin slices of brown bread and butter should be served with fried whitebait.

"So she makes", said Mr Barkis, after a long interval of reflection, "all the apple parsties, and does all the cooking, do she?"
I replied that such was the fact.
DAVID COPPERFIELD

Peggotty's Apple Pasties

2 cooking apples, large	A 'walnut' of butter
6 oz sugar	8 oz. puff pastry
3 cloves	White of egg

Peel the apples, cut into quarters and core. Cut into small pieces and put into a saucepan with the sugar, cloves and butter. Cook very slowly, with the lid on, so that the apple only just cooks and does not brown or burn. Then leave to get quite cold. Take out the cloves. Roll out the pastry to ⅛–¼-inch thick on a lightly floured surface and cut out rounds the size of a saucer. Put a tablespoon of the cooked apples on each round of pastry, dampen the edges and fold over in the form of a Cornish pasty. Crimp the edges with the finger and thumb. Brush over with white of egg, and sprinkle with sugar. Place on a greased baking sheet and bake in a hot oven, 400°F or Mark 6, until they are golden brown. Remove from the baking sheet and cool on a wire rack.

"Vere does the mince pies go, young opium eater?" said Mr. Weller to the fat boy, as he assisted in laying out such articles of consumption as had not been duly arranged on the previous night.
The fat boy pointed to the destination of the pies.
"Wery good", said Sam, "stick a bit o' Christmas in 'em. T'other dish opposite. There; now we look compact and comfortable, as the father said ven he cut his little boy's head off, to cure him o' squintin".
As Mr. Weller made the comparison, he fell back a step or two, to give full effect to it, and surveyed the preparations with the utmost satisfaction.

THE PICKWICK PAPERS

Dingley Dell Mince Pies

1 lb. cooking apples
A 'walnut' of butter
1 lb. mixed dried fruit
2 oz. blanched almonds, chopped
8 oz. soft brown sugar
2 oz. shredded suet
½ level teaspoon grated nutmeg
½ level teaspoon ground cinnamon
Sherry (optional)
The juice of one small orange and one lemon
Shortcrust pastry

Peel, core and chop the apples and cook in a little butter with the saucepan lid on, so as not to brown or burn them. Allow to cool. Add the other ingredients and mix well together with the juice of the orange and lemon. Add some sherry (if desired) if the mixture appears too dry, otherwise add a little more orange juice. Grease some patty tins and line with shortcrust pastry which should be rolled out thinly. Put a generous spoonful of the mincemeat into each pie. Cut suitable size lids, moisten the edges and put on firmly. Prick with a fork. Bake in a hot oven, 400°F or Mark 6, for approximately 10–15 minutes until golden brown.

COLLEGE YARD GATE, ROCHESTER
The Gatehouse home of Mr. Jasper in 'The Mystery of Edwin Drood.'

The concluding ceremony came off at twelve o'clock on the day of departure; when Miss Twinkleton, supported by Mrs Tisher, held a drawing-room in her own apartment (the globes already covered with brown holland), where glasses of white wine and plates of cut pound cake were discovered on the table.

THE MYSTERY OF EDWIN DROOD

Rich Pound Cake

8 oz. butter	4 oz. glacé cherries
8 oz. caster sugar	4 oz. ground almonds
8 oz. self raising flour	4 eggs
8 oz. currants and sultanas	A little milk if necessary
8 oz. seedless raisins	A few halved walnuts to decorate

Cream the butter and sugar together, add the eggs one at a time and mix well. Cut the cherries into quarters and mix with the other dried fruit and ground almonds. Fold in the flour and add a little milk if the mixture appears to be too dry. Lastly, fold in very carefully the fruit and ground almonds. Line a 9-inch round cake tin with a double thickness of greaseproof paper. Put the mixture in the tin and decorate the top with the walnut halves. Bake in a moderate oven, 325°F or Mark 3, for 2½ hours. Cool on a wire rack.

Letters from home had mysteriously inquired whether I should be much surprised and disappointed if among the treasures in the coming hamper I discovered potted game, and guava jelly from the West Indies. I had mentioned those hints in confidence to a few friends, and had promised to give away, as I now see reason to believe, a handsome covey of partridges potted, and about a hundredweight of guava jelly.

"Birthday Celebrations", THE UNCOMMERCIAL TRAVELLER

Potted Game

Cooked game of any kind	Salt and black pepper and
To each pound allow 2–3 oz. butter	cayenne pepper
Game gravy or stock	

Free the game from the skin and bone; chop finely. Pound in a mortar until smooth. Moisten gradually with strong game gravy or stock. Season well with salt, black pepper and cayenne pepper, and rub through a sieve. Press into small pots and cover with clarified butter.

English Country Fare

Ruth Pinch's Pudding

It was a perfect treat to Tom to see her with her brows knit, and her rosy lips pursed up, kneading away at the crust, rolling it out, cutting it up into strips, lining the basin with it, shaving it off fine round the rim; chopping up the steak into small pieces, raining down pepper and salt upon them, packing them into the basin, pouring in cold water for gravy;

Martin Chuzzlewit

He produced a very large tumbler, piled up to the brim with little blocks of clear transparent ice, through which one or two thin slices of lemon, and a golden liquid of delicious appearance, appealed from the still depths below, to the loving eye of the spectator.

..... Martin took the glass with an astonished look, applied his lips to the reed; and cast up his eyes once in ecstasy. He paused no more until the goblet was drained to the last drop.

"There, sir!" said Mark, taking it from him with a triumphant face; "if ever you should be dead beat again, when I ain't in the way, all you've got to do is, to ask the nearest man to go and fetch a cobbler." "This wonderful invention sir," said Mark, tenderly patting the empty glass, "is called a cobbler. Sherry cobbler when you name it long; cobbler when you name it short."

MARTIN CHUZZLEWIT

Sherry Cobbler

1 measure of fresh orange juice
A little sugar
1 measure medium sherry
1 tablespoon port
Ice
Slice of orange

Put the sugar into a tumbler with some crushed ice. Add the orange juice and sherry and stir. Place on top the slice of orange, with two straws through the middle. Pour the port over the orange and serve.

Here we have two Sherry Cobblers! One made with lemon, which is probably the American version, and one made with orange which comes from the Dickens family. The flavour of the orange blends so well with sherry that it is a really delightful drink.

Punch

2 lemons
Nutmeg
Cloves
4 tablespoons sugar
1 bottle sweet white wine
½ bottle brandy

Grate the outer rind of the lemons. Put the rind, with grated nutmeg and cloves to taste, with the sugar and the wine into a saucepan and bring gently to the boil, but do not let it continue to boil. Strain into a punch bowl, add the brandy and strained lemon juice. Decorate with thinly sliced orange rounds and serve.

"Why, what am I a'thinking of!" said Toby, suddenly recovering a position as near the perpendicular as it was possible for him to assume. "I shall forget my own name next. It's tripe!"

Tripe it was; and Meg, in high joy, protested he should say, in half a minute more, it was the best tripe ever stewed.

"And so," said Meg, busying herself exultingly with the basket, "I'll lay the cloth at once, father; for I have brought the tripe in a basin."

THE CHIMES

Tripe and Onions

1 lb. tripe	1 pint milk
1 lb. onions	¼ teaspoon salt
Black pepper to taste	

Cut the tripe in small strips about 2-inches long. Slice the onions. Put the tripe and onions into a stewpan with a tight fitting lid, or into a casserole, with the milk and seasoning. Cook slowly for 3 hours. Then thicken the gravy with a little cornflour and garnish with chopped parsley. Serve with potatoes that have been mashed with a generous amount of butter.

"I am a neat hand at cookery, and I'll tell you what I knocked up for my Christmas-eve dinner in the Library Cart. I knocked up a beefsteak pudding for one, with two kidneys, a dozen oysters, and a couple of mushrooms thrown in. It's a pudding to put a man in good humour with everything, except the two bottom buttons of his waistcoat".

Chapter III "Doctor Marigold", CHRISTMAS STORIES

Steak and Kidney Pudding

1 teacup shredded suet	1½ lb. bladebone steak
2 teacups self raising flour	¼ lb. ox kidney
Salt and black pepper	¼ lb. mushrooms
¼ pint cold water	1 dozen oysters (optional)

Mix the flour and suet with seasoning together in a bowl. Add water and mix together to form a soft dough. Cut the meat into small pieces, discarding any gristle or fat. Cut up the kidney after taking out the white core. Cut up the mushrooms. Toss all in seasoned flour. Grease a 1½–2 pint pudding basin. Roll out the suet pastry on a floured surface. Line the basin with two thirds of the paste, reserving one third for the lid. Put the meat, kidney, mushrooms and oysters, if desired, in layers in the basin, sprinkling a little flour with each layer. When the basin is full, add cold water nearly to the brim. Put on a pastry lid, moistening round the edge and pressing down well to make a good seal. Cover the top with greased greaseproof paper, and tie a cloth over it. Put the pudding in a saucepan of boiling water, not more than halfway up the basin. Simmer for three hours. Brown ale can be substituted for water in the pudding; it improves the taste of the gravy!

Every benevolent inhabitant of Mrs Crisparkle's dining-room closet had his name inscribed upon his stomach. The pickles, in a uniform of rich brown double breasted buttoned coat, and yellow or sombre drab continuations, announced their portly forms, in printed capitals, as Walnut, Gherkin, Onion, Cabbage, Cauliflower, Mixed, and other members of that noble family. The jams, as being of a less masculine temperament, and as wearing curl papers, announced themselves in feminine caligraphy like a soft whisper, to be Raspberry, Gooseberry, Apricot, Plum, Damson, Apple and Peach.
THE MYSTERY OF EDWIN DROOD

Mixed Sweet Pickle

2 lbs. cucumber	6 oz. sugar
1 lb. onions, peeled	2 teaspoons mustard seed
½ lb. cauliflower curd	3 cloves
2 oz. salt	1 teaspoon ground ginger
1 pint white vinegar	1 teaspoon turmeric

Dice the cucumber and onions into very small pieces and break up the cauliflower into small florets. Place all the vegetables into a pottery dish, sprinkle with the salt and leave for 3 hours. Drain and rinse thoroughly. Put the vegetables with the vinegar, sugar and the spices into a stainless steel or enamel saucepan (not aluminium) and heat gently, bringing to the boil. Remove from the heat, pack into hot jars and seal with vinegar-proof lids. Leave for 6–8 weeks to mature.

English Country Fare

Scrooge and Bob Cratchit

"A Merry Christmas, Bob!" said Scrooge, with an earnestness that could not be mistaken, as he clapped him on the back. "A merrier Christmas, Bob my good fellow, than I have given you for many a year! I'll raise your salary, and endeavour to assist your struggling family . . ."
A Christmas Carol

". . . we will discuss your affairs this very afternoon, over a Christmas bowl of smoking bishop, Bob!"

Scrooge; A CHRISTMAS CAROL

Smoking Bishop

6 Seville oranges   4 oz. sugar   Cloves
1 quart strong cheap red wine   1 bottle ruby port

Bake the oranges in a moderate oven for approximately 20 minutes until golden brown, and then place in a warmed glass or pottery bowl with 6 cloves pricked into each fruit. Add the sugar and pour in the wine, but not the port. Cover and leave in a warm place for a day. Then, squeeze the oranges into the wine and pour through a sieve. To keep for future use, bottle in sterilised bottles and seal at this stage, omitting the port. To serve, add the port to the liquid and heat in a pan, but do not boil. Serve in warmed goblets and drink hot. Or, pour into bottles and stand in a pan of simmering water; this keeps it hot and makes pouring easier. If Seville oranges are out of season, use 5 sweet oranges and 1 yellow grapefruit instead.

Whenever the Reverend Septimus fell a-musing, his good mother took it to be an infallible sign that he "wanted support," the blooming old lady made all haste to the dining-room closet, to produce from it the support embodied in a glass of Constantia and a home-made biscuit . . . and various slender 'ladies' fingers, to be dipped into sweet wine and kissed.

THE MYSTERY OF EDWIN DROOD

Savoy Biscuits or Ladies' Fingers

2 eggs   10 oz. plain flour
6 oz. caster sugar   ½–1 teaspoon lemon essence

Break the eggs into a basin over a pan of hot water, add the sugar and essence and beat well for ¼ hour until the mixture thickens and turns pale. Gradually sift in the flour, folding and cutting lightly into the mixture. Put the mixture into an icing bag and pipe the biscuits on to a greased baking sheet. Bake in a hot oven, 425°F or Mark 7, for a little less than 10 minutes. Watch very carefully as a few seconds over the proper time will scorch and spoil the biscuits. Cool on a wire rack.

English Country Fare

THE LEATHER BOTTLE, COBHAM
The inn to which Mr. Tupman retired, in disgust with life in 'The Pickwick Papers.'

"Splendid – capital. Kent, sir – everybody knows Kent – apples, cherries, hops, and women."
Mr Jingle; THE PICKWICK PAPERS

Kentish Apple Cake

¾ lb. apples
4 oz. mixed dried fruit
4 oz. butter
4 oz. sugar

8 oz. self raising flour
2 eggs, beaten
1 level teaspoon mixed spice
Sugar for sprinkling

Peel, core and cut up the apples into small pieces. Put into a saucepan with 1 oz. butter, 1 oz. sugar and the dried fruit. Cook very gently for about 5 minutes until the apple is soft. Leave to cool. Cream the remaining butter and sugar together, add the beaten eggs, fold in the flour and spice, and then the apple and fruit mixture. Line a 7-inch round cake tin with greaseproof paper and put in the cake mixture. Sprinkle with sugar and bake in a moderate oven, 325°F or Mark 3, for 1¼ hours. Or, the mixture can be baked in a small meat tin, and the cake cut into squares when cold.

With exemplary swiftness Bob Glibbery departed, and returned. Lizzie, following him, arrived as one of the two female domestics of the Fellowship-Porters arranged on the snug little table by the bar fire, Miss Potterson's supper of hot sausages and mashed potatoes.
OUR MUTUAL FRIEND

Sausages

8 oz. lean minced pork
4 oz. shredded suet
2 oz. white breadcrumbs
1 teaspoon mixed herbs

Half a nutmeg, grated
Salt and black pepper
2 eggs, beaten
Fat or oil for frying

Mix the pork and suet in a bowl, add the breadcrumbs, nutmeg and herbs. Season and mix in the eggs. Mix well. Form the mixture into sausages with well floured hands. Melt the fat or oil in a frying pan and fry the sausages for about 15 minutes, turning occasionally until browned all over. Drain on kitchen paper and serve hot, with mashed potatoes. To drink: Purl (ale warmed and spiced); one of the delectable drinks served at the Six Jolly Fellowship-Porters.

English Country Fare

The Friendly Waiter and I.

"Why you see," said the waiter, still looking at the light through the tumbler, with one of his eyes shut up, "our people don't like things being ordered and left. It offends 'em. But I'll drink it, if you like. I'm used to it, and use is everything. I don't think it'll hurt me, if I throw my head back, and take it off quick. Shall I?"

David Copperfield

I remember two pudding-shops, between which I was divided, according to my finances. One was in a court close to St. Martin's Church – at the back of the church, – which is now removed altogether. The pudding at that shop was made of currants, and was rather a special pudding, but was dear, two pennyworth not being larger than a pennyworth of more ordinary pudding.

DAVID COPPERFIELD

Special Bread Pudding

8 oz. stale bread
½ pint milk
4 oz. butter, melted
4 oz. currants or sultanas
3 oz. sugar
1 egg
½ teaspoon ground mixed spice

Soak the bread in the milk for at least an hour, then squeeze out the milk and put the bread in a bowl with the dried fruit, sugar and spice. Then add the butter, egg, and a little more milk if necessary. Mix well. Put the mixture into a greased 2–2½ pint baking dish and bake in a pre-heated oven, 350°F or Mark 4, for one hour.

Underneath the balcony, when we return, the inferior servants of the inn are supping in the open air, at a great table; the dish, a stew of meat and vegetables, smoking hot, and served in the iron caldron it was boiled in.

PICTURES FROM ITALY

Meat and Vegetable Stew

2 lbs. braising steak
1 lb. carrots
1 lb. onions
3 sticks celery
6 oz. button mushrooms
1 lb. tomatoes
½ teaspoonful salt
¼ teaspoonful black pepper
1½ pints good meat stock
1 bay leaf
1 tablespoon plain flour

Trim all fat from the meat and cut into cubes. Coat well with the flour, salt and pepper. Fry the meat in oil until browned. Set aside. Slice the vegetables, cutting the carrots and celery into small pieces. Put the meat and vegetables in layers in a large ovenproof casserole. Add the bayleaf and the stock and cook in the oven, 375°F or Mark 5, until the contents begin to boil, then turn down the heat to 300°F or Mark 2 for 2½ hours.

It was a substantial meal; for, over and above the ordinary tea equipage, the board creaked beneath the weight of a jolly round of beef, a ham of the first magnitude, and sundry towers of buttered Yorkshire cake, piled slice upon slice in most alluring order.

BARNABY RUDGE

Yorkshire Tea Cakes

¾ pint milk
1 egg
¾ oz. yeast
1 lb. strong white flour
1 level teaspoon salt
3 oz. butter
3 oz. sultanas
2 oz. sugar
Beaten egg for glazing

Warm the milk and beat in the egg. Cream the yeast with a little of the sugar, and add to the liquid. Rub the butter into the flour and salt and add the sugar and sultanas. Stir in the milk liquid to form a stiff and pliable dough. Knead well on a lightly floured surface and put into a bowl. Cover and put in a warm place until the dough has doubled in size; this takes approximately one hour. Return the dough to a floured board, knead, roll out half an inch thick and cut into 4-inch diameter rounds. Put the cakes on a greased baking tray, cover and leave to rise until puffy. Brush over with beaten egg and bake in a hot oven, 400°F or Mark 6, for 15 minutes.

Having again ordered his dinner, he went out, and was out for the best part of two hours. Inquiring on his return whether any of the answers had arrived, and receiving an unqualified negative, his instant call was for Mulligatawny, the Cayenne Pepper, and Orange Brandy.

Chapter IV, CHRISTMAS STORIES

Mulligatawny Soup

1½ lbs. stewing lamb
3 pints water
1½ oz. dripping
½ teaspoon salt
¼ teaspoon cayenne pepper
2 carrots
2 onions
½ lb. tomatoes
3 dessertspoons plain flour
3 dessertspoons curry powder
A glass of Madeira wine

Wash and slice the carrots. Peel and cut up the onions. Melt the dripping in a saucepan and fry the carrots and onions until lightly browned. Stir in the flour and curry powder and fry for a few minutes. Cut the lamb into small pieces, cut up the tomatoes, and add both to the vegetables. Add the water with seasoning to taste. Bring slowly to the boil. Remove the scum and simmer for about two and a half hours. Take out the meat and rub the soup through a sieve. Allow to get quite cold and then remove the fat from the top of the soup. Reheat the soup and adjust the seasoning. Before serving add the Madeira wine.

It was Christmas Eve, and I had to stir the pudding for next day, with a copper stick, from seven to eight by the Dutch clock.

Pip; GREAT EXPECTATIONS

Christmas Pudding

8 oz. raisins
10 oz. currants
10 oz. sultanas
4 oz. mixed peel
16 oz. soft brown sugar
2 oz. glacé cherries
8 oz. breadcrumbs
8 oz. plain flour
5 oz. shredded suet

5 oz. butter
5 large eggs, beaten
1 apple, grated
2 oz. ground almonds
1 orange
2 tablespoons brandy
½ teaspoon mixed spice
½ teaspoon ground nutmeg
½ teaspoon almond essence

½ teaspoon vanilla essence

Chop the raisins, quarter the glacé cherries and mix all the dried fruit together; add the grated apple, breadcrumbs, flour, spices, sugar, ground almonds and suet. Melt the butter and stir into the dry ingredients; grate the peel of the orange and add with the orange juice and the brandy. Add the beaten eggs and the almond and vanilla essence. Mix all very thoroughly. Put into greased basins. Cover each basin with greaseproof paper and kitchen foil. Stand in a saucepan of boiling water half way up the basin, and simmer for 7–8 hours. Remember to add more *boiling* water to the saucepan when necessary. When cooked, renew the greaseproof paper and foil. Steam again for 1½–2 hours before serving. Serve with brandy sauce or brandy butter.

English Country Fare

Mr Fezziwig's Ball

Away they all went, twenty couple at once; hands half round and back again the other way; down the middle and up again; round and round in various stages of affectionate grouping; old top couple always turning up in the wrong place; new top couple starting off again, as soon as they got there; all top couples at last, and not a bottom one to help them! *A Christmas Carol*

Dickensian Favourites

It was high time to make the Wassail now, therefore I had up the materials, and made a glorious jorum. Not in a bowl; for a bowl anywhere but on a shelf is a low superstition, fraught with cooling and slopping, but in a brown earthenware pitcher, tenderly suffocated, when full, with a coarse cloth . . . Having deposited my brown beauty in a red nook on the hearth, inside the fender, where she soon began to sing like an ethereal cricket, diffusing at the same time odours as of ripe vineyards, spice forests, and orange groves . . . This was the time for bringing the poker to bear on the billet of wood. I tapped it three times, like an enchanted talisman, and a brilliant host of merry-makers burst out of it, and sported off by the chimney – rushing up the middle in a fiery country dance, and never coming down again. Meanwhile by their sparkling light, which threw our lamp into the shade, I filled the glasses.

In the Old City of Rochester, CHRISTMAS STORIES

Wassail – apple

4 small eating apples with
2 cloves stuck in each
8 oz. soft brown sugar
1 pint medium dry sherry
1 cinnamon stick
4 pints brown ale
Thinly pared rind of 2 oranges

Put the apples in an ovenproof dish and pour the sugar over them. Pour in the sherry, add the cinnamon stick and bake in the oven, 350°F or Mark 4, for 20 minutes, or until the apples are just beginning to soften and brown. Do not overcook. Remove the contents from the dish into a large saucepan, and pour in the brown ale with the orange rinds. Heat the ale until it just begins to simmer; it is then ready to serve in heatproof glasses.

Wassail – orange

2 oranges
4 oz. soft brown sugar
1 pint medium sherry
2 pints brown ale
1 cinnamon stick
12 cloves
Thinly pared rind of 1 lemon

Put all the ingredients into a saucepan (except the oranges). Bring gently to the boil, but do not let it continue to boil. Leave to infuse for 10 minutes, then strain into a hot jug. Pour into glasses with a slice of orange on top.

RESTORATION HOUSE, ROCHESTER
The Satis House of Miss Havisham in 'Great Expectations'

"Look here", said Herbert, showing me the basket, with a compassionate and tender smile after we had talked a little: "Here's poor Clara's supper, served out every night. Here's her allowance of bread, and here's her slice of cheese, and here's her rum – which I drink. This is Mr Barley's breakfast for tomorrow, served out to be cooked. Two mutton chops, three potatoes, some split peas, a little flour, two ounces of butter, a pinch of salt, and all this black pepper. It's stewed up together, and taken hot."

GREAT EXPECTATIONS

Mr Barley's Breakfast

Ingredients as detailed in the quotation above.

Trim the fat off the chops and fry in a pan with the butter until browned on both sides. Add the flour and stir until thickened. Add the split peas, which should have been soaked overnight, the potatoes (sliced), and the salt and pepper. Add stock or water and cook slowly until the meat and vegetables are tender. Alternatively, the above ingredients can be cooked in a small casserole in the oven at 300°F or Mark 2 for two hours.

"A biled fowl, and baked bread-and-butter pudding, brought Mrs Walmers up a little; but Boots could have wished, he must privately own to me, to have seen her more sensible of the voice of love, and less abandoning of herself to currants."

The Holly Tree, CHRISTMAS STORIES

Bread and Butter Pudding

Thin slices of bread-and-butter   ½ pint milk
2 eggs   ½ a wine glass of brandy
1 oz. sugar   2 oz. currants
Grated nutmeg and sugar for sprinkling

Remove the crusts from the buttered bread and arrange around the sides and bottom of an ovenproof dish. Sprinkle the fruit over and cover with the remainder of the bread. Beat the eggs and sugar together, add the milk and brandy and pour over the bread and butter. Sprinkle a little sugar and grated nutmeg on the top, and bake in a moderate oven, 325°F or Mark 3, for about 30 minutes.

If I seldom saw better waiting, so I certainly never ate better meat, potatoes, or pudding. And the soup was an honest and stout soup, with rice and barley in it, and "little matters for the teeth to touch" as had been observed to me by my friend below stairs.

The Boiled Beef of New England XXV, THE UNCOMMERCIAL TRAVELLER

Oxtail Soup with Rice and Barley

1 lb. oxtail	2 pints beef stock
2 onions	8 peppercorns
2 strips of celery	2 cloves
2 oz. butter	1 medium carrot, grated
2 oz. lean ham or bacon, cut into cubes	1 tablespoon rice
	2 tablespoons barley
1 bay leaf	A small glass of sherry
1 bouquet garni	1 tablespoon cornflour

Roll the oxtail pieces in seasoned flour and fry in a pan, with the butter. Cut the onions and celery into small pieces and add to the pan with the ham or bacon, and fry all together until nicely browned. Add the stock and herbs, peppercorns and cloves; bring to the boil and simmer very gently for 4 hours. Strain and leave to get quite cold, preferably overnight. When cold, take off the fat. Cut up the lean meat of the oxtail into very small pieces and reserve. Put the strained soup into a saucepan and add one medium carrot, grated, the rice and the barley and simmer for 1 hour until the barley is well cooked. Mix the cornflour with the sherry, add to the soup and bring to the boil. Add the oxtail meat last of all, season to taste and continue to cook, to re-heat the oxtail. Serve hot.

Abernethy Biscuits

2 oz. sugar	8 oz. self-raising flour
3 tablespoons milk	3 oz. butter
2 oz. Lard	

Put the sugar and milk into a saucepan and stir over a low heat until dissolved. Allow to cool. Sift the flour into a bowl, rub in the fats and bind to a dough with the cooled milk liquid. Roll out the dough to ¼-inch thick on a lightly floured surface. Cut into rounds according to preference and place, a little apart, on a greased baking sheet. Prick each biscuit with a fork. Bake in a moderately hot oven, 375°F or Mark 5, for 15 minutes or until the biscuits are a pale golden brown. Cool on a wire rack.

After a little while, he opened his outer wrapper, which appeared to me large enough to wrap up the whole coach, and put his arm down into a deep pocket in the side.
"Now, look here!" he said. "In this paper," which was nicely folded, "is a piece of the best plum-cake that can be got for money – sugar on the outside an inch thick, like fat on mutton chops."

BLEAK HOUSE

Rich Fruit Cake

4 oz. glacé cherries, quartered	4 medium eggs, beaten
9 oz. plain flour	1 lb. 10 oz. mixed dried fruit
8 oz. butter	2 oz. chopped nuts (optional)
8 oz. dark brown sugar	Grated rind and juice of 1 orange

Cream the butter and sugar together in a large bowl until light and fluffy. Gradually add the beaten eggs. Add a little of the flour and fruit if the mixture begins to curdle. Then mix in the rest of the flour and fruit with the nuts, if desired, and the rind and juice of the orange. Line an 8-inch round cake tin with greaseproof paper and put in the mixture, making a slight well in the centre. Heat the oven to 300°F or Mark 2. Place the tin on a baking sheet and put into the oven, reducing the temperature to 275°F or Mark 1. Cook for approximately 4 hours, but start testing the cake about 30 minutes before the end of cooking time by inserting skewer; when the cake is ready it will come out clean. When cold remove from the tin. This cake improves with keeping. To increase keeping time and to improve the flavour, pierce the top of the cake with a skewer and spoon over a little brandy, sherry or rum. If it is intended to ice the cake, brush the surface all over with warmed apricot jam before applying the almond paste. Leave the paste to dry for two or three days before finishing with Royal Icing as desired.

English Country Fare

Mr. Bumble and Mrs. Corney taking tea

Mrs Corney rose to get another cup and saucer from the closet. As she sat down, her eyes once again encountered those of the gallant beadle; she coloured, and applied herself to the task of making his tea. Again Mr. Bumble coughed, – louder this time than he had coughed yet.

Oliver Twist

Dickensian Favourites

Christmas Eve in Cloisterham. Seasonable tokens are about. Red berries shine here and there in the lattices of Minor Canon Corner. Mr and Mrs Tope are daintily sticking sprigs of holly into the carvings and sconces of the Cathedral stalls, as if they were sticking them into the coat buttonholes of the Dean and Chapter. Lavish profusion is in the shops: particularly in the articles of currants, raisins, spices, candied peel, and moist sugar. An unusual air of gallantry and dissipation is abroad; evinced in an immense bunch of mistletoe hanging in the greengrocer's shop doorway, and a poor little Twelfth Cake, culminating in the figure of a harlequin – to be raffled for at the pastry-cook's.

THE MYSTERY OF EDWIN DROOD

Twelfth Cake

8 oz. butter	4 oz. mixed peel
8 oz. caster sugar	1½ lbs. sultanas
4 eggs, beaten	2 oz. blanched almonds
8 oz. plain flour	2 small glasses brandy

White of egg for glazing

Put the peel and sultanas in the brandy and leave to soak overnight. Next day, have the butter at room temperature and beat well with the sugar. Add the beaten eggs gradually. Fold in the flour gently, then add the fruit and mixed peel. Line an 8-inch round cake tin with a double thickness of greaseproof paper. Put the mixture into the tin and smooth over; decorate round the edges with the blanched almonds. Brush over the almonds with egg white before putting into the oven. Cook at 325°F or Mark 3 until a skewer inserted into the centre of the cake comes out clean. Cool on a wire rack

Cuxton Biscuits

6 oz. plain flour	2 oz. butter
2 oz. caster sugar	1 egg

A few drops of vanilla essence

Cream the butter and sugar together in a bowl. Add the egg and vanilla essence. Beat well. Work in the flour to form a stiff dough. Knead lightly on a floured surface, roll out to ¼-inch thick and cut into fancy shapes, according to preference or the availability of cutters. Put on to a greased baking sheet and bake in a moderate oven, 375°F or Mark 5, for 20–25 minutes. Cool on a wire rack.

The two caps, reflected on the window blind, were the respective head-dresses of a couple of Mrs Bardell's most particular acquaintance, who had just stepped in, to have a quiet cup of tea, and a little warm supper of a couple of sets of pettitoes and some toasted cheese. The cheese was simmering and browning away, most delightfully, in a little Dutch oven before the fire: the pettitoes were getting on deliciously in a little tin saucepan on the hob.

THE PICKWICK PAPERS

Pettitoes or Pigs' Trotters

Pettitoes are the little feet of suckling pigs, and are unlikely to be obtainable these days. The following recipe may be used instead, using one pair of pig's trotters. When cooked they may be eaten hot or cold. Ask the butcher to chop each trotter in half.

Leave the trotters to soak in brine overnight. Next day, wash them thoroughly in cold water. Put in a saucepan with just enough water to cover them. Add 1 bayleaf, 8 black peppercorns, 1 sage leaf and a sprig of thyme. Simmer gently for 4 hours. Remove the trotters and leave to cool. The liquid can be used for stock. Eat hot with parsley sauce.

Alternatively, when the trotters are cool, carefully bone them, coat with beaten egg and cover with fine breadcrumbs. Put into a baking dish with a little butter or margarine, sprinkle with grated cheese and cook in a moderate oven until golden brown.

Toasted Cheese

4 slices of bread	A shake of cayenne pepper
1 oz. butter, softened	¼ teaspoon Worcestershire
1 level teaspoon English mustard, made up	sauce
	6 oz. Cheddar cheese, grated
¼ level teaspoon salt	2 tablespoons milk or beer

Cream the butter well in a bowl and then stir in the mustard, salt, Cayenne pepper, Worcestershire sauce, grated cheese and the milk or beer according to preference. Toast the slices of bread on one side only. Spread the cheese mixture on the un-toasted side of the bread and brown under a hot grill until soft and bubbly. Serve very hot.

Dickensian Favourites

Turning into the town again, I came among the shops, and they were emphatically out of the season. The chemist had no boxes of ginger-beer powders, no beautifying sea-side soaps and washes, no attractive scents; nothing but his goggle-eyed red bottles, looking as if the winds of winter and the drift of the salt sea had inflamed them. The grocers' hot pickles, Harvey's Sauce, Doctor Kitchener's Zest, Anchovy Paste, Dundee Marmalade, and the whole stock of luxurious helps to appetite, were hybernating somewhere underground.

Miscellaneous Papers, OUT OF SEASON

Dundee Marmalade

2 lbs Seville oranges   Water
Preserving sugar

Wash the oranges in cold water, cut in half and squeeze out the juice. Carefully remove the pips and put into a separate bowl. Slice the oranges, fine or coarse as desired, and put into the preserving pan with 6 pints of cold water. To the pips add 1 pint of boiling water. Leave all to stand for 24 hours. Next day, strain the liquid and the jelly from the pips and add to the preserving pan with the pulp. Cook gently for 1½–2 hours until the pulp is tender. Remove from the heat and allow to stand for a further 24 hours. Next day, to each measured 1 pint of pulp add 1 lb. of preserving sugar. Heat gently until all the sugar is dissolved, then raise the heat to a rolling boil and cook until setting point is reached. This may be tested by dropping a very small amount on to a cold saucer, where it should form a stiff jelly as it cools. When the marmalade reaches this stage, remove from the heat, let it stand for a few minutes, stir to distribute the peel and pour into clean, hot jars; cover and seal.

CONVERSIONS

The weights, measurements and oven temperatures used in the preceding recipes can be easily converted to their metric or American equivalents.

Weights	Avoirdupois	Metric
	1 oz.	just under 30 grams
	4 oz. (¼ lb.)	app. 115 grams
	8 oz. (½ lb.)	app. 230 grams
	1 lb.	454 grams

Liquid	Imperial	Metric
	1 tablespoon (liquid only)	20 millilitres
	1 fl. oz.	app. 30 millilitres
	¼ pint (1 gill)	app. 145 millilitres
	½ pint	app. 285 millilitres
	1 pint	app. 570 millilitres
	1 quart.	app. 1.140 litres

Temperatures		Fahrenheit	Gas Mark	Celsius
	Slow	300	2	140
		325	3	158
	Moderate	350	4	177
		375	5	190
		400	6	204
	Hot	425	7	214
		450	8	232
		500	9	260

American			
	8 fl. oz.	app. 230 millilitres	1 cup
	10 fl. oz.	app. 285 millilitres	1¼ cups
	16 fl. oz. (American pint)	app. 460 millilitres	2 cups
	20 fl. oz. (Imperial pint)	app. 570 millilitres	2½ cups
	Sugar 8 oz.	app. 230 grams	1 cup
	Flour 4 oz.	app. 115 grams	1 cup

Plain flour: all-purpose flour
Self-raising flour: all-purpose flour with baking powder
Fat: any sort, usually butter or margarine: i.e. shortening
Caster sugar: fine granulated sugar
Demerara sugar: brown sugar
Sultanas: large seedless raisins
Golden syrup: corn syrup   Black Treacle: molasses

WHEN CROWBAR & BAYONET RULED

The Land War On The Belcarra Estate
Of
Harriet Gardiner & Susanna Pringle
1879-1910

Michael M. O'Connor & James R. O'Connor

ORIGINAL WRITING

© 2013 Michael M. O'Connor & James R. O'Connor

Front Cover Photo: Eviction of James Walsh & Family, Elmhall, Belcarra, 1886: Courtesy of the Wynne Private Collection.

All rights reserved. No part of this publication may be reproduced in any form or by any means—graphic, electronic or mechanical, including photocopying, recording, taping or information storage and retrieval systems—without the prior written permission of the authors.

ISBNS
PARENT : 978-1-78237-167-0
EPUB: 978-1-78237-168-7
MOBI: 978-1-78237-169-4
PDF: 978-1-78237-170-0

A CIP catalogue for this book is available from the National Library.

Published by ORIGINAL WRITING LTD., Dublin, 2013.
Printed in Great Britain by MPG BOOKS GROUP, Bodmin and Kings Lynn

Yesterday (Christmas day) when the High Sheriff, Mr. Alexander Clendining, and a few freeholders, were passing through Belcarra on their return home, the people who were assembled after mass, called out "No Browne." For this crime the police fired on them, killed one and wounded several. We are credibly informed the people were in the act of retiring, intimidated by threats, when the slaughter commenced. We regret to hear, with what truth we can't say, that Mr. Clendining gave the orders to fire.[1]

For our Parents Michael & Josephine

&

our Aunt Margaret T. Mitchell

Contents

Acknowledgements	VIII
Abbreviations	IX
Introduction	X
Part I: Gardiner & Pringle, their Origins & their Coming Together	1
Part II: Colonel St. George Cuffe, the Belcarra Estate & Tenant Families	21
Part III: James Daly, the Land League & the Land War in Mayo	45
Part IV: The Reign of Gardiner & Pringle at Belcarra Begins	61
Part V: Eviction Terror 1886	95
Part VI: The Evictions of 1887 & 1888	131
Part VII: The House of Gardiner, Pringle & Cuffe	155
Part VIII: Gardiner in Decline & the Rise of Pringle	169
Part IX: Nationalism on the Belcarra Estate	197
Part X: Grabbers & Graziers	209
Conclusion	235
Bibliography & Works Consulted	241
Appendix I: Townlands & Selected Tenants	246
Appendix II: Nationalist Demonstration at Belcarra, 28 November 1892: Attendees	253
Appendix III: Frenchill 1898 Centenary Meeting: Attendees	254
Appendix IV: Prison Treatment of Conor O'Kelly MP	257
Appendix V: Rev. Colleran CC., Letter concerning meeting with Pringle at Tully	260
Appendix VI: Summons Served on Tully Five	262
Appendix VII: List of Attendees at Court Appearances of Tully Five	263

*Appendix VIII: UIL Meeting at Belcarra, 19 October
  1907: Attendees* 264
Appendix IX: 1901 Census Tully 265
About the Authors 267
Endnotes 268

Acknowledgements

We wish to thank the following people for their assistance in the preparation of this publication: the staff of Castlebar and Westport Libraries and especially Ivor Hamrock; the staff of the Valuation Office, Dublin; the staff of the Office of the Registrar of Births, Deaths & Marriages, Castlebar; Genealogists John Hamrock and Aiden Ferick for their assistance in accessing and interpreting the Cancellation Books; the National Library of Ireland for granting permission to reproduce photographs from the Lawrence Collection; the Wynne Family for granting permission to reproduce photographs from the Wynne Private Collection; Sean Browne for guidance on structure and content; the Geraghty Family for granting permission to reproduce an impression of Gardiner and Pringle by the late Bridie Geraghty; artist Fionntan Gogarty for providing a copy of the illustration from *Le Petit Parisien*, 1898; and members of our own family for assistance with family records, photographs and papers and in particular our parents Michael and Josephine; our sister Pamela; and our aunt Margaret T. Mitchell, Columbus, Ohio. We would also like to extend our gratitude to all those we met with during the course of our research for their time, contributions and encouragement including Bernard Gibbons, Kathleen Nally, Pauline Keane, John Lavelle, and Stephen Connolly at the Connaught Telegraph, Castlebar.

Finally we would also like to acknowledge the enthusiastic support and encouragement we received from Caroline and Susan over the past three years.

Abbreviations

CC- Catholic Curate
CDB- Congested Districts Board
CI- County Inspector
CT - Connaught Telegraph
DI- District Inspector
FR- Father
FJ- Freemans Journal & Daily Commercial Advertiser
ILL- Irish Land League
INL- Irish National League
IPP- Irish Parliamentary Party
JP- Justice of the Peace
MP- Member of Parliament (Westminster)
PP- Parish Priest
QC- Queen's Counsel
RC- Roman Catholic
Rev- Reverend
RIC- Royal Irish Constabulary
RM- Resident Magistrate
RO- Relieving Officer
UIL- United Irish League

Introduction

Harriet Gardiner, whose "tactics".... seem to be opposite to those of Cromwell, for while the latter monster desired to hunt Irishmen "to hell or to Connaught" the former "man-fiend" or "she-devil" ...wishes to drive them, root and branch, out of Connaught.[2]

The story of the Land War of the late 19th and early 20th Century on the Belcarra Estate of Harriet Gardiner and Susanna Pringle has its origins in a marriage celebrated more than sixty years earlier and the loss of a family estate following the Great Famine. In 1819 Elizabeth Cuffe, daughter of James Cuffe, Baron of Tyrawley, married John Gardiner of Farmhill, Killala. Their daughter Harriet was born almost two hundred years ago in the summer of 1821. Harriet's mother died before Harriet's second birthday and nine years later her father John married Eleanor Knox Gore and they had a large family. Harriet thus grew up without her mother in the shadow of her father's second family. Sources tell us that she learned to fish, hunt, shoot and drink in the company of her uncle, Colonel St. George Cuffe, owner of Deel Castle, Crossmolina.

Five years after the birth of Harriet Gardiner and half a world away in the British East Indies, Susanna Pringle was born to Ann Elizabeth Dawnay and William Alexander Pringle. Susanna Pringle, a Presbyterian fundamentalist, joined the evangelical crusade to convert Catholics in Ireland and arrived in Mayo during the Famine. With her co-operation Gardiner gained control of her father's lost estate. The pair forged a bizarre and enduring friendship and together became two of the most notorious, eccentric and abhorrent figures in the history of Irish landlordism. At Farmhill and Belcarra they were reviled and ridiculed in equal measure by their tenants, the aristocracy and the authorities.

Gardiner's interest in the lands surrounding the small rural village of Belcarra, about six miles south east of Castlebar, arose following the death of her uncle, Colonel St. George Cuffe in 1883. Cuffe, a veteran of the Battle of Waterloo, lived in Deel Castle, Crossmolina and Dublin but he also had an extensive estate occupied by several hundred tenants in the Belcarra area. Gardiner came into her inheritance a few months before her sixty third birthday. Pringle was fifty seven. Neither was married. Gardiner had for some time been the subject of a boycott on her estate at Farmhill and so in 1883, accompanied by Pringle, and assisted by an entourage of bailiffs, emergency men, police, lawyers and the occasional doctor, she turned her attention to her inheritance at Belcarra. For the next 27 years tenants on the Estate were subjected to eviction, assault, attempted murder, imprisonment and forced emigration. The very fabric of the community in some of the townlands on the Estate was utterly shattered. Neighbour turned against neighbour and family members against each other as Gardiner and Pringle, master manipulators and orchestrators, used a small number of tenants and outsiders to further their ultimate objective of clearing the Estate. Tenants were evicted, their houses levelled, children were left on the roadside and prosecuted in the courts; women and their infants were imprisoned while the elderly and infirm were driven to the Workhouse. Land grabbing, beatings and boycotting became part of everyday life, the subject matter of numerous court proceedings, extensive coverage in the national and international press and debate in the House of Commons in London.

There is little by way of oral tradition concerning Gardiner and Pringle. This account of the events at Belcarra is based primarily on a number of contemporary sources including local, national and international press reports, land, tax, court and prison records. These records give a fascinating insight into what happened at Belcarra. But the story of what occurred is as much about the manner in which it was reported as it is about the events themselves.

Events on the Estate were reported across the English speaking world but the coverage given by one local newspaper, the Connaught Telegraph, was particularly extensive and the majority of this coverage is preserved at Castlebar Library. In the 1880s the paper's owner, editor and correspondents provided *"sky news"* like coverage as events unfolded on the Estate. The reporting is at times so extensive that it is possible to follow the tenants from one day to the next as they moved between their homes, their land, the rent office, the courts and in many instances the prison at Castlebar. From 1876 to 1888 local land activist, agitator, and Land League co-founder James Daly was both proprietor and editor of the Connaught Telegraph. Daly grew up on the Belcarra Estate at Coachfield two miles from Belcarra. From the moment he secured ownership of the paper he used it in his own personal war against landlordism and at times the Land League for its perceived failure to assist tenants on the Belcarra Estate. When it came to matters on the Belcarra Estate Daly never missed an opportunity to highlight the plight of the tenants and the shortcomings of the Land League in addressing their grievances. Under Daly's proprietorship the paper went much further than inform its readers, it moralized, it demonized, it judged and it did not pretend to be fair, it was absolutely the champion of the tenants.

At times the style of writing in the Connaught Telegraph makes it difficult to separate fact from fiction and raises questions about the reliability of the paper as a record of what really happened on the Estate. Daly's writing style was highly combative, uncompromising, at times decidedly satirical and at other times deadly serious. Occasionally the seriousness of the subject matter is lost in his extensive use of hyperbole. Daly's formal education at nearby Errew Monastery is also clearly evident in his frequent use of historical and literary references in his writing. The Connaught Telegraph contains a staggering thirty years of coverage concerning events at Belcarra. The most extensive coverage corresponds with Daly's period of ownership. Notwithstanding Daly's somewhat curious style, the material facts as reported by the Connaught Telegraph during that period and indeed after Daly sold the paper, stand up remarkably well to scrutiny. The tenants were evicted, they were taken before the courts at Ballyglass, Castlebar and Westport, they were imprisoned with their children and their houses were levelled. The accounts in the Connaught Telegraph are corroborated by other less colourful contemporary sources including the Valuation Records kept by the Rate Collector now known as the Cancellation Books, Petty Sessions Court Records, Castlebar Prison Records and the coverage in other newspapers that were often much less supportive of tenants and their interests and rights.

What happened on the Belcarra Estate also needs to be considered in the context of the wider changes that were taking place in Ireland at that time. Between 1870 and 1909 the Westminster Government introduced several major legislative measures to address the plight of tenant farmers in Ireland. Initial enactments were largely ineffective and by the time more progressive and workable schemes were introduced Irish tenant farmers and their representatives had changed their demands and were no longer seeking enhanced tenant rights, they wanted ownership. The Belcarra Estate is an excellent and complete case study in the application or misapplication of this body of legislation during the reign of Gardiner and then Pringle.

Not all of the legislation passed in this period was aimed at addressing the concerns of tenants. Legislation was also introduced with the objective of suppressing agitation in Ireland. One such enactment introduced by Gladstone was the Protection of Persons & Property Act, 1881. This act and other anti-coercion measures were the subject of heated debate at so called *monster meetings* at Belcarra and elsewhere on the Estate during this period. The 1881 Act and other criminal legislation was aimed at suppressing organisations such as the National Land League of Mayo founded by Michael Davitt, Belcarra man James Daly and others in 1879, its successor the Irish National League and the United Irish League founded by William O' Brien at Westport in 1898. The UIL in particular was very active on the Belcarra Estate in the early part of the 20th Century. Notwithstanding Daly's central role in the establishment of the National Land League of Mayo, Daly had, by the time Gardiner and Pringle arrived in Belcarra, sought to distance himself from the Land League and it's Executive. Daly was often openly critical of the Irish National League and it's Executive for failing to support tenants on the Belcarra Estate.

The rise in nationalism in the period is also clearly evident from many of the speeches delivered at gatherings on the Estate as is the debate on the issue of Irish Home Rule. MPs from the Irish Parliamentary Party were frequently in attendance at meetings in Belcarra, Tully and elsewhere on the Estate and Maude Gonne made more than one visit in the closing years of the 19th Century.

In the 19th Century elected Boards of Guardians managed Poor Law Unions. The Guardians employed a Relieving Officer tasked with the role of receiving applications for relief or making payments approved by the Guardians and issuing orders to admit people to the Workhouse. The Belcarra Estate was in the Poor Law Union of Castlebar and proceedings of the Castlebar Board of Guardians, of which James Daly was an active member, were reported in the Connaught Telegraph and other papers. During the mid 1880s the Castlebar Board of Guardians and the Relieving Officer were often concerned with what was taking place on the Belcarra Estate.

The number of cases concerning tenants on the Belcarra Estate that came before the Petty Sessions Courts and to a lesser extent the Quarter Sessions Courts is phenomenal. Many of these cases highlight the extensive squabbling that took place between tenants as well as the manner in which Gardiner and Pringle went about the business of securing and enforcing large numbers of eviction orders. The position of the Resident Magistrate in Belcarra is also very evident. The role of the Resident Magistrate was to sit alongside the justices at the courts. At Ballyglass Petty Sessions where many of the cases against Belcarra tenants were heard, the Resident Magistrate often sat alone. The Magistrates lived amongst the tenants on the Estate and whilst their role was very much a legal one it was not mandatory for them to have any prescribed legal instruction. Magistrates on the Belcarra Estate included former British Army Officers. Though they were expected to ensure that the law was applied fairly, they were not considered by the Belcarra tenants to be impartial and this is a theme that is addressed by the Connaught Telegraph on numerous occasions. The vast majority of cases concerning tenants on the Belcarra Estate were heard at Petty Sessions or Quarter Sessions. Petty Sessions were mostly concerned with what were perceived from the perspective of the authorities as minor crimes and local disputes. The men, women and children sentenced to periods of imprisonment by the justices and magistrates at Petty Sessions hearings at Ballyglass and elsewhere had no doubt a different perception of these courts. In each Petty Session's District there was a Justice of the Peace or JP and this role was usually filled by a local land holder. The Petty Sessions were the lowest courts and for cases of a more serious nature the JP was obliged to refer the case to the Courts of Quarter Session or the Assizes Court. There are several instances on the Belcarra Estate when this occurred.

The story of the Land War on the Belcarra Estate also illustrates how Gardiner and Pringle were able, notwithstanding the various legislative measures introduced to protect tenants, to use the law and the legal system to slowly grind down the tenants over time. Attempts by the Belcarra tenants to use the criminal law generally failed and the civil law and the specific legislation introduced in the last decades of the 19th Century to improve the position of tenants also provided no effective remedies or protection. Gardiner and Pringle, assisted by well paid and able lawyers, negotiated their way around the legislative obstacles set up to protect tenants. Gardiner was allowed to use large numbers of armed police, many of whom were Catholic, as her own private army and together with magistrates and bailiffs they secured numerous evictions and levelled homes. In this David and Goliath struggle there were occasional victories when tenants and their lawyers turned the tables on the pair but these were few and far between and were, more often than not, overturned on appeal.

This is also and indeed predominantly the tale of ordinary people. Tenant farmers such as John Garvey (Long) and Patrick Macken each of whom stood up to Gardiner and Pringle with very different outcomes; Mary Connor, imprisoned at Castlebar on numerous occasions with her infant child; Catherine Dunne, kicked and beaten by Gardiner's bailiff as the police and a magistrate looked on; bailiffs William (Billy) Cuffe and James Harte; tenant Oliver Canton who died a homeless pauper in the Castlebar Workhouse while his neighbours fought over the grass on his evicted holding: and our great-great grandfather, tenant turned bailiff, turned victim, John Connor who was subjected to a barrage of legal actions in the years and months leading up to his death after he had, in the words of one of his neighbours, decided to *"hang up his gun"* and cease to act as a bailiff. This is also the story of one Resident Magistrate who presided over evictions and passed judgment on tenants at the Petty Sessions and who as a consequence of mistaken identity was dragged from his carriage and beaten so badly that he would later die. The local clergy also played a very significant role at this time in protecting and furthering the interests of tenants. Men such as Canon Edward Gibbons delivered numerous politically charged speeches at large gatherings on the Estate and instructed tenants in the use of boycotting and other non violent measures.

In this account we have sought to the best of our ability to present the important facts as we have found them or as we have found them to be reported. In light of the ever increasing interest in genealogy and local and social history we have endeavoured to include as many names and place names as possible to facilitate and guide further research but we would caution the reader against slavishly following our conclusions but instead to look at the publicly available sources referenced in this publication and combine their findings with their own unique knowledge and understanding of their family history before reaching any final conclusions as to the role played by their family member or members in this story.

Part I

Gardiner & Pringle, their Origins & their Coming Together

Harriet Gardiner: Portrait of a Lady

In books you would never meet her type, probably, because there would lie a charge of exaggeration against any true description; in real life- if I except her mischievous shadow, Miss Pringle – you would not meet her like within the limits of an empire or the space of a century. Her appearance is the outward expression of her character. A squat figure, she tramps about in petticoats short enough to call for the interference of the lord chamberlain did she strut on any other stage but that of Irish landlordism. By no means tidy, nor, indeed cleanly, there is a brutal assertiveness about her carriage that boldly challenges your inspection; in fact, some of her gestures say as plainly as words "the devil may care, when it suits me". Her features, strongly marked by nature, are defined more rudely still by indulgence in stronger stimulants than are good for her or her tenants; her head is large, her hair split at the side in masculine fashion, and in her eyes there is constantly a strange, half-shirking, half angry look that is a mixture of suspicion and menace. She carries a revolver, but lest her own aim might be shaky two constables hold special watch and ward on her indoors and out.[3]

The Marriages of John Gardiner: 1819–1832

The Gardiners arrived in North Mayo in the early part of the 17th Century. They lived in the Parishes of Kilfian and Rathreagh, in the Barony of Tyrawley. The family residence at Farmhill, Killala was built in 1780.[4] By the late 18th Century, John Gardiner held extensive lands in Northern and Western Mayo. After the 1798 Rebellion the List of Claims of Mayo Loyalists who suffered losses in the Rebellion records that John Gardiner submitted a compensation claim of £2,322 18s. 7.5d. *"for damage to house, furniture, cattle, corn, trees and cloths."* John Gardiner held a number of senior positions in the County including High Sheriff of Mayo and Justice of the Peace.

In 1819 John Gardiner married Elizabeth, daughter of James Cuffe, 1st Baron of Tyrawley (1747–1821). It was this marriage that would bring Harriet Gardiner to Belcarra over sixty years later. James Cuffe was an Irish peer and politician. His father was James Cuffe of Elmhall and Ballinrobe Castle. His mother was Elizabeth, sister of Arthur Gore, 1st Earl of Arran. Between 1768 and 1797 James Cuffe represented Mayo in the Irish House of Commons. He became Baron Tyrawley in 1797 and was elected as one of the first representative peers for Ireland in 1800. He sat in the House of Lords until his death in 1821. On his death the title, *Baron of Tyrawley,* died out. Harriet Gardiner was his granddaughter.

Harriet was born in the Parish of Ballysakerry on 21 July 1821. Records show that other children were born to John and Elizabeth but they did not survive, a fact confirmed by Harriet many years later. On 19 June 1823 Elizabeth died. Harriet was not yet two years old. Nine years later, on 14 September 1832, John Gardiner married again. His second wife was Eleanor Knox Gore, the daughter of James Knox Gore (1774-1818). John and Eleanor had six children, two boys and four girls. Harriet's half siblings included Louise Anne (b. 1833); and John Charles (b.1844). Quinn paints a somewhat benevolent picture of the Gardiners and according to his account they had a good relationship with their tenants before Harriet Gardiner took control of Farmhill.[5] This is not a view shared by others. According to Becker it was said in North Mayo that John Gardiner was the first of the *"exterminators."*[6] In the normal run of things Harriet could not have expected to inherit the family estates as a large second family lay between her and any inheritance. John Gardiner's second family however failed to hold on to their inheritance. According to Quinn the Famine marked the beginning of the end for the Gardiners in Tyrawley. When profligacy led to the family losing Farmhill, Harriet stepped in and with the assistance of Pringle, took control of it.[7]

Gardiner's Early Years: 1821–1841
Little is known about Harriet's early life. George Moore in his somewhat controversial novel *Parnell and his Island*, written

over sixty years after her birth, relates that there were many legends surrounding her. Moore was born in 1852 at Moore Hall on the shores of Lough Carra, a short distance from the village of Belcarra. According to Moore it was said that she was once a pretty, graceful Irish girl. Her blue eyes and merry voice were the delight of her friends and in particular a young English painter whom she was passionately in love with. He was said to have painted her as Ophelia. Her father disapproved and sent her overseas with a travelling companion. On the death of John Gardiner, Harriet returned immediately to lay to rest her deceased father and marry the artist. He had however married someone else so she returned to Farmhill and talked of establishing a convent. Moore believed that there was some truth in this story as Harriet was undoubtedly born and lived as a lady. What Moore could not shed any light on is what he described as her *"decline into the sewer of debauchery."* According to Moore fortune was always on Gardiner's side and she inherited property from several relatives leaving her with vast wealth *"which she had no power or way of spending except in an occasional drinking-bout with her bailiffs and caretakers in a county town."*[8]

An account of the life Harriet Gardiner written by the Dublin Correspondent of the New York Catholic News in 1887 following an interview with the Bishop of Killala may throw some light on her early life.[9] According to this account, after the death of both parents a young Harriet Gardiner moved into the home of Colonel St. George Cuffe at Deel Castle. No decent woman would have entered that house as it was frequented by bachelors like Cuffe himself. Cuffe spent his time *"in hunting, sporting, fishing and debauchery."* He *"trained her under his own eye until she could ride, shoot and fish with the best of the set."* She learned to become a hard drinker and grew up *"strong and muscular, and had the constitution of an elephant."* The correspondent stressed that his account was based on solid fact and beyond dispute but as with everything else about Gardiner it is ultimately based on hearsay and written many years after the events in question. This is not to say that the account is not accurate but by the mid 1880s a significant body of folklore had already built up around Gardiner and it is at times difficult to see behind this.

What is certain is that by the age of 35 Gardiner had become a significant landowner in County Mayo. Griffiths Valuation of 1856-1857 lists her as a landowner in the townlands of Ballybeg, Farmhill, Rathreagh, Cloontykillew and Rathowen. She purchased Knox lands from the Encumbered Estates Court in 1854 and again in 1858. In 1867 she sold these lands in the Landed Estates Court.[10] By 1876 she owned 4,073 acres of land in Mayo.[11]

Portrait of a Lady

Gardiner's masculine appearance and dress, and her eccentric and repulsive habits were the subject of much comment. According to contemporary accounts she wore a man's felt hat and jacket, corduroy trousers and gaiters and parted her hair to the side after the fashion of men. She armed herself with a revolver and blackthorn stick. The former was frequently brandished at tenants; the latter employed to beat them behind the closed doors of her Rent Office. Her heavy and frequent use of alcohol was widely commented upon and this together with her habit of pipe smoking meant that her blue eyes were often bloodshot. The drinking and smoking were not confined to home and she was frequently drunk at fairs and on the roads and streets of Mayo. She had a dreadful temper and was uncompromising and hard of heart in all aspects of her dealings with her tenants. She was an accomplished herd's woman and had a good eye for the best cattle and horses at fairs. There was no aspect of animal husbandry that she was not expert in. She dealt directly with men buying and selling at fairs and markets. She checked animals before she committed to buying them and then closed the bargain herself. She frequently used language that was shockingly coarse and caused unpleasant scenes at fairs and other public places. With Pringle she spent much of her time on the road under armed police protection. She was regularly in court pursuing tenants for rent or trespass and seeking orders for possession and occasionally defending herself against allegations of assault. George Moore made the following observations on her dress and demeanour (Fearing the libel laws Moore referred to Gardiner as Miss. *Barrett*):

> Dressed as a man, in her dreadful corduroy trousers and felt hat, Miss. Barrett attends the fairs, and counselled by her herdsmen she buys and sells, spitting and swearing and drinking out of a flask, while she drives the bargain. The sexual economy of animals has no secrets for her; she goes down before the rams are turned into the fold, and it is she who often passes the usual coat of red paint over the animals' bellies. Miss Barrett is delighted as little as she is disgusted by the procreation of beasts; she merely declines to acknowledge the mystery with which we occidentals have surrounded such things, and having chosen to become a herdsman she accepts the duties in all their completeness. Against her virtue not a word has ever been said; she is execrated in the country in which she lives, but it is for drunkenness and cruelty that she is so violently and vehemently abused. To evict tenants is her one desire, to harass them with summonses for trespass is her sole amusement.[12]

Pringle shared many of Gardiner's unsavoury characteristics including her love of whiskey. Together they lived a life of penury and squalid filth. Their only extravagance would seem to have been alcohol and tobacco.

Attempted Assassination: December 1869

Gardiner was evicting tenants long before she arrived in Belcarra in 1883 and evictions at her Farmhill Estate prompted an attempt on her life in 1869. In a six month period in that year she secured several evictions and others were pending. In what is the only recorded attempt on her life, one (or possibly more), of her tenants chose Christmas morning 1869 to bring

Gardiner's reign of tyranny at Farmhill to an end. Gardiner was sitting in the kitchen at Farmhill when shots were fired through the window. Gardiner took several grains of shot in the head but the core of the shot hit a cabinet in the kitchen.[13] She was subsequently put under police protection. The incident was widely reported in Ireland and England as an agrarian outrage. According to the Aberdeen Journal, the Ballycastle constabulary was actively endeavouring to locate the perpetrator but no clue had been found.[14] Quinn's History of Mayo contains a lengthy account of the attempted assassination which, according to Quinn, took place not in December 1869, but in January 1870.[15] This however is not correct as at least one newspaper reported the incident on 31 December 1869. According to Quinn, citing the Tyrawley Herald as his source, the attack took place under the cover of darkness on a Friday night. Gardiner's life was saved by a lamp inside the window on a table at which two servants were seated. The lamp made the shot more difficult and the assassin missed. Gardiner took some shot in the forehead but the velocity of the gunshot was slowed and altered as it passed through the lamp. Gardiner had the presence of mind to call the servants to arms and together they waited out the night in the house fearing to go outside. In the morning Dr. Bournes was summoned from Ballycastle to remove the lead and dress the wounds. A reward was offered to anyone who identified the culprit but nobody came forward.

Shortly after the attack Gardiner and Pringle attended the Ballina Quarter Sessions. Pringle at this time owned property in Tyrawley district possibly at Ballinglen. Gardiner, armed with a revolver and a second gun in her belt, was in court seeking permission to evict tenants at Ballybeg. The revolver was brandished at Walter Bourke QC., Counsel for the tenants and the inevitable evictions followed.[16]

Farmhill Evictions: 1880
Long before Gardiner succeeded to the Belcarra Estate she had established her reputation as a hard and uncompromising land-

lord. In 1880 the Freemans Journal published the following extract from Becker's Disturbed Ireland:

> The owner's feud with her tenants began long before the Land League was known. It is said in Northern Mayo that her father was the first of the "exterminators", justly or unjustly so called, and that the traditions of the family have been heartily carried out by his heiress. There is perhaps very little doubt that Miss Gardiner, like Lord Lucan and the Marquis of Sligo, prefers large farmers as tenants to a crowd of miserable peasants striving to extract a living for an entire family from a paltry patch of five acres of poor land; but whatever her wish may be, she has undoubtedly a large number of small tenants on her estate at the present moment.[17]

Becker sought to justify Gardiner's actions by reference to the standards that applied in England at the time:

> It is therefore probable that she is somewhat less of an exterminatrix than the exasperated people represent her to be. In their eyes, however, she is guilty of the unpardonable crime of insisting upon her rent being paid. Her formula is simple, "Give me my rent or give me my land." In England and in some other countries such a demand would be looked upon as perfectly reasonable; but "pay or go" is in this part of Ireland looked upon as the option of an exterminator. Miss Gardiner merely asks for her own, and judged by an English standard would appear to be a strange kind of Lady Bountiful if she allowed her tenants to go on quietly living on her property without making any show of payment. But this is very much what landlords are expected to do in County Mayo, except in very good seasons.[18]

In April 1880 Gardiner evicted Thomas Goulden and his family of five.[19] On 8 October she obtained decrees allowing her to evict four other tenants. According to the Birmingham Daily Post the tenants in question had been evicted previously but had retaken possession at the instigation of the Land League.[20] The Liverpool Mercury reported the following exchange in the court:

> The court made an order for possession. There ensued a sharp crossfire of words between Mr. Muffery and Miss Gardiner. Mr. Muffery said this woman was better fitted for a fish stall than the position of a landed proprietress, - Miss Gardiner; I have no objection whatever to fish if they are good, and I will invite Mr. Muffery to dine upon them. – Mr. Muffery; I don't care for the company of such tyrants. Go and mend your ways. – Miss Gardiner; I suppose I can do what I like with my own property.- Mr. Muffery; it is not yours; it rightfully belongs to those poor creatures you are persecuting, and it will go hard with you if you do not change your conduct towards them. – Miss Gardiner; Go on I like to hear you preach. You are a grand preacher, but I care very little about you.[21]

Gardiner Mobbed in Ballina: December 1880

With the passage of time it became more and more difficult for Gardiner to conduct her business and personal affairs in North Mayo. On Friday 10 December, 1880, the Newcastle Courant reported that Gardiner had been mobbed in the streets of Ballina after she was turned out of a shop. Gardiner drew her revolver to defend herself and was subsequently taken into police protection. A more detailed account of the engagement can be found in the Williamsport Pennsylvania Daily Gazette and Bulletin.[22] According to that report, Gardiner had gone to Ballina on a Tuesday to do some shopping. She was accosted by a woman in the street and called some vile name. The woman then struck her across the face with a teapot. Later Gardiner was asked to leave a hardware shop by the owner, a man named Muffery, who refused to serve her. A crowd followed her through the streets yelling and hooting at her. Gardiner took out her revolver and called on them to stop shouting saying that she would use the gun if necessary. The police intervened and she was escorted to a local hotel.

Orange Expedition to Farmhill: January 1881

By January 1881 Gardiner had become a prisoner in her own home at Farmhill. She was under constant police protection and the subject of a boycott. The Glasgow Herald reported that for some time she was unable to get food supplies for the house without the assistance of the police.[23] Her servants had left her with the exception of one old steward and two policemen had moved into the house to provide her with protection.[24] Relief came unannounced on the midnight train that arrived in Killala on Monday 24 January. An expedition of Orangemen had travelled from Ulster to relieve Gardiner. According to the Bristol Mercury they were fully equipped and armed with modern weapons.[25] They were transferred from Killala to Farmhill on the back of carts provided by Gardiner. There is no record of how long they spent at Farmhill and if their mission was a success.

Fortress Farmhill: 1881

Notwithstanding that Farmhill was demolished in the 1950s, a number of contemporary descriptions of the house and estate have survived and these give an excellent impression of the bleak existence that Gardiner had created for herself at Farmhill. The following extract from Becker's Disturbed Ireland paints a particularly vivid picture of what Farmhill had become by the winter of 1880-81:

> There is something very "uncanny" about Farmhill. The first object which comes in sight is a police barrack, with a high wall surrounding a sort of "compound," the whole being obviously constructed with a view to resisting a possible attack. This stiff staring assertion of the power of the law stands out gaunt and grim in the midst of a landscape of great beauty. The only blot, if a white edifice can be thus designated, is the stern, angular police barrack. In the front enclosure the sergeant is drilling his men; and those not under drill are watching the domain immediately opposite, to the end that no unauthorised person may approach it. Like most of the dwellings

in a country otherwise sparsely supplied with trees, Farmhill is nestled in a grove. But the surroundings of the house are not those associated in the ordinary mind with a home. The outer gate is locked hard and fast, and the little sulky-looking porter's lodge is untenanted. Its windows are barred, and all communication with the house itself is cut off, except to adventurous persons prepared to climb a stone wall. From the lodge onward the private road passes through a poor kind of park, and subsides every now and then into a quagmire. It is vile walking in this park of Farmhill, and as the house is approached there is a barking of dogs. Oxen are seen grazing, and peacocks as well as turkeys heave in sight. The house itself is barred and barricaded in a remarkable manner. The front door is so strongly fastened that it is said not to have been opened for years. Massive bars of iron protect the windows, and the solitary servant visible is a species of shepherd or odd man, who comes slinking round the corner. No stranger gentlewoman's dwelling could be found in the three kingdoms. The spot reeks with a dungeon-like atmosphere. It is, according to the present state of life in Mayo, simply a "strong place," duly fortified and garrisoned against the enemy.[26]

Moore paints a similar picture drawing parallels between the decline in the Estate and the decline in Gardiner herself.[27] The house and grounds were, at one time, no different from the houses and estates of the other landed gentry but at the time of writing Farmhill was both *"dissolute"* and *"degraded."* The house was surrounded by thousands of acres of land from which tenants had been driven at different intervals. The lands had been stocked with herds of sheep and cattle. All the trees had been cut down and the hewn stumps were visible all around the gardens. Cement had fallen from the walls; windows were broken and barricaded on the inside with coarse boards. Large beams of wood and stone were scattered all around and the hall door was nailed up with the only entrance being at the rear of the property. The inside of the house was filthy; the drawing room was only identifiable because of the broken piano and gold cornices strewn around the floor. Little of the carpet remained and there was a deal table in the middle of the room. A wash tub was supported by a fragile Chippendale chair. The only furniture left in the bedrooms was the large four poster beds. Anyone going in to the bedrooms is met with *"foul earthly odours"* and all around there was damp, decay and dust. By 1882 Farmhill had become a desperate and desolate place and Gardiner had nowhere to go in North Mayo but Gardiner's good fortune would take her south a few short months later.

SUSANNA PRINGLE: FROM BENGAL TO BELCARRA

The tenants all state that they could have some rights out of Miss Gardiner were it not for the undue interference of an old fanatic spinster from the "Land o cakes"[28] who .... cut a rather sorry figure as an apostle in petticoats, ... Finding that thing of trying to convert the benighted papists of the Lagan of Tyrawly by bribes and soup a total failure in Connaught, she has abandoned the heretofore well paying scheme, and has turned her attention to the cork-screw, and the advisor of Miss Gardiner.[29]

Bengal, British East Indies: 1826

Susanna Pringle was of Scottish ancestry, born into a Presbyterian family in Bengal, British East Indies.[30] Her grandfather, father, three uncles, three brothers and a cousin all served in the British administration in India. Alexander Pringle (1747-1827), was the son of Alexander Pringle and Susanna Rutherford. He served in the Civil Service of the East India Company before returning to Scotland in 1783 and the family residence of Yair in Selkirkshire. In 1789 he married Mary, the daughter of Alexander Dick Cunningham and Mary Butler. They had 11 children including Susanna Pringle's father William Alexander Pringle (1793-1855).

Susanna was the fourth daughter born to William Alexander Pringle and Ann-Elizabeth Dawnay, daughter of John Dawnay of Aylesbury, Buckinghamshire, England. She was born on 20 August 1826 in the Bengal Presidency, East Indies.[31] Her siblings included Alexander; William John; Frances; Mary Ann; Anna Charlotte; Elizabeth Lindsay; Robert; George Stewart and Jane.[32]

Her sister Frances died young. The remainder of her siblings did what would have been expected of them as members of a family with status in colonial India. The men joined the army and the civil service; the women married men in the army and civil service. But not Susanna. Her brother Alexander died in 1854, an officer in the Madras Army. Her brother, Ensign George Stewart, was killed by mutineers at Allahabad in India on 7 June 1857. Her brother Robert was educated at Edinburgh University and subsequently enlisted in the Medical Department of the Bengal Army where he served from 1854 to 1884. He returned to London around the same time that Susanna arrived in Belcarra. From his home in Blackheath he continued to be involved in Indian affairs and produced papers on a number of medical subjects based on his experiences in India. Susanna's sisters Mary-Ann and Anna Charlotte married employees of the Bengal Civil Service. Mary-Ann married Archibald Spiers while Anna Charlotte married Edward Alexander Samuels. Susanna's uncle, Robert Keith Pringle (1802-1897), held various posts under the Government of Bombay including Secretary to the Revenue and Finance Department, Director of the Bank of Bombay, Master of the Mint, and Member of the Council. In 1847 he became Commissioner of Scinde. Following his retirement in 1854 he became Convener, Deputy Lieutenant, and Justice of the Peace for Selkirkshire in Scotland.

Evangelical Crusade: 1850

Against this background it is very difficult to understand how Susanna Pringle ended up in North Mayo as Harriet Gardiner's companion. At some stage in her childhood she must have returned to Scotland possibly to be educated. As to what happened after that, there are a number of helpful references in the Connaught Telegraph. In 1883 a correspondent (most likely James Daly), wrote of Pringle:

> ...an old Scottish lassie from the "Land o cakes" – a played out super anna noodle, as Mick M' Quaid so graciously described the evangelizers who had some years ago infested our native land, but with no effect.[33]

In the 1820s fundamentalists in the Church of Ireland and the Church of England embarked on an evangelical crusade to convert Catholics. The clergy men known as New Reformers pursued this campaign with significant vigour in Mayo where it was encouraged by the Right Reverend Thomas Span Plunket, 2nd Baron Plunket (1792–1866), Bishop of Tuam, Killala and Achonry. During the Famine the New Reformers offered food to starving Catholics. In return recipients were expected to convert. People who took the *"soup"* became known as *"soupers."* After the Famine many abandoned their new faith and converted back to Catholicism and consequently they became known as *"jumpers."*

A collection of papers at Durham University provide some clues as to the activities of Susanna Pringle in Mayo. The papers, which comprise for the most part of correspondence, are part of a collection of papers of Miss Elizabeth Copley. Elizabeth Mary Copley was born around 1801. In her lifetime she engaged in a number of charitable endeavours. One, a Protestant mission to the Catholics of Ireland was based around a Model Farm at Ballinglen a short distance from Farmhill. The scheme included a bible school. The correspondence, letters between Susanna Pringle and Copley in the period 1854 to 1872, concern matters at the Mission and indicate that Susanna Pringle was in Ireland at least as early as 1854 when she was 28 years old. There are also letters between Charlotte Pringle (Susanna Pringle's aunt) and Copley relating to the period 1850 to 1869. This suggests that Susanna Pringle may have been in Ireland as early as 1850 but based on commentary in the Connaught Telegraph it is likely that she was in North Mayo during the Famine. The correspondence indicates that the Pringles were heavily involved in the Ballinglen project but there is also evidence that they were difficult and quarrelsome.

The close proximity of Ballinglen to Farmhill would have meant that Susanna Pringle and Harriet Gardiner must have known each other. In 1887 the Dublin Correspondent of the New York

Catholic News, having spoken to the Bishop of Killala, wrote of Harriet Gardiner:

> When she came of age she fell in for her father's property. Shortly afterwards this wretched drunken creature took it into her head that she ought to become an apostle for the conversion of her tenantary from "the cross of Rome" as the proselytisers here gracefully say. She therefore set up a proselytising establishment at Ballinglen, which she purchased for the purpose. Being short of ready money she borrowed some from the Pringles, a Scotch family burning with zeal to turn good Catholics to bad Protestants. A Miss Pringle came over, ostensibly to help Harriet in the work of "evangelisation" but in reality to look after the prudent Scottish family's money. That happened some eighteen or twenty years ago but Miss Pringle never went back. She fastened like a parasite on Harriet and the two have lived together ever since leading lives of scandalous riot. [34]

The reference to *"eighteen or twenty years ago"* is clearly incorrect. The Pringles were in Mayo many years before 1867 as is evident from the Copley papers. Notwithstanding this, could Harriet Gardiner have taken the initiative to establish the mission at Ballinglen herself? It is unlikely. Harriet came of age in 1842 on her twenty first birthday. According to the History of the Congregations of the Presbyterian Church, the Reverend Brannigan was appointed in 1845 to take oversight of Irish Schools.[35] In 1846 he was requested to make Ballinglen the focus of his activities. In 1848 he presented a memorial signed by eighty converts requesting to be taken into the care of the Presbyterian Church. A collection was made for a new church and this was opened in 1850. Numbers subsequently declined and this was blamed on emigration. Thomas Armstrong writing about his *"Life in Connaught"* later wrote that the Scottish Ladies Society became very interested in Ballinglen and commenced mission operations there in co-operation with Brannigan. Charlotte Pringle was secretary of the society and considerable sums were raised. During the Famine aid was provided for spiritual causes and for relief of the destitute. A school and model farm was established at Ballinglen.[36] There is no reference to any Gardiner involvement in the establishment or management of the Mission. This ties in with the following commentary of a Canadian traveller touring Ireland in 1882:

> According to one commentator Harriet Gardiner was a near neighbour to a Model Farm at Ballinglen. The farm was managed by two Scottish ladies. Philanthropy collected the vast sums which bought and stocked the model farm. Their mode of management resulted in the Model Farm being significantly indebted to the two women, it was necessary to sell the livestock to pay one of the women and the farm itself to pay Susanna Pringle.[37]

Artist Bridie Geraghty's impression of Gardiner & Pringle (Reproduced with the kind permission of the Geraghty Family).

Part II

Colonel St. George Cuffe, the Belcarra Estate & Tenant Families

Colonel St. George Cuffe

He was, by long odds, the oldest gentleman in Mayo – in fact, we might say he belonged to the past generations. He oft times repeated that he believed the prayers and good wishes of his tenants were the means of giving him such a long life. His proudest boast through long life was that he never evicted a tenant, quenched a fire, or got pulled down a roof-tree. The good old Colonel is no more, and none will have greater cause to mourn and regret his demise than his tenantry. Interment will take place at Ballinrobe at the family burial vault at some future time, the body remaining in the meantime in a temporary mausoleum at Deel Castle.[38]

Acts of Settlement: 1653

Under the Acts of Settlement introduced by Oliver Cromwell in 1653, Sir James Cuffe was granted considerable holdings of land in County Mayo in the Baronies of Kilmaine, Carra and Tyrawley. His son Gerald Cuffe, a Collector of Quit Rents, bought land near the village of Belcarra, from Colonel John Browne of Westport and built a residence at Elmhall. Elmhall is a small picturesque townland to the west of the village of Belcarra. Today it is dominated by the imposing ruin of the Cuffe residence. The small village of Belcarra lies about six miles south east of the town of Castlebar. When Gerald Cuffe died he was succeeded by James Cuffe. In 1731 James married Elizabeth, the sister of Arthur Gore, 1st Earl of Arran. Their son James Cuffe of Ballinrobe became Baron Tyrawley of Ballinrobe in 1797.

In the 1770s Elmhall was leased to the Jordan family of Murrisk and subsequently to a branch of the Browne family of Westport from the 1780s until the early 19th Century. In 1837 Elmhall was described as being *'in ruins'* and the Irish Tourist Association File records that Elmhall is said to have been burnt in 1798.[39]

When Lord Tyrawley died most of his estate passed to his daughter Jane and her husband Colonel Charles Nesbitt Knox. A List of Landowners in County Mayo in 1876 shows that Colonel St. George Cuffe owned 3,205 acres in County Mayo at that time and this included the family estate at Belcarra. Most of the land in the Belcarra Estate was in the Parish of Drum but the Estate also included townlands such as Barney and Ballyshane in the Parish of Breaghwy and that part of the townland of Logaphuill located in the Parish of Ballyhean. It is this property that passed to Lord Tyrawley's granddaughter Harriet Gardiner when her uncle Colonel St George Cuffe died in 1883.

Deel Castle, (Photograph: James O'Connor & Michael O'Connor, 2012).

Cuffe Residence, Elmhall, (Photograph: James O'Connor & Michael O'Connor, 2012).

Death of George Cuffe: March 1883

Colonel St. George Cuffe died on Thursday 29 March 1883 at his home in Deel Castle, Crossmolina. The press were generous in their praise of him as a *"the most humane, hospitable, and generous landlord and gentleman, of the age."*[40] Cuffe, a veteran of the battle of Waterloo in 1815, served with the 4th Dragoon Guards in Paris after the capture of Napoleon and commanded the North Mayo Militia Regiment.[41] He was born in May 1795, the youngest son of Lord Tyrawley. During his life he had a keen interest in horses, guns and dogs. In 1876 George Cuffe owned 3,205 acres of land in Mayo.[42] He married a daughter of John Knox of Broadlands but they had no children. On several occasions it was suggested in the press that he had an illegitimate son William, also known as Billy. There is no evidence that George Cuffe acknowledged this. Billy Cuffe would play a central role in events at Belcarra but in 1883 he was trading as a publican in Ballina.

Under the 1832 Last Will and Testament of his elder brother, Colonel James Cuffe, the Belcarra Estate was left to George Cuffe. The terms of the will provided that in the event that George Cuffe died without an heir the Belcarra Estate was to go to the male children of George Cuffe's sister Elizabeth Gardiner (nee Cuffe) and in the event that there were no male children, then to the daughters of Elizabeth Gardiner. Colonel St. George Cuffe had no children. Elizabeth had died in 1823 leaving only a daughter Harriet and this is how Harriet Gardiner came into possession of the Belcarra Estate.

George Cuffe, the Landlord: 1883

Contemporary accounts suggest that George Cuffe had a good relationship with his tenants on the Belcarra Estate. In the three year period prior to his death Cuffe had accepted a reduced rent from tenants acknowledging that economic conditions were difficult. In 1879 Cuffe employed Robert G. Baxter, a Ballina Auctioneer, Valuator and Emigration Agent as his agent. It was reported that Baxter's acceptance of the position was conditional on him being given full control of the Belcarra Estate.[43] Following his appointment Baxter gathered the tenants together and told them that rents would be reduced. In November 1881, Cuffe instructed Baxter to reduce rents on his Belcarra Estate by 25 per cent. This was well received by the tenants and in many instances the reductions had the effect of bringing the rent payable below Griffith's Valuation of the land.[44] The lands had been let at the Griffiths Valuation amount but Baxter believed that this was not an appropriate criterion for setting rents. Baxter was widely condemned for this action by other landlords and agents because, in their view, it set a bad example that they were compelled by their own tenants to follow.[45] When Cuffe died Baxter retired and the scene was set for the arrival of Gardiner and her entourage from Farmhill.

The Belcarra Estate & Tenant Families

Everywhere the condition of the children was dreadful, having nothing but the Indian meal, badly cooked, to live upon, and the parents only too glad if the charitable funds provided the family with half enough even of that. Sometimes there was a miserable cow about the premises - for, in every case, I am referring to the class of small farmers, mostly residing on three to five acres of land.[46]

Tenants & Townlands

When Harriet Gardiner inherited the Belcarra Estate in 1883 there were between 350 and 400 tenants on the Estate distributed across townlands in the Parishes of Drum, Breaghwy and Ballyhean.[47] Though the hounding of tenants that followed the arrival of Gardiner and Pringle was widespread, the impact the pair had on the residents of the townlands of Tully, Logaphuill, Clogherowan, Tully Beg and Elmhall was particularly shocking. Between 1883 and 1893 a substantial number of the tenants in these townlands lived under constant threat of eviction, and many were evicted, imprisoned, threatened, beaten and had their homes demolished. Gardiner's last stand against her tenants was in fact at Tully where she lived with Pringle in the period leading up to her death. By the time she died the majority of tenants in Tully had been evicted and their houses levelled. The townland of Tully is therefore central to the story of the Land War on the Belcarra Estate. If there is any doubt as to this conclusion one has only to view the relevant pages of the Cancellation Books held at the Valuation Office in Dublin. As was the usual practice, on each occasion that the rate payer changed, the old name was struck out and replaced in manuscript by the new name in a different colour of ink. The extent of the multi coloured manuscript amendments on the pages for Tully (and the adjacent townland of Clogherowan), as a consequence of the evictions and demolition of houses, left the clerks in the Valuation Office with no option but to draw red crosses through the entire pages in 1901 and start new pages. The record that is left behind vividly illustrates the terrible impact Gardiner and Pringle had on this small village.

Townlands in Colonel St. George Cuffe's Belcarra Estate.

Tully, Parish of Drum: 1883

The townland of Tully lies in the Western part of the Parish of Drum, approximately two miles from the village of Belcarra and four miles from the town of Castlebar. The townland takes its name from the long hill or tulaigh that runs in a south north direction the length of the townland.[48] The Field Book for Tully and the adjacent townland of Clogherowan contains the following entry:

> Landlord, Captain Cuffe. There is a middle landlord. These townlands are occupied by a number of people who mutually

divide them among themselves and holding a certain proportional part of the whole- their houses are all grouped together. Tully-Total rent £104.6.00. Taken 20 years ago. There are no houses in this townland worth £5 a year.[49]

The middle landlord referred to is likely to be Christopher Baines but he was no longer the immediate lessor when Griffiths Valuation was published and Colonel St. George Cuffe is listed as the landlord. The extract from Griffiths Valuation of 1856-1857 below shows the position in Tully in the mid 1850s and the position changed little in the years leading up to 1880. Occupiers changed when son succeeded father, when tenements were split to accommodate children who did not emigrate or when outsiders married into the village.

VALUATION OF TENEMENTS.
PARISH OF DRUM.

No. and Letters of Reference to Map.	Names.		Description of Tenement.	Area.	Rateable Annual Valuation.		Total Annual Valuation of Rateable Property.
	Townlands and Occupiers.	Immediate Lessors.			Land.	Buildings.	
				A. R. P.	£ s. d.	£ s. d.	£ s. d.
1	TULLY. (Ord. S. 79 & 90.)						
a	Patrick Macken,	Capt. St. George Cuffe,	Land, house, & offices,		6 13 0	0 7 0	7 0 0
b	Patrick Malone,	Same,	Land and house,		3 7 0	0 8 0	3 15 0
c	John Connor,	Same,	Land, house, & office,		5 7 0	0 7 0	5 14 0
d	Thomas Connor, jun.,	Same,	Land and house,		4 2 0	0 6 0	4 8 0
e	James Garvey,	Same,	Land, house, & office,	118 3 35	5 2 0	0 8 0	5 10 0
f	Thomas Garvey,	Same,	Land, house, & offices,		5 2 0	0 10 0	5 12 0
g	Thady Higgins,	Same,	Land, house, & office,		5 7 0	0 7 0	5 14 0
h	Anthony M'Donnell,	Same,	Land and house,		4 7 0	0 7 0	4 14 0
-	Thomas Garvey, jun.,	Same,	Land,		4 2 0	-	4 2 0
-	Rose Litton,	Same,	Land,		3 11 0	-	3 11 0
i	Thomas Kelly,	Same,	Garden and house,	0 1 8	0 3 0	0 9 0	0 12 0
j	James Fallon,	Same,	Offices,	-	-	0 4 0	0 4 0
k	Patrick Walsh,	Same,	House,	-	-	0 4 0	0 4 0
l	John M'Donnell,	Same,	House,	-	-	0 2 0	0 2 0
m	Thomas Connor,	Same,	House,	-	-	0 2 0	0 2 0
n	Unoccupied,	Rickard M'Greevey,	House,	-	-	0 5 0	0 5 0
o	William Joyce,	Capt. St. George Cuffe,	House,	-	-	0 6 0	0 6 0
p	John Vahey,	Same,	House and office,	-	-	0 5 0	0 5 0
			Total,	119 1 3	49 3 0	4 17 0	54 0 0

Griffiths Valuation 1856-1857, Townland of Tully, Parish of Drum.

In 1883 sixteen tenants leased land from Gardiner at Tully. The Table below shows the position in Tully just before the evictions commence in 1885. The majority of the land (over 118 acres), is held as a rundale holding. Only John Kelly's small tenement is shown as a distinct holding for valuation purposes. The Cancellation Books do not record the rent payable by the tenants and to date research has not located copies of any leases. However, as rent was set by reference to the rateable valuation, it is likely that the rent was at one point in time at least equal to the specified valuation and possibly in excess of it. Prior to the arrival of Gardiner her uncle had offered a rent reduction to assist tenants and this had been gratefully accepted. Not surprisingly tenants expected Gardiner to honour the bargains made by her uncle but she had other ideas. By 1887 nine of the tenants in Tully had been evicted, some on more than one occasion and most permanently. Several houses in the village were levelled by Gardiner and her bailiffs to prevent tenants returning and a number of tenants, their wives and children had spent time in Castlebar prison. By 1901 there were only six tenants left in Tully and only four of these had a house in the village. To fully understand what happened at Tully, to the extent that this is possible, it is necessary to know something about the tenants and some of the key relationships in the village at the time Harriet Gardiner inherited the Belcarra Estate. Based on contemporary records it is possible to paint a picture of some of the key characters in the village and the interrelationships that existed at that time.

Cancellation Books: Townland of Tully; Parish of Drum; Union of Castlebar, 1885: Before Evictions Commence

Names Occupier	Immediate Lessor	Description	Area Note: Rundale Holding: Total 118a., 3r., 35p	Rateable Annual Valuation Land	Buildings	Total
Patrick Macken John Macken	Harriet Gardiner	House, Office, Land		£6, 13s	7s	£3.10 £3.10
James Deacy	Harriet Gardiner	House, Land		£2, 12s	8s	£3
Thomas Walsh	Harriet Gardiner	House, Land		£2, 15s	5s	£3
John Connor	Harriet Gardiner	House, Office, Land		£5,7s	8s	£5, 15s
Patrick Connor	Harriet Gardiner	House, Land		£4,3s	7s	£4, 10s
James Garvey	Harriet Gardiner	House, Office, Land		£5, 2s	8s	£5, 10s
John Garvey	Harriet Gardiner	House, Office, Land		£5,2s	10s	£5, 12s
Patrick Burke	Harriet Gardiner	House, Land		£2, 13	4s	£2, 17s
Robert Cardy	Harriet Gardiner	House, Land		£2,14s	4s	£2, 18s
Michael Lavelle John Kelly	Harriet Gardiner	House, Land House, Land		£4,7s	8s	£2, 8s £2, 7s
Thomas Garvey	Harriet Gardiner	Land		£4,2s		£4, 2s
Owen Vahey	Harriet Gardiner	Land		£3, 10s		£3, 10s
John Kelly	Harriet Gardiner	House, Office, Garden	1r., 8p	3s	9s	12s
James Fallon	Harriet Gardiner	Office			5s	5s
Total			119 a., 1 r., 26 p.	£49, 3s	£4,3s	£53, 6s

A map based on the authors' local knowledge, existing ruins, aerial pictures, old photographs, information in the Cancellation Books and other sources is set out below. It attempts to show the actual or likely location of tenant homes in the period 1883-1893. It has not been possible to pinpoint the location of a small number of houses.

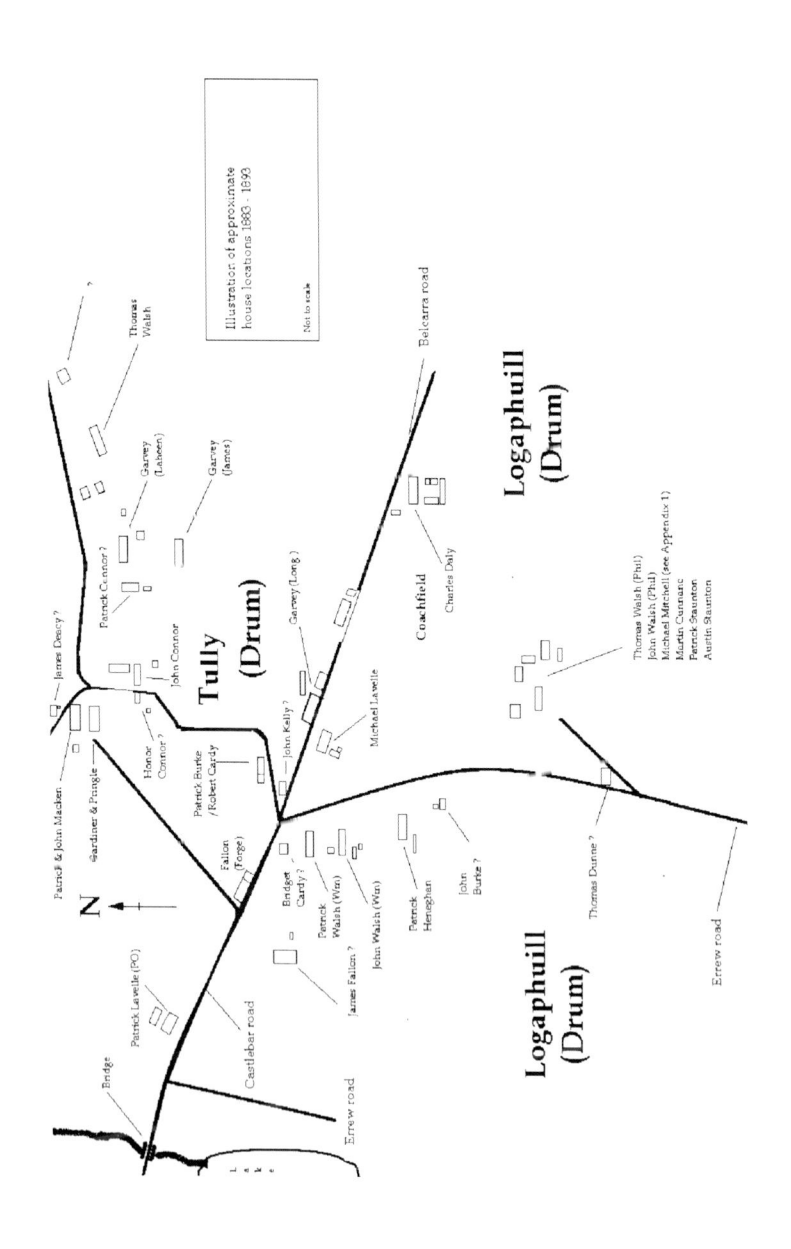

Illustration of approximate house locations 1880 - 1893
Not to scale

The Macken Family

Patrick Macken is one of the central characters in the story of the Land War on the Belcarra Estate. Patrick Macken's home was located near a cross roads at the centre of the village of Tully. He was born in 1816 in Tully and was approximately 67 years old in 1883. He was a relatively tall man at five foot nine inches. He had grey eyes, grey hair and a fresh complexion. He could neither read nor write.[50] Little is known about his early life save that in January 1856 he married Mary Garvey.[51] Their children included a daughter, Susan. The relationship between Patrick and the John Macken listed alongside his name in the Cancellation Books is not clear save that they were co-tenants and they shared a house. John may have been Patrick's brother. John Macken became Patrick Macken's co-tenant in the mid 1870s. John's wife was also named Mary. On 8 September 1858 a John Macken of Tully married Bridget Dunne. They had three children; Bridget, Mary, and John. Research to date has not revealed the relationship between these men. Part of the limestone gable wall of the Macken home remains today.

The Deacy Family

Though it is difficult to be certain it is likely that the home of James Deacy was located very close to that of the Mackens but on the other side of the road. Apart from some stones that may have formed part of the house there is no trace of the house today and contemporary maps and sources are inconclusive. James Deacy was born in the Parish of Aglish in 1839 to Martin Deacy and Honoria Handley and probably arrived in Tully in the spring of 1857 following his marriage to Catherine Malone in February of that year. Catherine was also born in 1839 to Anthony Malone and Bridget Connor so it is likely that she was related to Patrick Malone of Tully.[52] In 1868 the Cancellation Book shows that Patrick Malone's name is replaced by James Deacy suggesting that Patrick had died and that James succeeded to the tenement.[53] Between 1858 and 1873 James and Catherine had 9 children, Mary (b.1858); Patrick (b.1859); Owen (b.1861); Michael (b.1863); John (b.1865); Catherine (b.1867); Bridget (b.1869); Ellen (b.1872); and Julia (b.1873). By 1883 Catherine was a widow and lived in Tully with her son John and daughter Bridget.

The Walsh Family

A short distance from the home of James Deacy was the house of Thomas Walsh. This house, a thatched cottage, stood until relatively recently, when it was replaced by a modern bungalow. Walsh, the son of Michael Walsh from nearby Baile Cuill, came to Tully in 1876. The Cancellation Books show that James Deacy's tenement was divided with Thomas Walsh at this time and each took responsibility for a fifty per cent share of the rates. Thomas Walsh married Margaret Joyce, the daughter of William Joyce, a weaver from the village. Griffiths Valuation of 1856- 1857 records that at that time William Joyce leased a house in Tully from George Cuffe. In 1864 his son John married Bridget Connor. It is unclear where Bridget came from but her father's name was John. Twelve years later in December 1876 William's daughter Margaret married Thomas Walsh. They had at least two children: Patrick born in 1877 and Anne in 1880.

Ruins of house, Tully. (Photograph by Michael O'Connor & James O'Connor, 2010).

William Joyce's name and tenement were deleted from the Cancellation Books by 1879 suggesting that he had died or that the rate payer became his son in-law Thomas Walsh. In 1885 this house was the scene of a major raid by the Belcarra police. At the time the tenants had gathered for a station mass prompting local Catholic clergy to accuse the authorities of sectarian intervention.

The Connor Families

In 1883 there were two Connor families in Tully. The family of John Connor and the family of Thomas and Patrick Connor. Across the road and no more than one hundred meters from the home of Patrick Macken was the tenement of John Connor. Part of the ruins of his house stood until recently. Little is known of John Connor's early life though it is likely that he was born sometime between 1815 and 1820. Oral tradition suggests that he may have come to Tully to marry the niece or daughter of a man in the village. In 1850 he married Anne Higgins and in the course of the following 12 years they had five children; Martin, Mary, Thomas, Anne and John. It is not certain whether Anne Higgins was related to Thady Higgins of Tully though it seems very likely.[54] It has not been possible to establish either way whether John Connor was related to Thomas and Patrick Connor. By 1883 John Connor was living in Tully with his wife and two adult children, Martin and Anne. His sons John and Thomas were in America. The whereabouts of his daughter Mary at this time is not known though it is possible that she was also in America.

Close to John Connor's tenement was the tenement of Patrick Connor, the son of Thomas Connor. Patrick had succeeded to his father's tenement shortly before 1884 suggesting that his father had most likely died. In February 1844 Thomas Connor married Mary Macken.[55] It is likely that Mary was Patrick Macken's sister. Between 1844 and 1854 Thomas and Mary had four children, Bridget, Mary, Patrick and Nelly. Thirty five years later Thomas Connor's son Patrick and daughter

Mary and their respective spouses and children would occupy the front line in Gardiner's war against the tenants at Tully. Thomas and Patrick Connor's house has proved to be one of the most difficult to locate though a suggested location is indicated on the map above.

On 4 March 1878, a 28 year old Patrick Connor married Mary Philbin the daughter of Peter Philbin, a farmer.[56] Sometime during that year Mary died and eleven months later on 24 February 1879 Patrick married again. This time he married Mary Mulgrew, the daughter of James Mulgrew of Ballynamarroge, Islandeady and they had five children: Kate (b. 1880); Bridget (b.1881); Patrick (b.1883); John (b. 1885); and Thomas (b. 1887).

On 24 February 1868, Patrick's sister Mary married James Hopkins, a 26 year old shoemaker from nearby Frenchill. James was the son of John Hopkins a labourer. Between 1868 and 1885, James and Mary christened eight children; Ellen, Mary, Patrick, Honor, Thomas, Eleann, Bridget; and Margaret. James, Mary and their large family lived a short distance from Tully on the Cottage Road. The house is not listed amongst the Tully tenements in the Cancellation Books.

There was a third Connor house in the village at least up to 1876. This was the home of Thomas Connor Senior and Honor Connor (nee Shaughnessy). In 1885 Honor was in her eighties and Thomas (most likely Patrick Connor's grandfather) was dead. The house is not recorded in the Cancellation Books after 1876 but newspaper reports refer to the house of Honor Connor as late as 1886.

The Garvey Families

In 1883 there were three related Garvey families in the village. John and James Garvey had a house and land in the village. Thomas Garvey had land in the village but by the mid 1880s he also had a house. The three men were brothers, the sons of

Thomas Garvey. John Garvey (known locally as John Garvey (Long)), had succeeded to the tenement of his father Thomas at some stage during the mid 1860s.[57] It has proved difficult to establish his age at this time due to the significant disparity in the ages he gave to the authorities at different times in his life but it is likely that he was born in Tully sometime between 1831 and 1840. In 1864 he married 22 year old Bridget Egan from Rushill. Between 1865 and 1887 they had at least nine children. Significantly in the context of what was about to take place in the village, two of the children, Edward and Ann, were born after 1883. John Garvey (Long)'s house was close to the Castlebar-Belcarra road and according to contemporary sources was one of the finest houses in the district. John Garvey (Long) would prove to be Harriet Gardiner's most difficult opponent.

A short distance away across the fields and closer to the centre of the village was the home of James Garvey. In 1854 James married Alice Walsh in Aglish Parish. They had at least one son, John who became known locally as John Garvey (James) to distinguish him from his uncle. Close by was the home of Thomas Garvey. In September 1864 he married Bridget Leheen in Islandeady Parish. Their children included John, Maria and Thomas. John was known locally as John Garvey (Leheen), to distinguish him from his cousin and uncle.

Patrick Burke & Robert Cardy

Patrick Burke and Charles Cardy arrived in Tully shortly before 1876. A tenement held at that point by Catherine Higgins was divided between them. Catherine succeeded to the tenement of Thady Higgins shortly before 1874. She may have been his wife or daughter. Patrick Burke's wife's name was Catherine so perhaps he married Catherine Higgins. The Higgins house was split between Patrick Burke and Charles Cardy. The outline foundation of this house is visible on an aerial photograph taken some years ago.

Charles Cardy married Bridget Mitchell in 1844 in Balla. By the time Gardiner took over the Belcarra Estate in 1883, Robert Cardy (most likely Charles Cardy's son) had succeeded to the tenement of Charles Cardy. The Cancellation Books for Logaphuill, Drum show that Charles Cardy had two tenements in Logaphuill. A garden held under a lease from Patrick Walsh and a house. The markings on the Cancellation Books suggest that Cardy's interest in the house may have been a freehold interest. The issue of ownership of the house would become important two years later. It is likely that the two Cardy houses were located close to each other near the crossroads on the Castlebar - Belcarra road. In 1883 Robert Cardy lived on the Tully side of the crossroads. Across the road his elderly and widowed mother lived alone.

John Kelly & Michael Lavelle

In 1883 John Kelly and Michael Lavelle were co-tenants in Tully each holding land and a house close to the Castlebar - Belcarra road. Kelly separately held a second house and garden. Kelly was one of Gardiner's first adversaries.

James Fallon & Owen Vahey

On the Logaphuill side of the village near the junction with the Castlebar- Belcarra road, James Fallon, of Logaphuill had a forge adjacent to the main Castlebar- Belcarra road. Remnants of this structure existed up to the mid 1980s. Owen Vahey did not live in the village, he lived nearby on the Cottage Road but he rented land from Gardiner in the village.

A Troubled Townland: 1876–1883

Based on a review of newspaper reports alone it would be reasonable to conclude that the trouble at Tully began with the arrival of Gardiner in 1883. Oral tradition would also support such a conclusion.[58] The records however tell a very different story. There was trouble brewing at Tully for some time before George Cuffe died and it would appear to have had little to do with landlordism. Between 1876 and 1884 there were more than 100 legal cases before Ballyglass and Castlebar Petty Sessions concerning Tully tenants. Before 1876 there were occasional trespass cases but from 1876 onwards the number of cases increased dramatically and the nature of the cases themselves changed.

Between 1869 and 1875 the notorious Earl of Lucan[59] took several trespass cases against Patrick Macken, John Connor and Thomas Connor. The cases related to trespass by livestock on the Earl's land at Breaghwy adjacent to the townland of Tully. Nearby at Ballyshane another large landholder, James Daly, was also pursuing his neighbours in the courts for trespass. At this point in time the tenants themselves would seem, for the most part, to have settled their own differences outside the courts but for some reason this changed in 1876. In the autumn of that year and the spring of 1877 a series of trespass cases involving Tully tenants came before Ballyglass Petty Sessions. It would seem that the first volley was fired by Anthony Vahey who took a case against Bridget and John Macken who he accused of cutting and taking away grass from his tenement. John Macken took a case against William Joyce for trespass by goats and Thomas Garvey took proceedings against Thomas Connor and John Kelly for trespass on a cabbage crop. The defendants did not attend court in any of the cases. In early 1878 the Macken family turned on each other when John Macken took three cases for trespass and destruction of crops against Patrick Macken. Patrick Macken was ordered to pay damages and costs in all cases but succeeded in a case of his own against John Macken.

In February 1879 Oliver Canton of Frenchill took legal action against Patrick and Mary Deacy and Patrick and Ellen Connor of Tully for theft of turnips from his farm at Frenchill. At Castlebar Petty Sessions the cases were dismissed. The following month Patt Brennan, the Poor Rate Collector, sought judgments at Castlebar Petty Sessions against Thomas Garvey, John Macken and John Garvey for refusal to pay the Poor Rate.

The defendants made no appearance in Court. Throughout the remainder of 1879 and into early 1880 Thomas Garvey took a series of cases against John Macken for trespass and destruction of crops. Macken was ordered to pay damages and costs in many of the cases. Ellen Connor accused her brother Patrick Connor of forcibly taking and treshing a quantity of oats belonging to her. Patrick Connor did not make an appearance at Ballyglass Petty Sessions. In November 1880 John Bingham, a bailiff from Castlebar, had Bridget and Maria Macken from Tully before Ballyglass Petty Sessions for allegedly assaulting him while he was trying to enforce a court order. The cases were dismissed. No detail is given as to the nature of the court order he was seeking to enforce. At the same sitting of the Court, in a separate but undoubtedly connected case, Bingham was fined for assaulting Bridget Macken.

In 1881 the number of cases increased, more tenants became involved and the subject matter of the cases was no longer solely concerned with trespass. In April of that year John Connor was drawn in and took two cases against Patt Lavelle for trespass by sheep and damage to crops. In May and June, Patrick Macken took several cases against John Connor for trespass while in August Patrick Connor took an action against his brother in-law James Hopkins for assault and wilful and malicious breaking of a scythe. James Hopkins responded by accusing Patrick Connor of wilful trespass on his land and cutting grass having been warned not to do so.

In August 1881 Honor Connor (most likely Patrick Connor's grandmother), made a series of serious allegations against John Connor and his wife Anne. She accused the couple of violently assaulting her at Tully on 11 August. She also accused John Connor of taking stones, roofing timber and furniture from her home. The case was initially adjourned to enable a police report to be provided to the court. The following month the cases against John and Ann Connor were dismissed on their merits.

It would seem that at this time Patrick Connor was sub-letting land from his brother in-law James Hopkins and that this was the reason for the ongoing tensions between them. In 1882 there were several cases before Ballyglass Petty Sessions concerning the two men and allegations of assault and trespass. A woman named Mary Duffy who was employed as a servant in Tully took a case against Patrick Macken for assault accusing him of hitting her with a stone. The case was dismissed on its merits. In a separate case Duffy was cautioned for trespassing on Macken land.

Wednesday 1 August 1883 was a very busy day for the Tully tenants at Ballyglass Petty Sessions. John Macken had taken legal actions for trespass against Patt Lavelle, John Connor and James Hopkins. Damages and costs were awarded against Connor and Hopkins. Macken was also successful in a case against James Hopkins for destruction of his fences. John Connor failed in an action against John Macken to recover money for work done by him for Macken. A case taken by Anne Macken against John Connor for the recovery of wages was however successful. John Connor was also ordered to pay damages and costs in four cases taken against him by Patrick Connor for trespass by his livestock. The 12/- Patrick Connor recovered went a long way towards covering the judgment for 18/8 that Thomas F. Rutledge, Collector of Cess Rates, obtained against him later that day. Rutledge obtained judgments in the same amount against John Kelly, John Garvey and Thomas Dunne who lived nearby in Logaphuill. In the autumn of 1883 Patrick Connor took five cases against John Connor for trespass by livestock and damage to crops. He was successful in three of the cases and subsequently in a case against Thomas Garvey. Garvey was also successfully sued for trespass by Patrick Macken and Macken in turn obtained damages and costs against Patrick Connor for trespass.

What event or series events caused the tenants at Tully to turn against each other and against their own families? The answer is not apparent. What is known is that economic and social conditions had begun to seriously deteriorate in the late 1870s. Elderly people with no family support and people with large young families such as James and Mary Hopkins, John and Bridget Garvey and Patrick and Mary Connor would undoubtedly have found it difficult to feed their families and pay rent and rates as well. The market for livestock had declined and seasonal work in England and Scotland was not available to the extent that it had in the past. There is evidence that tenants from Tully travelled to England for seasonal employment. In the period between Griffiths Valuation of 1856- 1857 and 1880 the land in Tully was sub-divided with the arrival of several outsiders and to accommodate children who did not choose to emigrate. More farmers with more livestock farming the same area of land with no defined fences must have contributed to tensions in the village. It is likely that once one of the tenants had recourse to the courts it had a snowball effect and the tenants got used to making the trip by road to the courts at Ballyglass and Castlebar. The number of cases taken by Rate Collector Rutledge against tenants for recovery of rates would also suggest that tenants were struggling financially.

Clogherowan, Parish of Drum: 1883

Clogherowan is a townland of just over 145 acres in the parish of Drum east of Tully. From the mid 19th Century at least, Clogherowan was occupied and farmed by the people of Tully. In the distant past the area was known as Cowan's Stony Land. The various Censuses from 1841 show that there has been no habitation in Clogherowan since 1841 and there is no evidence of dwellings but it is undoubtedly an ancient place. In the 1980s author James O'Connor and Martin Connor discovered a section of Norman Chain Mail Armour on family land in the townland. The find was acquired by the National Museum. An old road traverses the bogs and woodlands of Clogherowan and this road is specifically mentioned in the Ordinance Survey Books of 1837. Notwithstanding various reclamation projects long stretches of this road still survive today lost in the trees.

The road has not been used in living memory but is clearly visible running through the trees between two parallel moss covered low limestone walls. At intervals there are stone structures that local farmers identify as rudimentary sheep pens.

Logaphuill, Parish of Ballyhean: 1883

The Western part of the townland of Logaphuill lies in the Parish of Ballyhean, the eastern part in the Parish of Drum.[60] The border is overlooked by the Monument at Frenchill erected to commemorate the events of 1798. In 1883 Gardiner inherited ten tenements in the part of Logaphuill that lies in the Parish of Ballyhean. A list of tenants is included at Appendix I. The ten tenements fell into three groups.[61] The first was a rundale holding at what is today the junction of the Cottage Road and the main Castlebar- Belcarra road. The tenants, Walter Mc Nally, Patrick Beirne, Patrick Hopkins and Oliver Canton, occupied an area of just over 45 acres and each had a house on the holding. The second group of houses was at the junction of the Castlebar road and the road to Errew at Frenchill, known today as Frenchill Crossroads. Here the tenants, Thomas Ward and John Ward occupied a rundale holding of just over 32 acres and each had a house. Apart from the two rundale holdings there were three separate tenements making up the third group. They were held by Julia Walsh (over 27 acres), Robert Nesbitt McAdams and Mary Reilly. Again each had a house. The McAdams holding is noteworthy as it comprised an area of just over 130 acres. A map based on the authors' local knowledge and showing actual or likely location of tenant homes in 1883 is shown below.

Logaphuill, Parish of Drum: 1883

In 1883 the Eastern part of the townland of Logaphuill comprised of just over 215 acres of land divided between 26 tenants.[62] There was in addition one freeholder, James Fallon. At Coachfield Charles Daly leased just over 8 acres. The valuation attributed to the Daly house and buildings was considerably higher than the valuation given to any other buildings in the area and suggests that Charles Daly occupied one of the better houses on the Belcarra Estate. Daly also leased a holding across the road in the townland of Gortaruaun. In the context of the arrival of Gardiner two other tenants require a mention namely Thomas Dunne and Charles Cardy. Dunne leased land and a house close to Coachfield. Robert Cardy leased a house and garden occupied by his elderly and widowed mother, Bridget Cardy. A list of tenants in the Townlands of Logaphuill and Gortaruaun is set out at Appendix I.

Other Townlands on the Belcarra Estate: 1883

Other townlands on the Belcarra Estate where evictions were carried out and houses levelled included Elmhall near the village of Belcarra and Tully Beg near the village of Errew. A list of tenants for both of these townlands is shown at Appendix I.

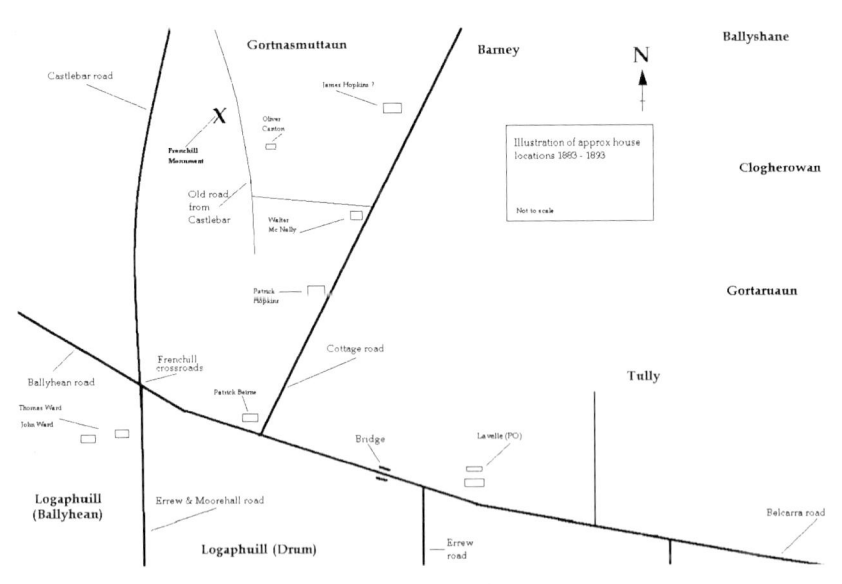

Part III

James Daly, the Land League & the Land War in Mayo

Policy & Legislative Change

The tenants should avail themselves of the Land Act, not such fools as to trust themselves to the mercy of the landlords or Land Leaguers. Resolutions should be passed expressing confidence in J. Daly and O'Connor Power, and calling on Parnell to purge the Executive of such men as Louden and a lot of other greedy vultures.[63]

The Land Acts

To put what happened on the Belcarra Estate into the broader context it is necessary to outline briefly some of the wider policy and legislative changes that were unfolding in the latter part of the 19th Century in response to Irish demands for change. Between 1870 and 1909 the Government introduced several major legislative measures to address the plight of tenant farmers in Ireland. Initial enactments were largely ineffective and by the time more progressive and effective schemes were introduced, Irish tenant farmers and their representative organisations had changed the nature of their demands and were no longer seeking enhanced tenant rights, they wanted ownership of the land. Since the Famine there had been an improvement in social and economic conditions but nationalism had reared its head once again. The fear of Fenian violence and political expediency motivated some to embrace the Irish Question. Foremost amongst these men was William Gladstone.

The Landlord & Tenant (Ireland) Act 1870

The Landlord & Tenant (Ireland) Act 1870 was a weak, complex and largely ineffective piece of legislation. To secure its passage through the House of Commons and House of Lords, Gladstone crafted a Bill that was so conservative it passed both houses with minimal opposition. The Act purported to confer compensation for improvements on the surrender of a lease, compensation for eviction or disturbance in circumstances other than non payment of rent and a mechanism to enable tenants to access Government funding to acquire their freehold but only where the landlord was willing to sell. Prevailing customs were also given the force of law. The Bill when introduced provided that rents must not be *"excessive"*. By the time the bill had become law *"exorbitant"* had been substituted for *"excessive"* thus enabling landlords to increase rent significantly and secure eviction orders when the tenant could not pay. The *"Report of her Majesty's Commissioners of Enquiry into the working of the Landlord and Tenant (Ireland) Act of 1870 and the acts amending the same"* more commonly known as the Bessborough Commission concluded that the 1870 Act was largely ineffective.

The Land Law (Ireland) Act 1881

In 1881 a second measure was introduced to give tenants greater security but by this time a severe economic depression had taken hold. Gladstone suggested that the new measure, the Land Law (Ireland) Act 1881, would make landlordism impossible but tenants had moved on and wanted ownership. The Act established the Land Commission and a Land Court. The former advanced money over a 35 year period to enable tenants to purchase their freehold, the latter enabled tenants to go to court to seek a rent reduction. The Act was amended by the Arrears Act 1882 and in 1885, in response to constant land agitation, the Irish Land (Purchase) Act 1885, otherwise known as the Ashbourne Act, was introduced. This instrument further enhanced tenant purchase powers and with each new enactment the number of tenants availing of funds to purchase their holding increased albeit slowly. All the time land agitation and the Plan of Campaign against landlords continued and further concessions were obtained in the form of the Purchase of Land (Ireland) Act 1891 otherwise known as the Balfour Land Act. The Wyndham Land (Purchase) Act 1903 followed and the number of tenants acquiring their tenements grew. Under the Balfour Land Act the Congested Districts Board was established to promote agriculture on the western seaboard and to amalgamate uneconomic land holdings by purchasing land. The transition from landlordism to full tenant ownership on the Belcarra Estate is a case study in the application or indeed misapplication of this body of legislation. Tenants and their lawyers sought to rely on the new measures as they were introduced to avoid eviction, secure reductions in rent and ultimately purchase the freehold to the land from the Congested Districts Board and the Land Commission.

Coercion Acts

Not all of the legislation introduced in this period was aimed at addressing the concerns of tenants. Legislation was also introduced with the objective of suppressing agitation in Ireland. One such enactment introduced by Gladstone was the Protection of Persons & Property Act 1881. This act and other anti-coercion measures were the subject of heated debate at so called *monster meetings* at Belcarra, Rosslahan, Tully, Frenchill and elsewhere on the Belcarra Estate during this period. The 1881 Act and other criminal legislation was aimed at suppressing organisations such as the National Land League of Mayo, its successor the Irish National League and the United Irish League founded by William O' Brien at Westport in 1898.

JAMES DALY

"I am a Land Leaguer myself, and I would not be a Land Leaguer if it had anything behind it like revolution. I would fight against it."[64]

James Daly: 1838

James Daly, the eldest of eight children, was born in Boghadoon near Lahardane, County Mayo sometime between 1838 and 1841. After his birth the family moved to Coachfield in the townland of Logaphuill about two miles from Belcarra and a few hundred meters from the village of Tully. His father Charles was a farmer and bailiff on the Belcarra Estate of Colonel St. George Cuffe. At Coachfield Charles Daly farmed 48 acres held under a lease from Cuffe. James Daly was educated by the Christian brothers at Errew Monastery a short distance from Coachfield.

Daly the Landholder: 1864

Little is known about Daly's early life. According to Feingold, he leased a farm from Harriet Gardiner at Ballyshane, Breaghwy during the 1860s.[65] This however is not strictly correct. Daly did rent land at Ballyshane in 1864 but not from Harriet Gardiner. Under a lease dated 24 February 1864, Daly leased just over 79 acres of land from Colonel St. George Cuffe at Ballyshane for a term of 31 years at a rent of £50. Up to that point the land had been leased by Michael Irwin of Ballyshane. On 28 November 1881, Daly took a new and longer lease from Cuffe for a term of three lives and 31 years, and significantly in the context of what was to happen at Belcarra, at a substantially reduced rent of £42.8s. Many years later in 1905 Daly would seek to have the rent reduced even further.[66] In that context he told the court at Castlebar that he had spent £185 on improvements to the land at Ballyshane.

Daly did not live at Ballyshane. The land he rented there was used for grazing cattle. There is evidence that his relationship with his neighbours at Ballyshane was not good and he frequently pursued them in the courts for trespass by their livestock. In November 1864 at Castlebar Petty Sessions he secured an order for damages and costs against William and Patrick Hynes for trespass by their sheep. The following month he obtained a similar order at Castlebar Petty Sessions against John Irwin. Irwin's cows had trespassed on Daly's lands. In May 1870, Daly had six cases for trespass by sheep against Ann Staunton. Staunton did not make an appearance at the hearing. In September 1873 Honoria Quinn took a case against Daly for trespass and cutting and taking grass from her land at Ballyshane. This time Daly did not appear. In December 1875 Daly had two cases for trespass against William Hynes at Castlebar Petty Sessions but Hynes did not put in an appearance.

Daly acquires the Connaught Telegraph: 1876
In 1869 Daly secured a seat on the Castlebar Board of Guardians and he became more and more outspoken in defence of tenants rights. In 1874 he succeeded his father Charles as a Poor Law Guardian for the Litterbrick Division in the Ballina Union.[67] Significantly in the context of what was to happen on Gardiner's Belcarra Estate, Daly was also the owner, editor and publisher of the Connaught Telegraph which he acquired together with Alfred O'Hea in 1876. Daly became the sole owner in 1879 when O'Hea died. Having taken control of the paper Daly made it the publicity mouthpiece of the Mayo-based land movement. Daly was also a town councillor in Castlebar.

Mayo Tenants' Defence Association: 1878
On 26 October, 1878 the Mayo Tenants' Defence Association was formed at Castlebar. Westport barrister J.J. Louden became Chairman and James Daly was appointed Secretary. John O'Connor Power MP was also in attendance. A few weeks later on 3 November Charles Stuart Parnell joined Daly, O'Connor Power, James Kilmartin and Matt Harris at the Ballinasloe Tenants' Defence Association meeting.

The Beginning of the Land War: April 1879

The Land War in Mayo began at a meeting held on Sunday, 20 April 1879, at Irishtown in County Mayo. James Daly's announcement in the *Connaught Telegraph* read:

> On to-morrow (Sunday) a mass meeting of the tenant farmers of Mayo, Galway, and Roscommon will be held at Irishtown for the purpose of representing to the world the many and trying ordeals and grievances the tenant farmers labour under. There will be several leading gentlemen present who will speak on the occasion, amongst whom will be John O'Connor Power, Esq., M.P., John Ferguson, Esq. Glasgow, and J.J. Louden, Esq. Westport. The meeting, it is considered, will be one of the largest ever held in Connaught.

Economic and social conditions in Mayo and Ireland significantly deteriorated in the period from 1877 to 1879. The prospect of another famine started to become a reality when the harvest failed in 1879. Cattle prices declined dramatically and prolonged periods of very cold and wet weather prevented the harvesting of grain, potatoes and fodder for livestock. The wet weather also made the drying of peat for fuel impossible. The Dublin Mansion House Committee reported:

> The harvest was the worst since the famine years. Two-thirds of the potato-crop were rotted and gone, and 250,000 people, to whom it was the staff of life, would, by the beginning of the new year, be without food or the means of buying it; 500,000 people more stood upon the verge of ruin.[68]

According to the Preliminary Report on the Returns of Agricultural Produce in Ireland in 1879, the potato yield in Mayo fell from 5.1 tons per statute acre in 1876 to 1.8 tons per statute acre in 1878. The fall in cattle prices left tenants short of cash to pay rent an issue addressed in the Connaught Telegraph in the spring of 1879:

> The Balla spring fair, held on Wednesday last, was fairly supplied with cattle in fair condition, but the prices that could be obtained were far from being remunerative to the seller. There was a fair attendance of buyers, but the majority left without buying a 'tail' to use a jobbers' phrase.[69]

Income from abroad also fell significantly during this period as a result of the drop in demand for Irish labourers in England and Scotland where economic conditions were also poor. The Dublin Mansion House Committee highlighted the collapse in available credit as a major contributing factor. Famine had initially been staved off by the existence of credit extended by food suppliers. But as time passed the traders could no longer advance food on credit. They were facing financial ruin because the tenants were unable to pay their debts.[70] In Mayo there were instances of typhus in the human population and cholera was destroying the poultry and pig populations. While some landlords responded positively to the calls from James Daly and others to abate rents, many large land owners did not.

The Irishtown Meeting: April 1879

There is some debate as to whether the Irishtown meeting was the idea of Davitt or Daly.[71] Whatever the truth of the matter the demonstration achieved its stated purpose locally when landlord Canon Burke desisted in his drive to evict tenants on his estate and reduced rents. The demand for similar demonstrations across Mayo and Ireland grew. As to the meeting itself the Connaught Telegraph reported:

> Since the days of O'Connell a larger public demonstration has not been witnessed than that of Sunday last. About 1 o'clock the monster procession started from Claremorris, headed by several thousand men on foot – the men of each district wearing a laurel leaf or green ribbon in hat or coat to distinguish the several contingents. At 11 o'clock a monster contingent of tenant-farmers on horseback drew up in front of Hughes's hotel, showing discipline and order that a cavalry regiment

might feel proud of. They were led on in sections, each having a marshal who kept his troops well in hand. Messrs. P.W. Nally, J.W. Nally, H. French, and M. Griffin, wearing green and gold sashes, led on their different sections, who rode two deep, occupying, at least, over an Irish mile of the road. Next followed a train of carriages, brakes, cars, etc. led on by Mr. Martin Hughes, the spirited hotel proprietor, driving a pair of rare black ponies to a phæton, taking Messrs. J.J. Louden and J. Daly. Next came Messrs. O'Connor, J. Ferguson, and Thomas Brennan in a covered carriage, followed by at least 500 vehicles from the neighbouring towns.[72]

Davitt & Parnell in Westport: June 1879
A meeting in Westport on 8 June 1879, chaired by Daly, was addressed by Michael Davitt and Charles Stuart Parnell. On 16 August of that year Daly became vice-president of the new National Land League of Mayo and he was elected to the committee of the Irish National Land League founded in Dublin on 21 October. On 2 November, 1879 Davitt addressed a land meeting at Gurteen, County Sligo, stating: *"...the time has come when the manhood of Ireland will spring to its feet and say it will tolerate this system no longer."* Daly added that *"if anyone was evicted it was the duty of his fellows to assemble in their thousands and reinstate him the next day."* James Bryce Killen concluded his speech by wishing that *"everyone at the meeting were armed with a rifle."* On 19 November Daly, Davitt, and Killen were arrested on a charge of using seditious language. Their arrest led to mass protest meetings and Parnell used it to launch a propaganda drive in Britain and the United States. The three were not convicted at their trial. Davitt, Daly and Killen became known as *"The Gurteen Three"*. In April 1881 Daly was imprisoned again, this time in Galway under the Coercion Act but he was released a few weeks later.

Daly addressing a Meeting at the Town Hall Sligo after his release on Bail. (The graphic, 6 December 1879: reproduced with the kind permission of Mayo County Library, Castlebar).

Outside the Assizes Court Sligo during the Trial of the Gurteen Three (The graphic, 6 December 1879: reproduced with the kind permission of Mayo County Library, Castlebar).

James Daly & The Land League: 1879–1882

With the passage of time Daly became dissatisfied with the League and with the manner in which it was managed. He gradually sought to disassociate himself from it and its executive and began to openly criticise it. Moran lists a number of reasons why Daly openly challenged the League.[73] In the context of events at Belcarra, Daly repeatedly criticised the League for failing to financially support evicted tenants and their families. In March 1882 he formally broke his ties and disassociated himself with his own role in the establishment of the League:

> Time was when I had hoped that something good might come of it. I was young and inexperienced then, and I had as little idea of the wire pulling and trickery by which a few of the nineteenth century artful dodgers can deceive millions, as they have of the honesty or fair dealing between themselves and the same deluded millions.[74]

The Irish National Land League became the flagship organisation for tenant rights up to 1882 when it was replaced by the Irish National League. From its foundation in 1898, the United Irish League targeted large land holders and graziers and called for a redistribution of land amongst small tenants. The UIL was very active on the Belcarra Estate in the early part of the 20th Century and became a thorn in the side of the political ambitions of James Daly.

The Rosslahan Demonstration

The depressed and disheartening state of affairs as presented at the Balla fair ...is a rather gloomy foreboding that the price of cattle is still likely to come lower. The consequent result will be that the value of land must descend in the same ratio....There is no alternative left the grazier and the tiller of the soil but to call on the land owners to abate their rents.[75]

The Rosslahan Demonstration: January 1881

Rosslahan is a small townland close to the village of Belcarra. On Sunday 31 January 1881 a large meeting was held there to protest against coercion laws.[76] There was a significant police presence and a government reporter at the meeting. John Barrett, a tenant farmer and chairman of the meeting, argued that it was only by peaceful and determined action that tenant farmers would succeed in their cause. The Freemans Journal reported:

> Mr. James Daly said that coercion laws instead of effecting the end of suppressing outrages would only tend to increase them. The outrages he said were the productions of the heated brains of Ireland's inveterate enemies. He proposed that it is the opinion of this meeting that coercion laws instead of putting a stop to outrages will only increase them. As landlords will avail themselves of the coercive measures.... being placed at their disposal by the Government to exact unjust rents, and evict tenants for nonpayment of exorbitant rents, we hereby say that it will be the means of creating a civil war in Ireland.[77]

Daly's resolution was seconded by Thomas Lally and passed as was the following resolution proposed by Thomas Kearns from Belcarra and seconded by H. Walshe:

> That we shall accept no settlement of the land question as satisfactory that will not make the tillers of the soil the owners thereof, and until such settlement we pledge ourselves not to pay more than Griffith's valuation.

The Freemans Journal reported that the following resolutions were also unanimously passed:

> That we hereby pledge ourselves never to take land from which a tenant has been evicted for the non –payment of an unjust and exorbitant rent, and not to buy from or sell to or hold any intercourse with any man who shall take such land. That if the Government pass unjust measures, which may aid landlordism to extort excessive rents, or to attempt to evict the tenant for the non –payment of any rents over Griffith's valuation, we pledge ourselves not to pay any rent, and if they succeed through coercive measures to evict the tenants that not one will be found to take those lands from which tenants will be evicted.

In light of the events that would follow the arrival of Harriet Gardiner, the resolutions passed at the Rosslahan meeting are very significant. Daly and the others present on that afternoon had set down a framework for dealing with unjust rents, eviction, vacated lands and *"grabbers"*. It is unlikely that any one present that day could have imagined that what had been decided would in a very short time be robustly tested on the Belcarra Estate. At that time however, the only connection between events at Belcarra and Farmhill was to be found in the Preston Guardian which reported:

> An orange expedition from the North arrived on Monday morning at Killala, and effected the relief of Miss Harriet Gardiner, of Farmhill House, who has been for some weeks past "Boycotted". All were fully equipped and armed with modern weapons. A Balla telegram states that the meeting which was announced to be held to-morrow at Rasslassan crossroads near that town has been prohibited.[78]

Part IV

The Reign of Gardiner & Pringle at Belcarra Begins

Gardiner's Inheritance

It is to be hoped that Miss Gardiner will see the wisdom of settling with her tenants, and save them and herself an enormous heap of legal expenses. She must bear in mind that the law has been considerably changed since the days of Farmhill and Deonadobe evictions. She will find some difficulty in rooting out the Belcarra tenantry, thanks to the passing of the Land Act.[79]

A Flawed Legacy: March 1883

When Gardiner took over the Belcarra Estate following Cuffe's death she discovered that the rent collected by Cuffe's agent Baxter was considerably less than the rent collected by his predecessor George Acton. A further difficulty encountered by Gardiner was that a number of 31 year leases granted by George Cuffe and which were due to expire in 1885 had been replaced by new longer leases at reduced rents in the years leading up to his death. One such new lease was granted to James Daly. On 28 November 1881, Daly exchanged his 31 year lease granted in 1864 at a rent of £50 for a new lease with a term of three lives and 31 years and at a substantially reduced rent of £42.8s. Gardiner immediately sought to challenge the validity of the leases.

Evictions at Carramore & Doonadoba: June 1883

Before Gardiner could concentrate on matters at Belcarra she had unfinished business at Ballycastle. On Friday 1 June 1883 Gardiner and Pringle assisted by Sheriff's Deputy Rodgers, a number of bailiffs and police carried out a series of evictions at Carramore and Doonadoba near Ballycastle. At Carramore the families of John Tige (a silver haired man nearly eighty years of age), Martin Mc Hale and Pat Kelly were evicted before Gardiner moved on to Doonadoba. There Martin Gouldin, James Mac Gurran and the Widow Duffey were turned out of their homes and the doors were fastened with padlocks. The Connaught Telegraph carried a detailed account of the evictions and there is no doubt that any tenants at Belcarra reading the account must have been concerned.[80]

Gardiner Assaults Pringle: June 1883

In June 1883 the Connaught Telegraph under the heading *"A Striking Display of Affection"* reported that Gardiner's escort Sub-constable Wynne came before W.H. Faussette, JP and Captain W.H. Bourke at Ballycastle Petty Sessions to apply for a summons against Gardiner for having, in his presence, committed an assault on Pringle. The details of the assault are not recorded but the magistrates refused to entertain the application.[81]

George Thompson Appointed Agent: July 1883

When George Cuffe died there were between 350 and 400 tenants on the Belcarra Estate.[82] Gardiner now set about taking control of her new property and appointed George Thompson of Ballina as her agent. The appointment was announced by the Connaught Telegraph noting that Thompson was, at that time, under police protection.[83]

The Connaught Telegraph made much of the fact that the relationship between the tenants on the Belcarra Estate and the Cuffe family going back to the days of James Cuffe, the first Lord Tyrawley, was so harmonious that the services of a policeman was never before required by a land agent. This is not however entirely correct and there is evidence that the Cuffe family did resort to the courts and eviction. Forty years earlier in January 1843, Colonel St. George Cuffe obtained decrees for possession at Castlebar January Sessions against Michael Walsh, Pat Mullins, Rose and Walter Walsh and fifteen others.[84]

James Daly undoubtedly knew what the arrival of Gardiner would mean for the tenants on the Belcarra Estate. His involvement with the Land League, Ballina Board of Guardians and the Connaught Telegraph meant that he was fully aware of what had happened at Farmhill. A Correspondent in the Connaught Telegraph had the following to say about the change in the regime at Belcarra:

We trust that the change of ownership, through the lamented death of the late Colonel Cuffe will not strain those friendly relations hitherto existing. If ever the Gordian knot is severed, it will not be found to be the fault of the tenants, and if ever it does, we believe that those tenants ever unaccustomed to anything but peace and unity with their landlords, will be found of sterner stuff than the class of white slaves this new land agent and her ladyship were accustomed to. We have no reason to anticipate that there will be any cause of disruption. On the contrary, we may, by way of advice, say, we trust there will be no cause given on either side. As far as we can learn, the Belcarra tenants are prepared to meet their landlord fairly, but that they are determined not to take grinding.[85]

Gardiner Calls for Payment of Rent: September 1883

But cause was given as Daly undoubtedly believed it would be and the resolutions passed at the Rosslahan Meeting would now be tested. By September 1883 Gardiner would appear to have dispensed with the services of Thompson and was acting as her own *"agent, bailiff, bill poster."*[86] She called for payment of rent for the period from November 1882 up to the end of May 1883. In the time of Cuffe the rent for this part of the year was not collected until November or December giving tenants time to harvest their crops and raise money. As the crops were still in the ground many tenants could not pay the rent demanded by Gardiner in September. For those that could pay, Gardiner was unwilling to give a receipt for the full period so the tenants refused to pay. The reason for this would seem to be connected with the fact that all but two months of the rent demanded related to the period before the death of Cuffe and was therefore due to his widow and not to Gardiner. Gardiner was also unwilling to grant the abatement that Cuffe and Baxter had granted in prior years. The following month Gardiner took legal proceedings for recovery of rent against several hundred tenants on the Belcarra Estate.[87]

Rent Office at Castlebar: October 1883

Notwithstanding that she had commenced legal proceedings against a large number of tenants Gardiner decided to hold a two day Rent Office at Castlebar. Tenants who had already received a civil bill attended in large numbers to pay their rent and avoid a court appearance. Pringle was also in attendance but Gardiner abruptly closed the office having taken rent from no more than half a dozen tenants.

Belcarra Tenants in Court: October 1883

On Wednesday 31 October the Belcarra tenants attended a crowded Castlebar Courthouse before J.H. Richards for the hearing of over 200 cases taken by Gardiner against them. In most of the cases the Judge granted decrees for the amount of rent claimed by Gardiner but did not award her costs due to the fact that the tenants had offered to pay the rent to her in advance of the court hearings but Gardiner had not accepted it. It would seem from the report of the proceedings in the Connaught Telegraph that the court was in a state of chaos due to the large number of people present and the fact that dozens of raised hands offering rent could be seen in the court room as the cases were called prompting the Connaught Telegraph to suggest:

> Better she would give the management of her affairs to some well disposed agent who would see justice done her by a tenantry, who do not want to take advantage of one farthing of hers. It is a delusion on her part to think that there is a holding cheaply let on the whole estate.[88]

In a case against John Cunniff of Ballyshane, Gardiner sought payment of £12 but the Court found that the rent had been reduced on the instruction of George Cuffe to £9.10s. Gardiner's lawyer John Garvey argued that the Commissioners had decided on a higher rent in the case of Cunniff but when asked to produce the order of the Commissioners Garvey explained that Gardiner had lost it. Separately Gardiner got a decree for

£9.10s against John Cunniff's brother Michael. The battle between Gardiner and the Cunniff family would continue for the next nine years.

In an action against Pat Staunton of Belcarra, Baxter gave evidence that the rent was £18 per annum but that it had been reduced to £15 per annum by George Cuffe. The Court decided that the rent was £15 but Gardiner refused to accept the lesser amount. An adjournment was granted when Gardiner agreed to pay the costs. Gardiner did not want the Court to uphold the lease at £15. She had obtained a legal opinion that the new leases granted by Cuffe were not valid and she wanted the matter determined by a higher court. Twelve months later Gardiner had Staunton before the High Court seeking £27 rent. Staunton argued that documents existed which showed that the rent had been reduced from £18 to £15. Gardiner sought discovery of these documents.[89]

A case against James Daly broke down into a farce when he threatened to take a case against Gardiner for intimidation. She had threatened to drive the Connaught Telegraph out of Connaught. The Judge suggested that being driven out of Connaught might be a change for the better. Other cases included cases against the deceased J. Blouke, Larry Muldoon and a case against Patrick Corless that was dismissed. The paper once again drew comparisons between the *"humane and generous"* Cuffe on the one hand and Gardiner on the other quoting Gardiner's promise to *"put her foot through"* the favourable leases granted by Cuffe. The correspondent concluded that:

> To our certain knowledge every leaseholder on the estate would be glad to get divorced from the leases and go into the land court to have fair rents fixed had that court due regard for the value of the tenant's labour and improvements.[90]

Gardiner appealed all the cases in which the Judge did not award her costs. Pending the hearing of the appeals at the next sitting of the Court, the Connaught Telegraph had a number of recommendations for the authorities:

> We would recommend that special sessions be appointed for Miss Gardiner; she will also require a special assizes to hear all her appeals. We would recommend her solicitor to apply for police protection, in order to keep the amazon and her jack-in-the-box – Miss Pringle – from gobbling him up entirely. There is one thing certain; the Belcarra tenants are subjected to treatment that they were heretofore unaccustomed to.[91]

Gardiner was not happy with the role played by Baxter in having the rents on the Estate reduced and made this known during the proceedings.

Calm before the Storm: January 1884

Gardiner and Pringle spent December 1883 collecting rents at a rate of three or four tenants per day. Sometime during that month the pair were thrown out of a public house due to their excessive drinking and behavior.[92] Between November 1883 and December 1884 reporting of activities on the Belcarra Estate ceased. It may have been the case that Gardiner and Pringle were focusing their activities elsewhere or that Daly was otherwise preoccupied. The more likely explanation is that there may not have been matters worthy of reporting. In any case this period represented the calm before the storm for the tenants on the Estate and in particular those in the townlands of Tully, Logaphuill and Elmhall. In the eight year period from the end of 1884 the pages of the Connaught Telegraph would be overflowing with tales of intimidation, violence, eviction, imprisonment, death and emigration and much of this would relate to the Belcarra tenants. It is interesting to note that in 1884 the tenants at Tully ceased their pursuit of each other in the courts. The arrival of the strange pair of ladies from North Mayo undoubtedly caught their attention.

An Angel of Darkness[93]

Monday last was as beautiful a spring day as could possibly be desired, but in the townlands of Logafoil and Tully, heart rendering scenes were witnessed that might be well calculated even to "make angels weep" over the callous barbarity of things in human form. For some days previous it had been known that the notorious old Gardiner animal had selected that day for a monster swoop on the tenantry of the above hamlets and had served notice on the board of guardians that she would have no less than thirteen evictions! [94]

Oliver Canton goes to the Workhouse: December 1884

If 1883 was about using the legal system to collect rents that Gardiner seemed reluctant to collect, twelve months later she was using the legal system to pursue what was undoubtedly her true purpose. Towards the end of 1884 she served eviction notices on a significant number of her Belcarra tenants. According to Thomas Ward of Frenchill, a decree for possession was given against him at Westport Petty Sessions in January. He offered to pay one year's rent, amounting to £7, both before and after the hearing but he owed three and a half years rent so Gardiner refused to accept the lesser amount.[95]

In December 1884 the Connaught Telegraph reported that a Frenchill man had voluntarily left his home and gone to the Workhouse at Castlebar.[96] The report does not name the man but it is almost certain that it was Oliver Canton. The Connaught Telegraph reported that the man had said *"he would rather do so than bear to be looking at her, with her police escorts, daily turning the corner at Frenchill."* Gardiner was not however satisfied with Canton's self eviction and was determined to close matters out legally and finally:

> Still the poor man, who evicted himself, and chose the poorhouse for his dreary abode, was not let die in peace even there. The civil bill ejectment (an unpleasant Christmas offering) was presented to him while sheltered from her ire, on

a bed of sickness, under a poorhouse blanket. Folks may talk of the records of landlord tyranny, but this is surely one of the hardest cases yet made public. This self-evicted tenant of Miss Gardiner, flung from her cruelty, is hunted down, literally hounded to death, and served with an ejectment, while under medical care and treatment in that inhospitable palace of grim despair, and on a poorhouse straw pallet. Under these sad circumstances, the wretched man gets his legal death notice, on this close approach to the holy festive season of peace and goodwill to all men.[97]

In the same report the paper highlighted the fact that many tenants believed that Gardiner would not have been as difficult if it were not for the fact that she was, to a certain extent, under the tutelage and influence of Susanna Pringle.[98]

Oliver Canton was born at Frenchill in 1807. In 1840 he married Anne McNally the daughter of his neighbour Walter McNally. They had two daughters, Ann and Elizabeth. Ann's date of birth is not recorded but Elizabeth was christened on 23 May 1852. There is no evidence of further children though other records from the 1860s show that a John and Mary Canton also lived at Frenchill. Oliver Canton was a carpenter and farmed land at Frenchill. Griffiths Valuation shows that he occupied a rundale holding of just over 45 acres at Frenchill with neighbours Walter McNally, Bridget Beirne and Mary Hopkins. As was the case with his neighbours, he was a regular visitor to the Petty Sessions. In September 1859 he took a case against neighbour Thomas Ward for an assault committed at Castlebar on the night of 10 September 1859. The case was heard at Castlebar Petty Sessions and was dismissed on its merits. He was involved in several trespass cases in the 1860s and 1870s. In 1862 he succeeded in a trespass case against neighbour Samuel McAdam. In 1879 he took an unsuccessful legal action against Ellen and Patrick Connor and Mary and Patrick Deacy of Tully for theft of turnips. On 24 October 1880 his daughter Anne married Thomas Davis a Dealer from Thomas Street, Castlebar and it would seem that by 1883 a very elderly Oliver Canton was living alone at Frenchill.

Search for Missing Land at Lakelands, Manulla: January 1885

At some point during 1884 Gardiner engaged John Connor of Tully as her bailiff. The reason for selecting Connor, who at that point was at least sixty five years old, is not known. There is no evidence that he had previously acted as George Cuffe's bailiff though this cannot be ruled out. Perhaps it had come to Gardiner's attention that the tenants at Tully were engaged in their own trespass war and she seized the opportunity to exploit this to her advantage.

In January 1885 the people of Manulla, a short distance from Belcarra, witnessed what was undoubtedly a peculiar entourage making its way through the bitter January weather. Gardiner, Pringle and John Connor accompanied by a number of police including two by the name of Campbell and Hughes embarked on an expedition to locate what the Connaught Telegraph described as a missing piece of land somewhere between Belcarra and Cloonagh.[99] In the bitter January cold and in the midst of a hail storm, the land was located on the north side of the railway track near the bridge that spans the river at Lakelands near Manulla Junction. According to the Correspondent, the land was of little value being *"a small strip or belt of snipe land beautifully situated as a kind of roosting ground for the waterfowl of the surrounding lakes"* and was not likely to yield enough in seven centuries to cover the costs of the expedition including the brandy consumed. Hughes, it was reported got a strip of land for his trouble.

Gardiner Seeks Court Orders for Possession: March 1885

A few weeks later Gardiner sought and obtained Court Orders for possession against several tenants on the Estate for non payment of rent. As was the case in 1883, a number of the tenants had offered to pay some rent but Gardiner refused to accept it.

The cases were heard in late March or early April 1885 and a comprehensive account of the proceedings can be found in the Connaught Telegraph.[100]

Redmond Reilly represented by a lawyer named Tuohy got an adjournment when he explained that there were two sub-tenants in possession of his property. A decree for possession for non payment of rent for two and a half years was granted against Patrick Biggins of Elmhall who it was alleged was seen running from his house to avoid the authorities. Decrees for possession were also granted against Michael Garvey, James Walsh, Pat Bourke, Thomas Ward, Walter Mc Nally, and another tenant named Garvey (most likely John Garvey (Long) of Tully).

The Court also granted a decree against Dominic Bourke who it was alleged had been seen running from his house. In this case Gardiner was asked for more time as Bourke, an old, feeble and deaf man, was not present in Court and was not represented by a lawyer. The Court was told that he had offered to pay one of the two years due but Gardiner refused to accept it. Tenant Thomas Dunne argued that he had transferred his land to Dominick Byrne. This was confirmed by Byrne and his name was added to the ejectment notice. This was the beginning of a protracted struggle between Thomas Dunne and Gardiner, a struggle that would have devastating consequences for Dunne, his wife Catherine and their children.

Notwithstanding that he had evicted himself, a decree for possession was granted against Oliver Canton. He was not in Court as he continued to reside at the Workhouse and the ejectment notice was served on him there. The next case to come before the Court concerned a group of tenants from Tully namely Patrick Macken, Honor Connor, James Hopkins, and Patrick Connor. Honor Conor was possibly the widow of Thomas Connor Snr., listed in Griffiths Valuation and grandmother of Patrick Connor.

The tenants, represented by M.J Kelly, sought to avoid eviction by arguing that Gardiner's bailiff, John Connor, had forcibly taken possession of the Macken's land four years earlier when John Macken went to England to get work. According to Kelly, Connor held forcible possession of the land by building a hay barn, piggery and other buildings on it. Connor testified that he was Gardiner's bailiff; he was 35 years in possession and had never paid a shilling to the Mackens. He explained to the Court that he had been before the Ballyglass Petty Sessions Court over the issue but was not convicted of assault or forcible possession. Mary Macken explained that she was 35 years married and that her husband was in possession of the land until he went to England four years earlier after which John Connor took forcible possession and built a piggery on the land. Patrick Connor gave evidence in support of Mary Macken as did James Hopkins. The Judge held that Gardiner was only suing for the part in Macken's possession. Connor denied holding possession of any Macken land. The decree was granted.

Had John Connor built *"a hay barn, piggery and other buildings on the land"* as was suggested, the new buildings would undoubtedly have had a valuation attributed to them and be included in the Cancellation Books by the Rates Collector. However, no additional buildings appear on the Cancellation Books for Connor or Macken in the period. It is likely that there is a connection between the events of August 1881 when Honour Connor accused John and Ann Connor of assaulting her and taking stones, roofing timber and furniture from her home. The cases against the Connors were dismissed on their merits. Whatever the truth of the matter things were about to get much worse for the Macken, Connor and Hopkins families.

Tully & Logaphuill Evictions: March 1885
Once Gardiner had obtained Court Orders for possession she did not delay enforcement. Four weeks later, on Monday 30 March, Gardiner set about evicting thirteen tenants at Tully and Logaphuill. The events of that day were widely reported in

Ireland and England. The most detailed account is to be found in the Connaught Telegraph.[101] The tenants had advance notice as Gardiner, in accordance with legal requirements, had served notice on the Castlebar Board of Guardians of her intention to carry out the evictions.

The Connaught Telegraph reported that it was a beautiful spring morning when Gardiner and John Rodgers, the Sheriff's Deputy, supported by a large police force from Castlebar, Belcarra and Ballyhean, arrived in Logaphuill. A great crowd of people gradually assembled. According to the report the only violence the crowd resorted to was verbal in nature and was directed towards Gardiner, Pringle and a man named Hoban from Westport who was assisting them in clearing the homes. John Connor, whose role it was to point out the different gardens of the evicted, was also subjected to verbal abuse from the crowd. The Castlebar Board of Guardians was represented by Gordon RO and in the afternoon by James Daly.

The first house visited was that of Oliver Canton. The house, which had no roof, was unoccupied as Canton was still in the Workhouse. Gardiner took possession. This was symbolically achieved by Gardiner taking a handful of clay from Rodgers and handing it to Pringle. At the home of Thomas Ward, Hoban, assisted by a companion, cleared the house and barn. A request to allow Ward and his family to be readmitted as caretakers was refused by Gardiner. Evicted tenants were often readmitted as caretakers. By doing this the landlord sought to change the tenant's status from that of tenant to that of employee. Legislation introduced to protect tenants did not protect employees so that it was considered legally easier to remove a caretaker by dismissing him. The property was locked and Ward and his family were left on the roadside with their furniture. Ward and his family did however re-enter the house sometime after they were evicted. Gardiner and her party then moved on to the home of Paddy Bourke of Logaphuill. Dominic Byrne had an interest in the property and endeavoured to make a deal with Gardiner promising to make a payment when they got to Castlebar. This was refused and the house was cleared. In the evening Dominick Byrne paid the rent of £8. 7s to Rodgers and the family were readmitted.

Bridget Cardy, the widow of Charles Cardy, was next on the schedule. According to the report she lived in a small cottage on waste land at a cross roads. She was, according to the Connaught Telegraph, removed from the cabin in a *"fainting condition,"* and required assistance from neighbours. Gardiner and her entourage then moved down into the village of Tully. The homes of Honor Connor, Patrick Macken, Patrick Connor, James Deacy and John Garvey (Long), (reported to have nine or ten in family), were next to be cleared. The Connaught Telegraph reported that:

> ...the same heart stirring scenes enacted, amid the piercing cries of women and children, and the stern gaze of the assembled multitude, who, of course, could only bestow looks of sympathy, but were powerless to stay the exterminating hand of the ruthless despoiler, who, with her despicable shrivelled-up companion- the once ranting, proselytizing brandy- swilling Pringle- is a filthy caricature on the very name of woman![102]

Two of the children in John Garvey's house were ill and following the intervention of Gordon and Daly the eviction was postponed and the family allowed to return. According to an account given to the Connaught Telegraph by John Garvey some years later, his combined holding at Tully and Clogherowan consisted of about 20 acres at a rent of £ 7. 15s. About 8 acres of the land were fertile; the remainder was covered with rocks and bushes. He owed 2 years rent and 10/- costs at the time of his eviction. He offered to pay one year and the remainder in instalments, but this offer was refused. [103]

At the home of James Hopkins (which the Connaught Telegraph reports was an English mile from Garvey's), three or four of the children were sick. There is a ruined cottage and out buildings in a boggy wooded area on the Cottage Road that was the home of the Hopkins family up to the middle of the 20th Century and this may have been Gardiner's target. Gardiner took the view that the children were *"shamming"* illness and sought to proceed with the eviction. She refused however to enter the cabin to see them in their sick beds and called for a doctor to be sent for. Daly told her that no doctor of the Union would come and if she wanted one she would have to pay his fee herself. The eviction did not take place.

James Daly's arrival at 3pm that afternoon was greeted with immense cheering from the assembled crowd. The day finished with Daly addressing the crowd and telling them:

> ...above all things to avoid anything like a violation of the law, painful as were the proceedings they were called on to witness. Let them blame nobody, but let the lands from which the people had been evicted, remain waste and unoccupied; and Miss Gardiner would be made to see that, by having to pay county cess, and seed and poor rates for them, without receiving any rent, it would be better for her to have dealt reasonably with her poor tenants than have recourse to those harsh measures. Let there be no man got to take another man's holding and thus the lands will remain there idle and waste, useful only to the birds of the air, and the hungry donkeys of the country. Let them remember that not Miss Gardiner, or any one of her class, is their worst enemy-the low, mean, base land-grabber is the person they should most detest, as such wretches are the greatest curses of Ireland and enemies of her people. As they were assembled there on a trying occasion, and for a serious purpose, he would read for them the following resolution, which, he well knew, would meet their views, and for the requirements of which he was sure, they would strictly adhere:

Resolved- That having regard to the attitude taken by Miss Gardiner in putting her many violent threats into execution- by a system of wholesale eviction of her tenants, and persistent refusal to give them any terms, save outside doors, despite their willingness to pay her just rents, we, in public meeting today pledge ourselves to look upon any land grabber, who will take the lands of the evicted upon any terms, as an enemy of his fellow men, and a traitor to the interests of his country.[104]

The resolution was, according to the Connaught Telegraph, received with applause, with all present exclaiming that the land grabber was the enemy of the people.

Time for Redemption not yet Expired: April 1885
The pages of Cancellation Books for the townland of Tully show extensive markings for the period 1885 -1893 as the names of the tenants are struck out and replaced by the name of Harriet Gardiner. In the margin there is a very faint note written in pencil which reads: *"Tenants evicted six months for redemption not yet expired. 29/4/85."*

Gardiner Serves Notice of 13 Evictions: May 1885
In May 1885 the Guardians of the Castlebar Union received notice that Gardiner intended to evict thirteen tenants on the Belcarra Estate. Gardiner was required by law to give notice to the Guardians in advance of any evictions.[105] One of the tenants included on the list was Thomas Dunne of Logaphuill. An error was however made in preparing the Notice and Dunne's address was given as Tully. The error would be the subject of court proceedings almost two years later in January 1887. The Dunne house was actually located near a small group of houses across the fields from the Daly residence at Coachfield.

The Case of John Connor's Sheep: June 1885
The next instalment in the struggle between the Connors and the Mackens was the subject of a lengthy satirical letter to the

Editor of the Connaught Telegraph in June 1885.[106] The letter is signed *"Your obedient servant, Frenchill."* The satirical style and some of the references in the letter suggest that the author may have been James Daly himself. In light of his role as Gardiner's bailiff it is not surprising that John Connor should have had concerns for his safety and the safety of his family. In the course of 1885 Connor was subjected to several scathing attacks in the form of letters to the Connaught Telegraph and also in reports written by Connaught Telegraph correspondents. The letter of June 1885 deals with an incident that occurred on a warm Sunday morning in early June when John Connor discovered one of his sheep dead. His suspicions immediately turned to his neighbours. On finding the animal dead the letter tells us that Connor went to Belcarra in a state of extreme agitation calling on the sergeant of police for protection. The allegation was that the sheep had been killed by his neighbours or, as was suggested in the Connaught Telegraph, by the people that he had assisted Gardiner in evicting the previous month. According to the letter Connor believed that he would be next.

The matter was reported to the police in Castlebar and at 3pm District Inspector Moore and the police arrived in Tully. The scene and dead sheep were examined and, according to the letter (and this is where reality may have been abandoned), it was decided that a post mortem should be carried out on the dead animal. VS Ryan and the O'Connor family butcher were sent for. A jury was assembled with Patrick Macken as foreman. The sheep was dissected but no external wound could be discovered so it was concluded that the animal had died of old age. According to the letter Patrick Macken disagreed with the coroner's verdict suggesting instead that the sheep was too well fed on the grass of the evicted tenants land. It was also suggested that the complaint against the tenants was motivated by a desire to claim compensation from the authorities for malicious damage perpetrated against Connor's property. Did the letter record actual events or an embellished version of events or was it simply intended as a message to John Connor to mend his ways and end his association with Gardiner? If the latter, John Connor did not get the message, at least not yet.

Patrick Macken & John Connor: June-August 1885
Matters came to a head between the Mackens and the Connors later that month. A lengthy letter from the *"O'Beirne"* Frenchill to the Editor of the Connaught Telegraph informed him that Patrick Macken had clashed with John Connor and his son over cattle grazing on evicted lands. Macken was, according to the letter, saved by the intervention of his wife Mary and daughter. It is clear from the letter that the tenants, including the Mackens, were sheltering in their evicted homes which were now without doors. But the time for redemption had not yet passed and the O'Beirne accused John Connor of acting prematurely in trying to seize the lands for grazing. It suggested that Patrick Macken would seek redress in the courts against John Connor and his son and this he did.[107]

On Wednesday 1 July Patrick Macken had two cases for assault against John Connor at Ballyglass Petty Sessions. The alleged assaults were stated to have occurred at Tully on 15 June. The cases were adjourned but came up for hearing again on Wednesday 12 August when the Court dismissed both cases. The 22 August Edition of the Connaught Telegraph published another lengthy letter to the Editor from *"The O.B. Frenchill"* on the subject of the case. According to the author the case was dismissed due to the lack of evidence, the wounds were healed and the bloodstains washed out of the Macken's clothes.

The Belcarra Grabber: July 1885
In July 1885 a Belcarra tenant wrote to the Editor of the Connaught about a man who had *"graduated from the crowbar brigade of Mr. Thomas Ormsby"* and who had tried to purchase the farm of George Coghlan, Belcarra. Gardiner had advertised the land for sale to recover arrears of rent.[108] The attempt to purchase the lands was not successful.

Malicious Injuries: July 1885

Later that month a number of claims for compensation for malicious injuries and damage came before the courts. Gardiner sought compensation in respect of a house on her estate that had been burned down. The tenant had disputed the amount of the rent but had left for America and Gardiner took over the 35 acres and house. The tenant's name is not reported. In a separate action James Philbin sought compensation for three sheep that had been stabbed and beaten about the head. Philbin was under police protection as he had taken the holding of an evicted tenant. Compensation was awarded in both cases.[109]

The Trial of Bridget Cardy, Logaphuill: July 1885

On Wednesday 29 July Gardiner and Pringle were back at Ballyglass Petty Sessions for another court appearance of the widow Bridget or Biddy Cardy. Cardy had been evicted on 30 March and was, according to the Connaught Telegraph, a woman in her eighties who had spent most of her life in the cabin.[110] Following her eviction she had re-entered her home to shelter from the wind and rain and was now in court for this offence. Gardiner's lawyer MJ Kelly explained that many of the tenants evicted in March had re-entered their homes. John Rodgers, assistant to the Deputy Sheriff, testified that he had been present when Cardy was evicted on 30 March and that she had strongly resisted arguing that the land was not part of Gardiner's Estate. The house was on a triangular plot at a cross roads and was separate from the land which was in a different townland.[111] M.J. Jordan, lawyer for Cardy, argued that the cabin was not part of Gardiner's land and was in a different townland. The entry on the Cancellation Books would support the conclusion that the house was not indeed part of Gardiner's Estate. Colonel Blake and Major Neild choose to avoid the complicated issue of ownership and sided with Gardiner finding that if Cardy had been wrongly evicted in the first instance she should take proceedings against the Sheriff. In the end Cardy was given the choice of six hours in prison or a fine of 1d. She elected to pay the fine.

Arrest & Imprisonment of Tully Women: August 1885

Three weeks later in August the police were back in Tully in force. The tenants evicted in March were back in their homes and Gardiner was intent on clearing them. After the evictions some of the men had gone to England to raise money to redeem their homes and land. The women and children left behind sought refuge in their houses once the police had left the scene. The Connaught Telegraph reported that a number of women, children and one man, were taken to the police barracks in Belcarra leaving behind young children without food or anyone to care for them. In the absence of the men it was suggested that their crops were at the mercy of the bailiff's cattle.[112]

A letter to the Editor of the Connaught Telegraph from the *"O.B. Frenchill"* contains further details of the arrests.[113] According to the O.B, John Connor had sought warrants for those who had re-entered their homes following their eviction. The women and children were sleeping at night in the houses and hiding in the ditches during the day to avoid the Belcarra police. On Thursday 20 August, the police ambushed three women in their beds. They were arrested and taken along with an infant and an eighteen month child, in an awaiting car to the police barracks at Belcarra and on to Towerhill for a bail hearing. The women arrested were Mary Macken, Catherine Deacy and Mary Connor, wife of Patrick Connor, and her two young children. All would, according to the OB, have gone to jail if they had not been bailed by a *"kind hearted neighbor."* Instead they were ordered to appear at Ballyglass Petty Sessions the following Wednesday. The letter concludes with O.B asking *"Where are Parnell and the Land League? And what are they doing for the poor evicted creatures? might be fair questions to ask."* The identity of the *"O.B. Frenchill"* is not revealed. The style of the letters written suggests that they were all written by a single person and it is likely that this person was James Daly himself. The only other obvious candidate by virtue of his name is Patrick Beirne who lived at Frenchill.

On 26 August at Ballyglass Petty Sessions, Mary Connor, Catherine Deacy and Mary Macken were each fined 5/- and ordered to pay costs. In the alternative they would each spend seven days in Castlebar Prison. They were given one week to come up with the money. According to the O.B., jail was the outcome but the tenants would return to their homes afterwards. In the course of the Court hearing John Connor gave evidence that the women were sleeping in the houses at night. In yet another letter to the Editor of the Connaught Telegraph, the OB gave the following account of the proceedings:

> The Pringle hag kept, jack-in-the-box like, jumping up and down in her seat the whole time, grinning and working her worn out chops, much after the fashion of a Cheshire cat mumbling at sour cheese, and all the time nodding at the bench, who seemed to take no notice at all of her. This whole time the Gardiner hag seemed to be just recovering from a fit of somnolence, evidently brought on by the long drive from Farmhill to Ballina, the shaking of the train to Balla, and the jostling of the rickety car to Ballyglass – or, perhaps she was suffering inwardly for the want of a "hair" from "the dog" that had bitten her late the previous night, or early that same morning.[114]

On 9 September the Connaught Telegraph published a third letter from the OB telling the Editor that the women were taken by the Belcarra police on a two horse car to Castlebar Prison.[115] Mary Connor had an infant child in her arms when she was committed. Her three other children were left behind in the ditches. This suggests that Mary's husband Patrick may have been elsewhere working. OB also explained that Gardiner had purchased the benefit of the judgments previously obtained by the widow of the late George Cuffe against the tenants for non-payment of rent and by doing so now had another whip to beat the tenants with.

The Castlebar Prison Records show that on 8 September three women from Tully; Mary Connor (with an unnamed male child), Mary Macken and Catherine Deacy were committed by John O' Gaye, RM., to seven days imprisonment for the crime of wilful trespass. It was their first time in prison. Mary Connor is described as a woman of 30 years of age, five foot four inches in height with dark hair, grey eyes and a fresh complexion. The child was most likely her son John. Mary Macken is described as a woman of 49 years of age, five feet tall with grey hair, blue eyes and a sallow complexion. Catherine Deacy is described as a woman of 46 years of age, with fair hair, grey eyes and a fresh complexion. All three were Roman Catholics, housekeepers and illiterate. They were released on 14 September and duly returned to their homes because they had nowhere else to go.[116]

Seizure of Connor & Leheen Cattle: August 1885

In August cattle belonging to John Connor and a lady referred to as Biddy Leheen by the Connaught Telegraph Correspondent were seized by the Rates Collector. Biddy Leheen was the wife of Thomas Garvey. The OB of Frenchill once again felt the need to keep the Editor of the Connaught Telegraph in the picture and for reasons that are not apparent he embarked on a savage attack on Leheen in two letters published in the paper. The letters suggest that Leheen, from Aughagower, believed that she and Pringle shared Scottish ancestry. After the cattle were seized, Leheen could be heard at night, as far away as Frenchill, calling to her father and mother even though they had been dead for ten years:

> ...upbraiding them for ever bringing her with her "big means and fortune of cows and cattle" to be the second- hand wife of a "brock" in Tully "braddagh" [117]

It would seem that following the seizure Leheen made a significant racket in the village. The OB reported that:

During the past week, ever since the cattle seizure, we have a pretty lively time of it here, for the poor dear woman talks in the highest key that could be imagined for 36 hours out of 24. She could be heard at all times to make the valleys ring to Knockspologathaun, with the exuberance of her eloquence – at one time threatening the unfortunate tenants that she will eat the grass of the evicted holdings despite the poor rate collector.

On the night of the seizure she *"serenaded"* the people of main street Castlebar with her threats against the rate collector. These actions did not succeed in getting her cow back. Accompanied by John Connor she went to visit the *"talented and rising lawyer"* Mr. Tuohy who in return for two half crowns examined the relevant laws and wrote a letter *"threatening all sorts of pains and penalties on the poor – rate man"* though with no success. Following this she pleaded directly with the Rate Collector and secured, on payment of a sum of money, the return of the cow. According to OB she regretted not having tried this tactic before paying over the money to the lawyer and pound keeper.

The Rate Collector pursues John Garvey (Long): September 1885

Occupiers of land were liable to pay a rate known as the Grand Jury Cess. The Grand Jury was made up of landowners selected by the County Sheriff. The Grand Jury Cess or rate collected from occupiers was used for works or purposes authorized by the Grand Jury including the construction of public buildings such as court houses, the repair of infrastructure such as roads and the upkeep of hospitals. On 23 September Thomas F. Rutledge, Cess Collector of Castlebar, obtained a judgment at Ballyglass Petty Sessions against John Garvey in the amount of 17/8 plus costs for refusal to pay his Grand Jury Cess.

Belcarra Meeting: October 1885

On Sunday 11 October a mass meeting was held at Belcarra to denounce the activities of Gardiner; to call on the Government to intervene and restrain her; to call on the Government to provide employment for people to help them through the looming depression and finally to call for a reduction in rents.[118] The meeting was chaired by the Balla Parish Priest, Canon E. Gibbons. Also present were Charles Daly, James Daly, Rev. J. Healey and W. Brennan. The full text of Canon Gibbon's speech was reproduced in the Connaught Telegraph which also reported that there was a large contingent from Balla at the meeting together with a fife and drum band.[119] Canon Gibbons instructed the crowd on the subject of boycotting Gardiner and Pringle:

> I do not know anyone in Castlebar, or elsewhere, who would be bound by any law that I know to supply them with anything they may require. Do not touch a hair on their heads. Do not molest them in any way. Do not interfere with them. If your faith and piety be not too much trespassed upon I would even ask you to pray for them. This may be called Boycotting, well I don't admire boycotting, I don't say it is, but even were it so, it violates no law and if you like, at most it would only be an easy remedy for a desperate disease.

James Daly then came forward to deal with the resolutions before the meeting. It was resolved that the Government should restrain Gardiner in her persecution of tenants and introduce a program of works such as arterial drainage as a means of putting money in the pockets of tenants who could not otherwise pay their rents or keep a home over their heads due to the large influx of foreign meat and produce which had the effect of driving down the price of domestic meat and produce and reducing the income of tenants.

The Time for Redemption is Passed: October 1885
Daly's speech at Belcarra specifically addressed the plight of some of the evicted Tully tenants. According to Daly, Mary Macken had been evicted and was now in America. This is likely to be a reference to Mary Macken wife of John Macken, Tully. Castlebar Prison Records show that Mary Macken wife of Patrick Macken, Tully was committed to 7 days imprisonment on 10 October. Her co-tenant could not pay the rent and redeem both holdings and as a consequence would also need to go. His wife an aged woman was in Castlebar jail. Though not referred to by name the co-tenant referred to was Patrick Macken. Reference is also made by Daly to a woman and her baby who were also in Castlebar Prison (the second time since the birth of the child two months earlier). The woman was Mary Connor, the child her infant son John.

Daly also referred to a hearing of Ballyglass Petty Sessions the previous Wednesday 11 October, when Colonel Blake intervened and called for a settlement of the matter between Gardiner and her tenants. Gardiner in response exclaimed: *"No, no, never, the time for redemption is passed, they shan't be let in at all-no, no."* According to Daly, Gardiner had boasted that she had only twelve tenants on the Gardiner Tyrawly estates and she would have as few on the Belcarra Estate. Daly concluded his speech by advocating the observance of peace and order and calling for civil measures and boycotting as the way forward.

Police Raid on Tully: October 1885
Two days after the meeting in Belcarra the police response came. The Connaught Telegraph reported that on Tuesday 13 October, the Belcarra police surrounded the house of William Joyce while the local priest was holding a station for mass and confession.[120] William Joyce's name had been removed from the Cancellation Books many years earlier. It is however likely that the house in question was that occupied by William Joyce's daughter Margaret and her husband Thomas Walsh. While Father Healy was celebrating mass the house was surrounded

and a number of evicted tenants in attendance were arrested. The raid was led by Sergeant McEvoy from Belcarra. Father Healy protested strongly at the timing of the raid and the conduct of the police. The Connaught Telegraph Correspondent likened the activities of the police to those of the notorious Shawn Na Sagarths.[121] Of the five people arrested one subsequently escaped while the remaining four were marched to Towerhill where they were granted bail to appear the following Wednesday at Ballyglass Petty Sessions. A letter to the Editor published in the Connaught Telegraph highlighted the fact that:

> ...public feeling runs very high in the locality over this wantonly insulting piece of contemptible officiousness and people of all creeds and shades of opinion feel ashamed of the conduct of the wretched little "Catholic" sergeant who planned and carried out the surprise in a manner so contemptuously insulting to religion and shamefully outrageous to the feelings of the people. [122]

On 19 October Canon Edward Gibbons wrote to the Freemans Journal complaining about the activities of the police.[123]

John Kelly & Harriet Gardiner: October 1885

The day after the raid the focus of attention moved to Castlebar Petty Sessions. John Kelly took a case against Gardiner and Pringle for assault arising out of a visit by Kelly to Gardiner's Rent Office at Ellison Street, Castlebar. There are two contemporary sources for the events of that day. A letter to the Editor of the Connaught Telegraph in September from the *"The OB Frenchill"*[124] and an extensive report in the Connaught Telegraph. On Wednesday 30 September the case came before D.A Browne and H. Jordan at Ballyglass Petty Sessions but it was adjourned. On Wednesday 14 October the parties and their lawyers were back in court this time at Castlebar Petty Sessions before D.A. Browne and J.F.B Tardy. Kelly was represented by G.F Tuohy, Gardiner by J.C. Garvey. The alleged assault had occurred just over one month earlier on 12 September.

Saturday 12 September was market day in Castlebar. John Kelly made his way from his home to Gardiner's office on Ellison Street to pay six month's rent. The money was taken by Pringle and Kelly left with his receipt in his pocket and made his way down town. After he had departed Pringle sent a messenger, a lady by the name of Margaret Gallagher, to ask Kelly to return. When he arrived back at the office Pringle and Gardiner were there along with their bodyguard Constable Patrick Reilly and Margaret Gallagher. Pringle sought to serve a notice on Kelly in relation to arrears of rent owed to the widow of George Cuffe. Kelly would not accept it and the pair sought to force it on him. The Connaught Telegraph reported:

> As he refused to accept the precious paper, the attenuated Pringle animal vowed he should not leave the premises without it - the two legged creature called Gardiner laid her wrinkled hand on her aged breast, and threatened that there was a sharp-shooting revolver there, which would be employed in the enforcement of service if, he longer persisted in refusing acceptance of the document!. The "beautiful" Susan threw her ancient frame against the front door, to prevent the possibility of escape, while both of the " gentle" animals dragged and hauled and tore and scratched, and mauled him, till, on leaving the blessed establishment, where the pair of maiden "graces" have fixed their hallowed abode, his appearance was that of one who had just emerged from some little trouble, in which sharp finger-nails had been used with no slight effect, as their visible trade-marks were left on his neck and countenance.[125]

In the course of the court hearing Kelly gave evidence that he did not actually see the revolver but he was frightened as both women were under the influence of alcohol and both physically assaulted him. Gallagher and Reilly gave evidence that supported Gardiner's account of events that Kelly was not assaulted. Garvey, for the defence, said that Gallagher proved no violence had occurred while *"the constable, the only disinter-*

ested person" examined, cleared up the matter satisfactorily, and showed that no assault or attempt at assault was committed. According to Garvey:

> These bogus prosecutions might be made use of on public platforms, but the law must not be used to sustain them. In these trumped up cases, any menial or tenant may bring respectable ladies into court, but the magistrates will see justice done by dismissing the case.

Browne and Tardy agreed, there was no assault and the case was dismissed.

Harriet Gardiner & Thomas Ward: October 1885

Later that same day Gardiner was back in court for the hearing of a trespass case against Thomas Ward. Gardiner had obtained a decree for possession against Ward in January and she had him evicted in March. She now contended that he had re-entered the house following the eviction. Gardiner was again represented by J.C Garvey. Ward was very ably represented by P.J. Kelly who made matters very difficult for Gardiner in the witness stand. Kelly questioned the proper authority of the acting Sheriff on the day and whether Gardiner had actually taken possession of Ward's house or that of his neighbour, Beirne. This suggests that Patrick Beirne had also been evicted a fact not recorded in the Cancellation Books.

John Connor testified that on the 1 October, he was going to Castlebar on horseback when Thomas Ward came out and asked him to tell Gardiner that he was going into the house for the purpose of threshing the oats to be able to pay a year's rent. On his return that evening, Connor told Ward that he had mentioned the matter to Gardiner, and that she replied that she would summon him. Kelly explained that under the legislation if Gardiner was to succeed it was necessary to show that Ward had been warned by Gardiner and that he neglected or refused to leave after the warning.[126] Tardy and Browne found against

Gardiner. The words used by Connor did not constitute a warning within the meaning of the law. Tardy found it difficult to get answers from Connor and Browne concluded that Connor did not tell Ward to leave. This was one of the few occasions when a tenant succeeded against Gardiner in Court. It was also a turning point for John Connor and a mere nine months after his appointment his time as Gardiner's bailiff was coming to an end.

Constable Patrick Reilly & John Kelly: October 1885
John Kelly failed in his action against Gardiner and Pringle but that was not the end of the matter. The next case before Browne and Tardy that day was a charge of disorderly conduct against Kelly. Patrick Reilly had him before the court for using *"scandalous expressions to Miss Gardiner and Miss Pringle."* Kelly denied the charge but for the second time that day Tardy and Browne did not believe him and he was fined 5 shillings and ordered to pay costs.[127]

Tully Tenants Fined & Imprisoned: October-November 1885
Through the months of October and November Gardiner had the Tully tenants and their families back in court for trespass on their houses and in most cases imprisonment was the outcome. At Ballyglass Petty Sessions on 7 October Major Thomas Kent Neild fined Mary Connor 10/- plus costs or in default of payment she was to be committed to seven days imprisonment. She could not pay the fine and the Castlebar Prison Records show that she was accompanied by her male child when she was committed to prison. Neild made a similar ruling against Mary Macken. She too went to prison for seven days rather than pay the fine. Cases for trespass against Catherine Deacy, Bridget Deacy, John Deacy, Susan Macken and Patrick Macken were adjourned by Blake at Ballyglass Petty Sessions on Wednesday 21 October and again on 4 November. The cases came before Major Neild on Wednesday 18 November at Ballyglass Petty Sessions. The cases against Bridget Deacy and John Deacy were adjourned. Catherine Deacy was fined 10/- and ordered to pay costs or in default she was to be committed to Castlebar Prison

for seven days. Susan Macken, daughter of Patrick Macken, was fined 10/- and ordered to pay costs or in default she too was to be committed to Castlebar Prison for seven days. Both elected to go to prison as no doubt they did not have the money to pay the fine. It was Susan Macken's first time in prison and she is described in the Prison Record as a woman of 19 years of age, five foot four in height with brown hair, brown eyes and a fresh complexion. She was a Roman Catholic, a labourer and illiterate. The cases against John and Bridget Deacy came before Ballyglass Petty Sessions again on 16 December but neither turned up for the hearing.

John Connor gives up his Gun: December 1885

On Stephens Day the Connaught Telegraph published a letter from the *"O'Byrne"* Frenchill informing the Editor that John Connor had given up his gun and was refusing to continue to act as Gardiner's bailiff as he feared for his life. According to O'Byrne he had handed up his gun fearing *"he should be mistaken for the wren, and hunted as one by the boys, on St Stephen's Day."* Some suggested that he had been sacked while others believed he had resigned on the arrival of Gardiner's newly appointed bailiff Billy Cuffe. During the 12 months or so that Connor had acted as Gardiner's bailiff he was subjected to regular attacks in the Connaught Telegraph and in letters published by the paper. Whatever the reason for his ending his arrangement with Gardiner the last ten years of John Connor's life would prove to be difficult as Gardiner and Pringle supported by their bailiffs would use every available opportunity to bring him before the justices at Ballyglass Petty Sessions.

William (Billy) Cuffe appointed Bailiff: December 1885

By late 1885 it was clear that Gardiner was not making progress. Over two years had elapsed since the death of her uncle. In that time she had succeeded in obtaining multiple court orders against many of the tenants, some had been evicted and others imprisoned more than once. However, with the exception of Oliver Canton (workhouse) and John and Mary Macken (emigrated) most of the tenants had re-entered their homes. Against this background, Gardiner engaged William (Billy) Cuffe as her new bailiff and emergency man. Cuffe, from Ballina, was the proprietor of a public house at Hill Street in the town.[128] He later explained that he did an extensive provision trade but gave up the public house to better his position which had improved after he moved to Tully.[129] He arrived in Tully in December 1885. It is not clear where he resided initially but he would eventually take over the home of Patrick Macken. The Connaught Telegraph frequently reminded readers that Cuffe was the illegitimate son of George Cuffe and this, if true, would mean that he was Gardiner's cousin. Other than the fact that she employed him as her bailiff there is no evidence that this was ever acknowledged by Gardiner or indeed by George Cuffe. Based on the 1901 Census Records which shows Cuffe's age as 75, he was born around 1826 and was a Catholic.[130] On 30 March 1858 he married Mary Kilcullen and they had five children; four boys (James, Pat, George and William) and a daughter Mary Jane. In 1864 when George was born they were living at Bridge Street, Ballina. The arrival of Cuffe marked a significant change in tactics by Gardiner and the beginning of the end for many of the tenants on the Estate.

PART V

Eviction Terror 1886

Eviction & Imprisonment: Spring & Summer

Those who read of the cruel and wholesale evictions, personally superintended by Miss Gardiner in Mayo may picture to themselves a reckless young heroine driven to extremities by distress. What would they think of the true picture – a blue-eyed, filthy, middle-aged woman dressed in man's hat and clothes, that would disgrace the most reputable scarecrow; a woman of enormous wealth and no means or thought of spending it, save in occasional drunken bouts with her companion in-arms Miss Pringle – bouts which sometimes end by being arrested by the police – a woman crazed by whiskey, greed, and cruelty.[131]

Castlebar Rent Office: January 1886

With the arrival of the New Year many tenants owed Gardiner three years rent. She had refused the rent with the objective of *"breaking their rotten leases."*[132] As time passed and the amounts owing increased substantially, it became more and more difficult for the tenants to pay the full amount outstanding. The situation was exasperated by the economic difficulties and the decline in tenant income. Notwithstanding Gardiner's stance of not accepting rent, she announced that she would hold a Rent Office in Castlebar on Wednesday 6 January. She arrived at Castlebar train station with Pringle on the Monday before and they were:

> …seen trudging into town with police men in front of them, policemen in rear of them, and the hailstones mercilessly playing pranks on their wixened faces, disheveled head-gear, and besotted black encasements [133]

Sixteen tenants turned up at the Rent Office where they were met by Gardiner, Pringle and a large number of police. Gardiner refused to accept anything less than the three years rent so the tenants left pledging that they would lodge the money to a bank.[134]

John Irwin & James Daly: January 1886

On the same day James Daly appeared before the Justices at Castlebar Petty Sessions for the next engagement in the Ballyshane trespass war. On Christmas Day 1885, 25 head of cattle belonging to Daly trespassed on a cabbage crop belonging to John Irwin. The matter was referred by the parties to arbitration by Michael Cunniff and William Hynes of Ballyshane. The outcome is not reported.

Evictions in the Snow: January 1886

The following day, Thursday 7 January, was a bitterly cold day with snow on the ground in the Belcarra area. In many ways it was a perfect day for Gardiner and Pringle to strike at the tenants and they took full advantage of it. The Connaught Telegraph reported:

> With some three inches of snow on the ground and the temperature of the weather far below freezing point, or, in other words, the temperature was as low as to be fit to test the nerve of a Polar Bear; yet it was not too hard or cold in the estimation of the heartless Pringle and Gardiner, to leave, on the roadside some 30 souls of all ages, from the septuagenarian to the three months old child.[135]

At 10 am a contingent of at least fifty police men left Castlebar by way of Spencer Street in the direction of Belcarra. The Connaught Telegraph reported that at the tail of the procession were two rickety old cars the property of an old soldier named Collins and driven by two young men by the name of Cosgrave. Gardiner and Pringle occupied one of the cars with *"Smash all"* Mc Dermott in the other.

> Precisely at ten o clock the stentorian voice of that big man with the long sword, called the county inspector, could be heard at the corner of the county courthouse marshalling some 50 mail-clad buckshot warriors. At the tail of the procession could be seen the pair of old screws, lame, blind, and

spank as they were in tow of two rickety old cars, the property of an old solider named, Collins, and driven by a pair of young scamps named Cosgrave, and on the cars were the wizened but doubled remnants of fallen humanity in the shape of the pair of inebriates – Pringle and Gardiner. Next came the car of the flaming McDermott, alias "smash all" he and the Gardiner Pringle pair scarce knew where they were going further than that they were following the police. The solemn procession wended its way through Spencer Street where they were scared with no small amount of horror, sad loathing, particularly the camp followers and pair of "children of the regiment" who were greeted by many a "may you never come back" which did not apply to the police, who, of course did not at all like the duty they had before them. The tryating ground was Belcarra.[136]

At Belcarra the convoy was joined by 80 policemen from Ballyhaunis, Claremorris and Balla under the command of Sub-Inspector Magee and Major Thomas Kent Neild. A further 40 constables from Ballinrobe and Partry joined the group bringing the total to at least 170 in number. Neild would play an important role as events unfolded at Belcarra that day.

James Walsh of Elmhall was their first target. Walsh and his family occupied a tenement at Elmhall comprised of land, a house and out buildings.[137] According to the report in the Connaught Telegraph the Sheriff, a man named Rutledge, was so shocked by *"the sad and sickening sight of poverty depicted in human faces"* that he decided not to evict the family and instead went through a process of turning them out and allowing them back in as caretakers contrary to the instructions of Gardiner. When the work was completed at Elmhall, the convoy turned back in the direction of Castlebar towards Tully. There is no report of the actual house or houses visited though it would seem likely that John Garvey (Long) was amongst those evicted and possibly allowed to re-enter as a caretaker though this is unclear. Once again Rutledge acted humanely:

They next proceeded to Tully, where a more sad and sickening sight of old age and poverty, coupled with the innocence of youth met them. The sheriff acted equally as magnanimous amidst the prayers and, blessings of the poor victims and a crowd of neighbours who had assembled.[138]

It is likely that those evicted at Tully included the Mackens, Patrick Connor and his family, Catherine Deacy and her family and Bridget Cardy. Similar scenes played out at Logaphuill and Tully Beg before the different garrisons went their separate ways. The Connaught Telegraph reported that they:

> ...got leave to go back to their different garrisons without one to say "boo" to them save that a few snow-balls were hurled at them, and for which one young lad was arrested and kept in custody for some time by an antiquated sub who could be often found tripping himself, if the people cared to show him up for it.[139]

The boy is not named but he may have been one of the sons of John Garvey (Long). At the end of the day the number evicted stood at 30 persons ranging from a 70 year old to an infant of 3 months. Though not reported those evicted at Logaphuill included Thomas Dunne and his family.

Police Hut at Tully: March 1886

Billy Cuffe arrived in Tully sometime between the months of December 1885 and January 1886.[140] Gardiner installed him in Patrick Macken's home though the precise timing of this is not certain. To provide protection for Cuffe, Gardiner decided to have a hut built at the front of the Macken house and to station members of the RIC there. For the construction Gardiner purchased three thousand bricks from P.M. Henry, a contractor from Ballydrum, Swinford. The bricks were delivered and construction commenced. The Belcarra, Balla and Bohola branches of the INL were not happy that Henry had facilitated Gardiner in this way and each passed a resolution censuring him. The resolution passed by the Balla branch read:

> That we, the Balla branch of the I N League, agree with our brothers of the Bohola and Belcarra branches in considering the erection of a police hut at Tully, in the western division of this parish a very ill advised proceeding; that, considering the high character for peaceableness, industry, and religion of the people of the Belcarra district we cannot regard the superfluous proceeding otherwise than assault and an outrage upon such a people, to whom no crime can be imputed nor any violence of the civil law; that, while we sympathise with our respected neighbours, so inconsiderately and unjustly treated, we must record our strong disapproval of any aid or assistance given towards the maintenance of that standing injury by anyone who respects his creed and country; and finally, we believe the Government would exercise their functions much more appropriately in protecting the people against creed and ferocious tyranny that oppresses them, than in planting a police hut among them of which there is no need, and which they did not provoke. It is a wanton symbol of war, not of peace.[141]

The Bohola branch resolved:

> That we learn with surprise, astonishment and regret that respectable persons in our parish was decoyed by the so called contractor, Mr. P M Henry of Ballydrum, parish of Swinford, in getting them to deliver three carts of bricks to the RIC hut now erected in Belcarra at the suit of the notorious Misses Gardiner and Pringle, against the poor unfortunate people, and that we condemn his conduct.[142]

Henry wrote to the Connaught Telegraph alleging that the Belcarra branch had been duped into passing the resolution by the Bohola branch.[143] In his opinion, the object of the Bohola branch in getting the Belcarra branch to move such a resolution was to injure his chances of getting elected as a Guardian of the Swinford Division. Henry admitted to selling the bricks but said that a man named Vahey from Claremorris had ordered him to deliver the bricks which he partly delivered but once he learned what they were to be used for he refused to deliver any more. The Bohola branch appears to have accepted the explanation at a subsequent meeting chaired by Rev. James Cullen. John P. O'Connor did not however accept it and wrote a lengthy letter on the subject to the Connaught Telegraph.[144] In his opinion Henry was not telling the truth. O'Connor produced a letter from Thomas Mc Nicholas of Bohola. According to Mc Nicholas, Henry had employed two of his carts to transport bricks to a man named Mc Cormack of Castlebar. Henry accompanied Mc Nicholas and the load. When they reached Castlebar Henry asked Mc Nicholas to take them outside the town. When Mc Nicholas discovered that he was near Tully he threatened to dump the load on the roadside. Henry opened up to him and told him that he did not want anyone to know where he was taking the bricks. This according to O'Connor contradicted the Vahy from Claremorris story put forward by Henry. O'Connor also dealt with a suggestion made by Henry that the Tully Hut was in fact a structure known as Scanlon's Hut that had been taken from Bohola to Belcarra by six National Leaguers of the parish. According to O'Connor, Scanlon's hut had been removed to Foxford two years earlier but not by anybody from the parish. O'Connor acknowledged that an allegation that he had acted as a bailiff between 1874 and 1878 was indeed true but since those days he had nothing to do with landlordism and he had not, as Henry had suggested, served a writ on a dying neighbour. Notwithstanding all the resolutions, accusations and counter accusations, construction of the Tully Hut proceeded.

Letters to Gladstone, Parnell & O' Brien: February-March 1886

In early 1886 the Balla branch of the INL wrote to Gladstone on the issue of the Land Question. On 23 February the branch received a letter from E.W. Spenser Lyttleton confirming that

Gladstone had received their communication.[145] On 23 February the branch wrote to James F.X. O'Brien enclosing a declaration for the enlightenment of Gladstone.[146] The response from O'Brien was sympathetic but not entirely supportive; there was now something much more important than the Land Question at stake, namely self government:

> Permit me to assure you and the Balla branch of the League that the anxiety of the members of the Irish Parliamentary Party respecting the very great danger our poor country is exposed to, and, in fact is daily suffering from, in consequence of terrible depression, and the landlord "death sentences" cannot be greater than it already is. It is clear to anyone, not wilfully blind that a reduction in the value of agricultural products of say 40 per cent must have swept away the whole profits from farming, out of which profits, of course, farmers usually calculated to pay rents. But, while realizing this terrible state of affairs, we have to bear in mind that we are promised by Mr. Gladstone a full statement of his policy towards Ireland on or about 22nd March, and if in the interim we give special prominence to the Land Question we would be playing into the hands of our enemies, and the Land Question would get precedence with the result of possibly great risk to the vital question of Self –Government. It is therefore, necessary to be very prudent and patient during the coming few weeks. At the same time, reference to the proceedings in Parliament will make it evident that our party is careful to seize upon every opportunity of calling attention to the malignant conduct of Irish Landlords and there is reason to hope that a discussion on that subject i.e., evictions carried on by the aid of military and police which took place on Friday night last, will show good results.[147]

On 7 March the Balla branch wrote to Parnell enclosing resolutions that the branch had passed concerning the eviction of tenants. Later that month Parnell responded:

I have read the views expressed by your members with much interest. The question of suspension of evictions in Ireland is one that is receiving the most anxious consideration of my colleagues and myself at the present moment.[148]

Gardiner & Pringle seek to Evict 26: June 1886

Three months later on 11 June, Gardiner and Pringle appeared before the County Court Judge at the Westport Land Sessions seeking to evict 26 tenants. The strategy employed by Gardiner is summarized in the Connaught Telegraph:

> The stratagem they resorted to was to refuse rent for over three years, from tenants holding under leases from the late Col Cuffe, on the plea that that gentleman was only a tenant at will, and had not power to grant leases, they then unmercifully pounced on them for three and a half years rent up to May day last; but the tenants who at all times had offered their rent as it fell due, very properly resisted the ejectments. Cheques were produced in court which were returned by Gardiner and Pringle, which plainly went to show that Miss Pringle was reckless in her swearing when she repeatedly swore that they were never tendered payment, such was invariably, in each case, on, cross-examination.[149]

The Judge put a stay of execution for six months in those cases where the tenants had offered two years rent.

Eviction of John Connor & Thomas Walsh: June 1886

There is very little recorded information concerning the eviction of John Connor and his family. The fact of the eviction is however noted in the Cancellation Books. By 1887 his name had been struck from the books and replaced by Gardiner.[150] His name was however back in the books by 1888. It is therefore likely that he was evicted as part of the January or June 1886 eviction drives. A report some years later refers to Gardiner having *"kicked"* Connor out but it does not give a date. Many years later in 1901 the Connaught Telegraph would include

John Connor among the list of Tully evicted tenants that were the victims of a local land grabber. John Connor's neighbour Thomas Walsh and his family were also evicted at this time and like Connor they were back in possession by 1888. Neither Connor nor Walsh would be evicted again which suggests that they paid the rent demanded. That was not however the end of matter for John Connor and Gardiner and Pringle would continue to pursue other avenues against him.

Tully Police Hut: June 1886

By June of 1886 the construction of the Tully Police Hut was complete. The Hut would remain in situ for a number of years until Gardiner decided to build a more permanent home for herself and Pringle at Tully. The Connaught Telegraph again questioned the need for the structure as no one in Belcarra would have harmed the *"spawn of disputed illegitimacy"* (a reference to the fact that Billy Cuffe was reputed to be the illegitimate son of the late Colonel St. George Cuffe), and argued that the Belcarra rate payer should not have to pay for it.[151]

Imprisonment of John Garvey (Long): August 1886

On Sunday 8 August John Garvey (Long) was committed to serve one month's hard labour at Castlebar Prison for the offence of forcible possession of a house. He had either resisted eviction or re-entered the house following his eviction which must have occurred sometime in June though this is not certain as it is unclear whether he and his family were spared eviction when Sheriff Rutledge intervened out of pity during the 7 January evictions. Based on subsequent events it would seem that they were spared eviction at that time and re-admitted as caretakers. He was released on 9 September but he would be back in prison before the end of the year.[152] At this time Castlebar Prison was located on the site of what is now Mayo General Hospital.

Belcarra Tenants Prosecuted: August 1886

Three days later on Wednesday 11 August, Gardiner had a dozen Belcarra tenants before Ballyglass Petty Sessions. Actions taken against John Garvey (Long), Thomas Dunne and James Walsh, in each case for refusing to give up possession of their homes when demanded by Billy Cuffe were all dismissed because the summonses were defective. Garvey was at the time serving a one month term in Castlebar Prison. The Court records show that all three were living in their homes as mere caretakers and not tenants. This confirms that Garvey was more than likely readmitted as a caretaker following his eviction on 7 January. Two cases against him for damage to property by cutting grass and turf were also dismissed because the summonses were defective. The turf and grass was taken in June of 1886 from land at Tully that Garvey held as a tenant. But Garvey was no longer a tenant and Gardiner claimed that as a caretaker he was not entitled to take either.

A number of cases for trespass and forcible entry were prosecuted by John Garvey, Solicitor. The tenants were defended by P.J. Kelly. For trespass on 19 July, Patrick and Mary Macken, their daughter Susan, together with Bridget and John Deacy were each fined 2/6 and ordered to pay costs. In default they would be committed to Castlebar Prison for 7 days. A similar order was made against Catherine Deacy for trespass on 20 July. It would appear that the tenants were not imprisoned at this point and were back in court a few days later. The Connaught Telegraph reported that when the women had been imprisoned before, the local Land League supported their families. When the funds were exhausted an application was made to the National League but assistance was refused prompting the Correspondent (most likely Daly himself), to write:

> Their replies to fair and legitimate demands to monies entrusted to those avaricious would-be leaders was vague and hollow bombast, and a kind of idle subterfuge. A member of the Belcarra branch who called on those at the office in

Dublin was not alone refused but grossly insulted. This is what the custodians of funds, to relieve the evicted poor in Ireland have been doing for those poor creatures, on Belcarra estate of the viciously –disposed tyrant, Gardiner.

Castlebar Prison – From the Lawrence Collection of Photographs 1870–1910 (Courtesy of the National Library of Ireland).

Case against Thomas Ward Dismissed: August 1886

Thomas Ward of Frenchill was evicted in March 1885. He returned to his home after the eviction. In October 1885 Gardiner failed in a legal action against him because the Court found that Gardiner's Bailiff, John Connor, had not given the requisite warning to Ward to vacate the property. He remained at the house with his family and in August 1886 he was prosecuted for wilful trespass. P.J. Kelly, representing Ward, had the case which came before D.A. Browne and H.W Jordan dismissed. Gardiner and Pringle were represented by their solicitor John Garvey.[153]

Cases against the Dunne, Connor & Deacy Families: August 1886

At Ballyglass Petty Sessions on Wednesday 25 August Gardiner was drunk and a picture of misery.[154] She had arrived from Ballina the day before with Pringle and was reported to be drunk, stubborn and unmanageable as she staggered across the Mall in Castlebar accompanied by Pringle. The following day the pair attended court with Billy Cuffe for the hearing of cases against a number of Belcarra tenants.

The first case heard by Francis Blackburn Henn R.M., and Major Neild was against Thomas Dunne.[155] Dunne occupied his house in Logaphuill as a mere caretaker. When Billy Cuffe demanded possession of the house, Dunne refused to give it up. Pringle gave evidence that on 7 January 1886 Dunne had been evicted and readmitted as a caretaker. Dunne explained that he had offered the rent one week after the time for redemption had expired but it was refused. Henn said that it was Gardiner's right to do so. Billy Cuffe gave evidence that he had demanded possession. Dunne pleaded with Henn not to put his five children out on the road. Henn said that it had nothing to do with him and granted a decree for possession against Dunne. Billy Cuffe was appointed Special Bailiff by the Court to deliver possession to Gardiner.

In a case against Bridget Deacy, described as a girl of seventeen or eighteen years, Cuffe gave evidence that he had seen her in the family home at Tully on 13 August following the eviction of the family. She explained that she had gone to see her mother who was ill. Neild reminded her that he had previously cautioned her not to go there. Henn wanted her to prove where she had been the night before. She explained that she had been with family at Frenchill. She was fined 2/6 and ordered to pay costs in the same amount. Her mother Catherine was fined a similar amount. In a case against Mary Connor (wife of Patrick Connor), for wilful trespass on a house, Cuffe gave evidence that he had found her in her home at Tully on 12 August. Mary Connor pleaded with Henn but he responded by reminding her that:

It's not your land woman! You were turned out of it, what are you talking of?

She was fined 2/6 and in default of payment she was to be committed to prison for seven days. She was given two weeks to pay but according to the Connaught Telegraph the police were sent out to take her into custody and she was in Castlebar Prison that evening. The Castlebar Prison records show that when Mary Connor was committed by Nield she was, once again, accompanied by her unnamed male child. They were released on Tuesday 31 August.

Cases taken by Gardiner against James Walsh and John Garvey (Long) for refusing to give possession to Billy Cuffe when he demanded it were dismissed as neither summons had been served. Two cases for wilful and malicious damage taken by Gardiner against John Garvey (Long) were similarly dismissed. Garvey was still in Castlebar Prison at this time. These cases related to the cutting of grass and turf on his holding after he was allowed to re-enter as a caretaker. Mary and Patrick Macken were each fined 10/- for wilful trespass at their house. In default of payment they were to spend seven days in Castlebar Prison.

Imprisonment of the Macken Family: September 1886
On Wednesday 8 September Susan Macken was fined for wilful trespass at the Macken house in Tully. Billy Cuffe appeared as a witness for Gardiner in proving the trespass. Susan Macken could not pay the fine of 10/- and she was committed by Neild to Castlebar Prison for 7 days. Her parents Patrick and Mary were committed at the same time as they had not paid the fines imposed on 25 August by Neild. When they were released on Tuesday 14 September they returned to their home in Tully to find their furniture outside and Billy Cuffe inside. A scuffle broke out between Cuffe and Patrick Macken and Cuffe was forcibly removed from the house by Macken.[156] At some point after this Cuffe did get possession of the house and took up residence in it as a caretaker for Gardiner.

Cases against John Garvey (Long): September 1886

At the same sitting of Ballyglass Petty Sessions there were four cases heard against John Garvey (Long). Garvey was serving the final day of a one month term in Castlebar Prison but was in court for the hearing. The first two cases concerned the taking of grass and turf from his holding after he had been evicted and allowed to return as a caretaker. Billy Cuffe testified as to the value of the turf taken by Garvey from the land. Garvey explained to Neild that his father and grandfather had cut turf in the same place. Neild said that the right to cut turf ended when Garvey ceased to be a tenant. Garvey was fined 2/6 for the trespass and ordered to pay Gardiner 10/- compensation or one half the value of the turf. If Garvey refused to pay he would spend seven days in Castlebar Prison. On the charge of cutting grass, Neild asked Gardiner to withdraw the case. He obviously concluded that Garvey had been punished enough for one day. Gardiner refused. Neild adjourned the case stating that whilst a caretaker had no legal right to cut grass he had that right as a matter of custom. There was also a case against Garvey's son who it was reported, was not yet in his teens. Neild held that the boy had acted on the direction of his father. Gardiner's solicitor John Garvey challenged this and the case was adjourned. Cases against John Garvey (Long) and James Walsh for refusing to give up possession of their homes when it was demanded by Billy Cuffe were adjourned as only one RM was present. As with Garvey, James Walsh had been readmitted to his Elmhall holding as a caretaker following his eviction.

The Connaught Telegraph reported that Gardiner and Pringle had been transported to and from the Ballyglass Petty Sessions by:

> "Billy Pethaghawn" Walsh – a land-grabber and expelled member of the League in Balla ., as no other car owner would pollute his vehicle with the dirty animals.[157]

CATHERINE DUNNE & BILLY CUFFE

On Tuesday last, from an early hour Castlebar was swarmed with carloads of policemen, thronging in from various parts of the county; and, up to about 9 o'clock am, droves of vehicles might be seen passing through Spencer St, in the direction of the railway station. The cause was known to all – this was the day, the evil minded old Gardiner wretch had selected for the execution of her hellishly conceived designs on the unhappy tenantry, in Tully and adjacent villages that are cursed with the infliction of her inhumanly despotic sway. On arriving at the crossroads of Logafoil, we perceived long files of policemen (about 100 in all) ready for business, and under the command of Mr. Dobbin, C I Westport, with Messrs Mc Gee, D I, of Claremorris, and Mr. Chambers, D I, of Castlebar, Major Neild R M, had charge of all, There were sergeants and constables there from Ballina, Ballinrobe, Ballindine, Ballyhaunis, Castlebar, Claremorris, Foxford, Hollymount, Kiltimagh, Kilkelly, Louisburg, Newport, Swinford, Westport.[158]

Catherine Dunne & Billy Cuffe: September 1886

Tully Beg is a small townland a short distance from Tully. Bridget Dunne was one of the seven tenants in the townland in 1883. She leased a house and land from Gardiner. Adjacent to her tenement Thomas Dunne (most likely Bridget's relative), also leased a plot of land. John Gallagher of Errew leased land from Gardiner close to the Dunne holdings. In nearby Logaphuill not far from the Daly residence at Coachfield, Thomas Dunne leased a house, buildings and land from Gardiner, and this is where he and his wife Catherine and their five children lived in 1886. On Tuesday 7 September of that year they were violently evicted and their home was rendered unfit for habitation. Thomas Dunne and his family had first been evicted by Gardiner in May 1885 but she had allowed them to be re-admitted as caretakers.

On that Tuesday in September one hundred members of the RIC arrived in Logaphuill in support of the eviction effort. The police were under the control of CI Dobbyn, Major Thomas Kent Neild RM, DI Chambers from Castlebar and DI Magee from

Claremorris. A large crowd of people had assembled to witness the eviction. Cuffe was assisted by two men by the name of Killeen one of whom was missing a hand. When they arrived at the Dunne home they found the door locked. Thomas and Catherine Dunne and their five children were inside. At that point the battering ram was not used in evictions and there is no evidence that it was ever used on the Belcarra Estate.[159] The Connaught Telegraph reported the following dialogue between Billy Cuffe and Thomas Dunne after James Daly had suggested that Cuffe should go down the chimney:

> Billy then began to use "soft soap", and thus addressed Dunne – "Now, Thomas, the easy way is the best; if you don't open I'll have to force the door" – to which the other, spurred to desperation, replied, "You hanging boned dog, you may thank the law, or you wouldn't come this way to my door; I'd scatter your brains on the street, you dirty bloodhound and nameless bastard. My father and grandfather were reared here, and you want to put me out of it – a fellow who couldn't tell who was his own father. When your old mother called you after Col Cuffe, to try and knock money out of him, he always denied that you had a drop of his blood in you, and you have Na Billeen Sollagh![160]

Cuffe had no crowbar and when he failed to break the door with his shoulder he used a limestone rock instead. When the door was opened the Freemans Journal reported:

> The bailiffs Killeen were set to work and soon cleared out the furniture, which was of a most miserable description. The children, five in number, and the father were removed without any trouble, but the mother, a woman who was for some time past in delicate health, declined to leave, and a little force had to be resorted to.[161]

More than *"a little force"* was however used, as Catherine Dunne was subjected to a violent assault by Billy Cuffe assisted by Killeen. The assault, which amongst other things involved Cuffe kicking Catherine Dunne in the abdomen, was subsequently the subject of a legal action taken by Catherine Dunne against Cuffe. The case was heard on Wednesday 29 September at Ballyglass Petty Sessions. Both Gardiner and Pringle were in attendance. Catherine Dunne was represented by C. O'Malley (instructed by her solicitor P.J. Kelly) and Cuffe was represented by J.C. Garvey. The case was widely reported in Ireland and in England.[162] The testimony given by Catherine Dunne was reported in the Connaught Telegraph:

> She deposed that, on the 7th September, Cuffe came to her house with the police; she was standing at the chimney with a child in her arms; the furniture and her husband and the other children having been removed, Cuffe told her to leave, and she said she would go when she "had cried enough before bidding a last farewell to the house;" he said if she would not go out quickly he would make her go; he seized her by the right arm, as she held the child on her left, and dragged her from the fire to the door; he then kicked her in the sides and on the belly; the first kick was on the belly near the heart; he kicked her several times, and she fell on her right side, in a faint; she did not know what became of her, but remembered being taken out by somebody she thought was Major Neild; she was left sitting outside under the wall on a mat that one of the police brought to her; she was afterwards removed on a car to Mr. Charles Daly's where Dr Jordan examined her....[163]

Major Neild gave evidence that he did not see the assault, that he had seen Catherine Dunne sitting on the floor with her back to the wall looking very faint and weak and he assisted her by getting her a drink of water. James Daly who attended the eviction in his capacity as a Poor Law Guardian gave evidence in support of Catherine Dunne and specifically that he had witnessed Cuffe kicking her in the stomach. Dr. William De Exeter Jordan who had attended to Catherine Dunne testified that:

I found a mark on the right side of her abdomen below the ribs, one on the right hip, and a slight abrasure over the right knee; the palm of the left hand was discoloured and swollen; and her stomach so enlarged that I thought she was pregnant, but she denied that, the wound on the abdomen was a serious one, but the others were slight; when I first saw her, she was sitting by the wall, hysterical, rather weak and very nervous.[164]

On cross examination the Doctor said that he was of the opinion that the wounds were caused by kicks.

Cuffe's defence took the form of a counter claim against Catherine Dunne that she had kicked him several times. He was Gardiner's bailiff and Killeen, who he described as an *"off-handed man"*, was his assistant. He testified that he did not kick Catherine Dunne and that she had kicked him at least twenty times after he took her by the arm to escort her outside. When he arrived at the house Thomas Dunne refused to let him in. Cuffe forced open the door and removed the furniture. After Thomas Dunne had left he asked Catherine Dunne to leave but she refused. Sergeant John Elliot of Ballinrobe and Sergeant Thomas Frisell of Cloghans both gave evidence that Catherine Dunne kicked Cuffe but they did not see him kick her. Constable John Hayes and Constable Patrick Hughes both of Tully Hut gave evidence that they did not see Cuffe kick Dunne but that it might have happened.

The presiding justice, Francis Blackburn Henn RM, found that in light of the conflicting evidence and the seriousness of the charges against both Cuffe and Dunne he would send both cases for trial to the next Castlebar Quarter Sessions on Tuesday 2 November. In a separate action James Daly was fined 10/- and ordered to pay costs for assaulting Billy Cuffe leading the Connaught Telegraph Correspondent to conclude:

>…seeing the treatments the rascal had given the poor woman, with a child in her arms, it was not easy for any person to

restrain his feelings of disgust at the brutality displayed by the vile spawn of bastardy.[165]

The following week the Connaught Telegraph took issue with a report of the proceedings that appeared in the Western People. The Telegraph alleged that the Western People had no reporter within thirty miles of Ballyglass Petty Sessions and that the report was biased in favour of the Cuffe and Gardiner faction. The report in the Western People could have been:

> penned either by the woman slayer Billy Cuffe, the old jade Pringle or their partisan, the little acrobat Henn, who could not restrain his feelings of sympathy with tyrant Gardiner, or conceal his sour temper while on the bench.

The Dunne eviction was also the subject of a lengthy article in the Freemans Journal.[166] The report contains an excellent explanation of how Gardiner and her bailiffs approached the task of attacking the structure of the Dunne home to ensure it could not be lived in again:

> On the last particle of furniture having been cleared out, the bailiffs were ordered by Miss Gardiner to commence the work of unroofing. One of the bailiffs here refused to have anything to do with such proceedings, and was loudly cheered by the crowd. The other two then proceeded with a crowbar and other implements, entered the dwelling house and soon the sound of the crowbar smashing the walls could be heard. At the door partially closed stood Miss Gardiner, superintending the work going on inside, but when spectators attempted to look in, she closed the door indignantly. Occasionally she opened it inquiring how they were going on, and gave peremptory instructions. All the time the crowd of people who had gathered outside, notably women and children, heaped a torrent of abuse upon her and her associate Miss Pringle, but to all that she turned a deaf ear, and a smile of satisfaction sometimes appearing on her face as she listened to their

condemnation of the evictions. At length the bailiffs made their appearance, and one of them gave up possession to Miss Gardiner, and the door was locked, and she, apparently satisfied, intimated to Major Neild her readiness to proceed to the next house, which she declared was empty. A large hole was made in the side of Dunne's house, and some of the rafters destroyed.

George Moore in his novel *Parnell and His Island* devoted an entire chapter to the Dunne eviction.[167] Fearing libel laws of the time he changed Gardiner's name to Miss Barrett, Pringle to Miss McCoy and Billy Cuffe became Mr Pratt. In broad terms the account accords with the reported facts; the merciless alcohol bloated landlord accompanied by her bailiffs and the police brutally terrorizing the Dunne family, evicting them and demolishing their house. Moore's description of the Dunne home is truly shocking and while Moore may never have seen the house it is likely that he based his description on one or more of the dwellings of other tenants in the locality at the time:

> So horrible is the place that it seems a mockery, a piece of ferocious cynicism to suggest that the possession of it is about to be contested, and that to restore it to its rightful owner an army has to be gathered together. It lies under the potato-field, and the space between bank and wall is a stream of mud and excrement. The incessant rain has rotted the straw of the roof, and at one end it droops ready to slip down at every moment. The week walls lean this way and that, and their foundations are clearly sinking away into the wet bog. Hard by the dung-heap, in front of the door, where the pig strives to find a place dry enough to lie in, the mud and filth have lapsed into green liquid where some ducks are paddling; under the thatch there is mould and damp, about the door and window- holes blackness and ooze, mud permeates and soaks through every crevice; the place seems like a rat's nest built on the edge of a cesspool. Not a tree is to be seen, not even a bush.[168]

The eviction of the Dunne family in September 1886 was not the end of the matter. Thomas Dunne and his family had nowhere to go so they would, notwithstanding the state of disrepair of the house, continue to return to their home when they had the opportunity and Gardiner would have to resort to more force to break their resolve but this would take time.

Eviction of John Gallagher & Bridget Dunne: September 1886

Though the eviction of Bridget Dunne and John Gallagher of Tully Beg does not appear to have been picked up by the press or by other commentators, their names had been struck from the Cancellation Books by 1887 and replaced by Gardiner. It would seem therefore that they were evicted at the same time as Thomas Dunne.[169]

Autumn Evictions at Tully & Elmhall

There were ten families living together in a kind of hamlet at this district which is about 4 miles to the east of Castlebar and among them Miss Gardiner and her boon companion appeared on Saturday last for the purpose of evicting five of them. In some cases perhaps I should say re-evicting because the poor foolish people imagined they had a sort of claim to shelter themselves in the houses they had themselves built, and had the hardihood, in a few instances at least, to re-enter their little homes even after the base dogs of the rent-office had stripped them bare and put the sign manual of desolation on their hearths.[170]

Attempted Eviction of Catherine Deacy: September 1886

Following the eviction of the Dunne family and the destruction of their home on 7 September, Gardiner, her bailiffs and the police moved on a short distance to Catherine Deacy's home in Tully. The Freemans Journal Reported:

> From Dunne's they proceeded to the house of a woman named Mrs. Deasy; but instead of this house being empty, it was found that Mrs. Deasy was in occupation, and in such a critical state of health, that her death was hourly expected, and reluctantly she was obliged to proceed to the next house. Here also disappointment awaited her. The house was locked and barred and completely deserted. This was the last on the list, and she again turned her steps towards the dwelling of the Emergency man,[171] which she entered, and remained there for a considerable time.[172]

The second house visited was that of Mary and Patrick Connor.

Use of Police in Mayo Evictions: September 1886

On Friday 17 September the issue of the use by Mayo landlords of the RIC to secure evictions in the County was raised by Mayo West MP., John Deasy in the House of Commons:

I find that in Mayo there have been 100 men, under the direction of a County Inspector and Sub-Inspectors, sent out to enforce evictions. I think it is high time the right hon. Gentleman the Chief Secretary should take the practice of utilizing the Royal Irish Constabulary for the purpose of carrying out evictions into his serious consideration. A hundred men have been sent where five or six constables are quite enough to preserve order, and I fail to see why the taxpayers of the country should be annually robbed of a very large sum of money which might well be disposed of in another way. On the West Coast of Ireland the poverty and destitution of the people is notorious, and they are at present altogether unable to pay rent. I trust that the right hon. Gentleman will give these matters the attention they deserve. I would also point out to him that some of the evictions now taking place are being carried out in cases where the unfortunate tenants have actually been obliged to receive relief from the Guardians. Therefore, I ask the right hon. Gentleman, in the case of the county of Mayo, to withdraw the extra police, and to refuse to lend the assistance of the ordinary police to the landlords in carrying out these cruel evictions, leaving them where it is apparent that the victim is unable to pay to carry them out as best they can. There is a widespread fear that in the coming winter the destitution of the people will be far more severe than it has ever been before, and that they will be obliged, in many cases, to enter the workhouse in order to prevent themselves and their families from being actually starved......... Since the commencement of the Sitting in this Parliament there were, in several instances, more than 100 men employed in evicting tenants in the county of Mayo and other counties, and the only people who have not received protection are those unfortunate persons who have suffered at the hands of the police. In a case which occurred recently at Castlebar, in the county of Mayo, more than 100 policemen were employed to carry out evictions, and they made a savage attack upon defenceless people, and the Medical Officers of the district had to attend both women and children who had suffered from ill-usage at the hands of the police. In order that something may be done to prevent similar occurrences in the future, I would ask the right hon. Gentleman and the Government to put a stop to evictions, or, at any rate, take steps to prevent brutal assaults being made by the police upon women and children.[173]

Billy Cuffe dragged from Belcarra Church: September 1886

On Sunday 12 September Billy Cuffe was dragged from Belcarra Church by a group of women. According to the *"O' Beirne"*, in another of his many letters to the Connaught Telegraph, the priest subsequently admitted Cuffe and his bodyguard by the side door. O'Beirne issued the following warning to the priest:

> It is strongly on the cards that Father John will soon have to choose between the masses of the people and Billy and his bodyguard for a congregation. It is to be hoped it will never come to that, but it is looking very like it. [174]

Gardiner Boycotted: September 1886

On the same day the Belcarra branch of the INL passed the following resolution:

> Resolved – That we, as Irishmen, ask the car owners throughout this county not to give the use of their cars in future, for the purpose of assisting in carrying out such heartless evictions as took place on Miss Gardiner's property at Logafoil on Tuesday last, when she superintended in person the leveling of the roof –trees of her unfortunate victims, and left them without home.[175]

Five days later on 17 September while the House of Commons was debating the use of police to enforce evictions in Mayo, Edward Gibbons, PP., Balla was writing to the Connaught Telegraph to complain that Sub-Inspector of Police, Chambers from Castlebar, had visited a number of businesses in Balla and warned the proprietors that if they continued to refuse to make a car service available to transport Gardiner around the countryside, their spirit licenses may be objected to.[176]

Mary Connor & Catherine Deacy: September 1886

Wednesday 22 September was another eventful day for the Belcarra tenants at Ballyglass Petty Sessions and Billy Cuffe was in the witness box. He had discovered Mary Connor in her home on 31 August and Catherine Deacy in hers on 8 September. Both women were fined 1/6 and costs were awarded against them. They could not pay so later that day Mary Connor, her baby and Catherine Deacy were imprisoned in Castlebar Prison. Neild and Henn committed them for seven days. They were released on 28 September. It is not clear whether they returned to Tully after they were released and where they were a few days later when Gardiner finally concluded her crusade against Catherine Deacy.

Later that day an action against Patt Deacy for trespass on 10 September was adjourned. Two cases against Susan Macken were also adjourned. She was charged with entering the Macken home with force and strong hand on 14 and 15 July. The cases were on the list for hearing again on 6 October but Susan Macken did not appear in Court. Notwithstanding their best efforts including physical force on the part of both Patrick Macken and his daughter Susan, the Mackens could not hold on to their home and their long occupation at Tully was finally brought to an end. Just over three years after Gardiner had taken control of the Belcarra Estate, Patrick Macken and his family disappeared from the records in Tully. Their house was not however demolished.

John Garvey & James Walsh: September 1886

On 22 September Neild and Henn also granted decrees for possession sought by Harriet Gardiner against John Garvey (Long) and James Walsh of Elmhall. The Connaught Telegraph reported that there were also several cases against children of evicted tenants but the cases were dismissed. There is no record of the latter in the Ballyglass Petty Session Records.

Demolition of Homes at Tully: October 1886

A few days later Gardiner's army of destruction was back in Tully. On Saturday 2 October a large contingent of police numbering between fifty and sixty men arrived in the village. Their purpose was firstly to demolish the homes of tenants that had re-entered following eviction and secondly to evict a number of others. On this occasion the police were under the command of Major Thomas Kent Neild RM. He was accompanied by DI Huddy and DI Chambers, Gardiner, Pringle and Billy Cuffe.

The first action of the party was to evict John Garvey (Long). Garvey's eviction in March 1885 was postponed when it was realised that two of Garvey's children were ill. Garvey had been evicted in January 1886 but was readmitted as a caretaker. Thereafter Gardiner had pursued him in the courts for trespass and damage to property. He was released from Castlebar Prison on Thursday 9 September having served one month for forcible possession of his house and he returned to Tully and now, less than a month later, he had been evicted once more with his family. His relatives and neighbours, James and Thomas Garvey were among a small number of tenants not evicted by Gardiner. Shortly after the 1886 evictions James Garvey died and was succeeded by his son John Garvey (James). A third John Garvey (son of Thomas Garvey), and known as John Garvey (Laheen), was growing up in Tully at this time also. The three men would play a significant role in one of the most celebrated cases in the Land War not only in Belcarra but in County Mayo generally. However that was still 16 years away. The Cancellation Books show that by 1887 John Garvey (Long)'s name was replaced by Gardiner.[177] Unlike the Macken, Deacy and Connor families, John Garvey (Long) and his family did not go away.

Following the eviction of John Garvey (Long) Gardiner's attention switched to the nearby cabin of Catherine Deacy's and it was levelled. Catherine Deacy's name never appeared on the valuation records so her husband's name was struck out and replaced by Gardiner. The amount of rates payable by Gardiner was reduced to reflect the fact that there was no longer a house on the land. The house was, according to the record *"down."*[178] This was the end of the Deacy family at Tully. The family would continue to have an interest from a distance in the evicted holding as no other tenant would take it or if they were minded to do so they would be labelled a *"grabber"* and their neighbours would operate against them.

Cuffe then took the police to Elmhall where James Walsh leased a house, buildings and land from Gardiner. Walsh and his family were evicted. James Walsh paid annual rates of £5. 16s and a rent of a similar if not greater amount was payable to Gardiner. James Walsh, the son of John Walsh, married Margaret Devaney of Kilnageer on Wednesday 2 March 1864 in Belcarra Church. Margaret was the daughter of Michael Devaney. In the period 1865 to 1887 they had ten children. Between 1997 and 1999 the ruins of the Walsh cottage at Elmhall were restored and the cottage is now operated as a Heritage Centre by Belcarra Community Co-Op.[179]

The following week the Connaught Telegraph reported:

> On Saturday last, the savage crew, composed of Gardiner Pringle, Cuffe and 50 or 60 policemen, with three or four officers and a paid Magistrate attended at Tully and Elmhall and succeeded in evicting two wretched families and tumbling the miserable cabin of Mrs. Deasy. There is nothing remarkable to be noted in the proceedings further than we mentioned last week –that John Garvey and James Walsh were turned adrift, and that the heartless wretch Gardiner, assisted her bastard relative in removing the furniture from the cabins. In fact it was laughable to see the unfortunate old hag (Gardiner) tussling with tables and boxes, as the "respectable" Billy was alone in his dirty work, and so the "gracious" Harriet should come to the rescue of her dear relation. They were truly a pretty pair of animals engaged at nice kind of work! [180]

A number of photographs taken on the day are now part of the Wynne Family Collection:

Photograph of the eviction of James Walsh, Elmhall- Gardiner assists with the removal of furniture (centre). (Courtesy of the Wynne Family Private Collection).

Photograph showing the large police force present at the Elmhall eviction. (Courtesy of the Wynne Family Private Collection).

Meeting of Castlebar Guardians: November 1886
At a meeting of the Castlebar Guardians on 20 November the Guardians decided, based on legal advice obtained from A.B. Kelly, to take legal proceedings against Gardiner in respect of her failure to comply with the notice requirements prescribed by the law when she evicted six tenants on the Belcarra Estate. James Daly remarked:

> The treatment Miss Gardiner's tenants were subjected to was something awful. Even that week on the return from gaol of a poor woman, after serving seven days there, she was met on her way home by the notorious Billy Cuffe, who served her with a summons, which was tried at last petty sessions, and the poor woman, with her husband, got 7 days more.[181]

Imprisonment of Thomas Ward: November 1886
The Ward family of Frenchill can be traced back to the late 1700s and almost certainly to 1798. At the time of Griffiths Valuation of 1856-1857, Thomas Ward and Thomas Ward (Senior) each rented a house, buildings and land from George Cuffe. The combined area of land held by the family was just over 32 acres. Their tenements were located at Frenchill crossroads. By the mid 1870s Richard and John Ward had succeeded to Thomas Ward senior's tenement and John Ward would seem to have converted the out buildings into a home for himself. Gardiner had evicted Thomas Ward in March 1885. He re-entered and Gardiner failed in two subsequent legal actions against him and Ward and his family continued in occupation. On 22 November 1886, James F.B. Tardy sentenced Thomas Ward, then aged 59, to seven days imprisonment in Castlebar Prison for the crime of trespass on a house.[182] Ward was released on Sunday 28 November.

Mass Demonstration at Tully: November 1886
The following day, Monday 29 November, a mass national demonstration was held at Tully. According to the Connaught

Telegraph the Balla fife and drum band were there playing national airs and there were a large number of people from surrounding towns.[183] John Deasy MP.,[184] and Thomas Mayne MP.,[185] were in attendance having arrived from Balla in a carriage followed by a parade. A platform was erected for the speakers but the Government note taker was denied a position on it.

The Connaught Telegraph reported:

> At three o' clock, on the motion of Mr. Charles Daly, Seconded by Mr. E Cannon, the chair was taken by the Very Rev. Edward Canon Gibbons, PP, VF Balla. The following resolutions read by Mr. Deasy MP, as secretary to the meeting were passed with acclamation –

> That we declare our continued confidence in our leader, Mr. Parnell and his colleagues, and pledge ourselves to persevere in our efforts for the restoration of our National Parliament. That, in view of the unprecedented depression in the price of agricultural produce and the unproductiveness of the seasons, we hereby call upon the landlords of Mayo to meet their tenants in a fair and reasonable spirit, taking such rent as tenants can afford to pay, after providing for the necessities of themselves and their families. That we express our unqualified approval of the plan of campaign put forward by "United Ireland."

There then followed a lengthy speech by Fr. Gibbons in which he called for support for the political aims of Parnell who has:

> ...proved himself an able leader, a sagacious strategist, a courageous soldier. He has made demands that have been called revolutionary.

He addressed the crowd on the threatened imprisonment of Dillon,[186] the demand for a native parliament, the impact of emigration; the end of landlordism and the aristocracy in Ireland and the tactic of boycotting. The speech was periodically interrupted by cheers, applause and (at the mention of landlords, aristocracy and such), groans from the crowd. John Deasy was then introduced to great cheering. He also spoke of Dillon's threatened imprisonment and the actions of the Tory Government in Ireland. On the dealings of Gardiner and the plight of her tenants he declared:

> Miss Gardiner has thrown out 13 of her tenants within the past few months, and the remainder will probably meet the same unless you make the necessary provision. Enter into combination, and do not by any means touch an acre of their evicted farms. Let them adopt the plan recently formulated for their guidance and offer fair rent, and if she refuses they can easily adopt the rules laid down, and she will soon yield to the offer. The tenants should offer a fair proportion of the rent the landlord asks. If he refuses to accept the rent offered go home with your rent. You have Parnell with you in your difficulty. They cannot arrest us all. We will have men ready in the breach and on the battlements. They will have no jails for us all. We must protect the tenantry, and bring about a satisfactory settlement if possible. The strength of our cause is in our righteousness and we must not sully its banner. We are on our trial, and we will stand to our guns in the face of the landlords. Have no connection with landlords, but offer them fair rent, and if you do this we need not care for the Government, and in time to come we hope to place the old flag over the old house in College Green.

Thomas Mayne continued on similar themes. After the meeting Mayne and Deasy were entertained by Fr. Gibbons at Belcarra.

Mary-Ann Ward & John Garvey (Long): December 1886

On 2 December James F.B. Tardy imprisoned Mary-Ann Ward, wife of Thomas Ward, for seven days at Castlebar Prison for the offence of trespass on a house. This was a mere four days after the release of her husband. Mary-Ann (nee Conway), was born in Buncom, a short distance from Frenchill. The Castlebar Prison Records show that Mary-Ann was 51 years old when she was imprisoned. She was 5ft 1" tall, 6s. 12lb with brown-grey hair, grey eyes and a sallow complexion. She was released on 8 December.

John Garvey (Long) was released from prison on Thursday 9 September having served one month for taking forcible possession of his house. On 2 October he and his family were evicted. On Friday 3 December Major Neild sentenced Garvey to seven days imprisonment for damage to a bog on the land he had been evicted from. It would be the last time that Major Thomas Kent Neild would sit in judgment over a tenant from Tully or indeed preside over the eviction of tenants and their families. Fate had other plans for him. Daly was again critical of the lack of support from the INL:

> The persecution that those tenants, evicted on the Belcarra estate, have been receiving; at the hands of the "Battered beauties", Gardiner and Pringle is something awful to contemplate. During the past week, one poor woman was imprisoned for a second time in the last month, and the husband once; yet they have not got one shilling as succor from the N League. That same body have made grants to some of the tenants residing in Drum parish, but up to the present they have refused to give any to those evicted in the Ballyhean portion of the estate.[187]

Hunting the Wren: December 1886

Billy Cuffe, accompanied by *"a pair of burly looking policemen"* spent St. Stephens Day at their *"favorite game of 'hunting the wren' by chasing evicted tenants."* In the morning, amongst the ruins of Thomas Dunne's house, Cuffe found Dunne, his sick wife Catherine and their children.

> It appears that poor Dunne, who, since the date of his eviction, was trying to earn an honest shilling to support his sick wife

and little children, visited the ruins of his once happy home to spend the Christmas under the old but lately dismantled rooftree, the possession of which has been kept since the date of the eviction, by a trio of hardy little urchin children. The rascally, old Billy, finding Dunne, his sick wife, and the little Dunnes in the ruins, bellowed and swore that he would have them at Ballyglass petty sessions, and would never feel content until he would give Thomas Dunne penal servitude. What a happy state of things, when Salisbury's paternal Government can make the people pay a half dozen of policemen to aide and abet the degraded scoundrel, Cuffe, in his barbarous work of hunting on, St Stephen's day poor half starved and wholly-famished evicted tenant serfs, for the crime of sheltering themselves on Christmas night in the ruins of their once comfortable home. How long, O Lord, how long? [188]

Restored ruins of the Walsh Cottage at Elmhall now operated as a Heritage Centre by Belcarra Community Co-Op. (Photograph: James O'Connor & Michael O'Connor, 2012).

PART VI

THE EVICTIONS OF 1887 & 1888

ASSAULT, EVICTION & IMPRISONMENT: 1887

The duty of the moment is clear......it now remains for us to prove for the thousandth time that as slaves we can be formidable foes. I assert here today that the Government of Ireland by England is impossibility, and I believe it to be our duty to make it so. [189]

Attack on a Resident Magistrate: January 1887

Saturday 1 January 1887 was New Years Day and a holiday. At Charlestown in East Mayo, a large crowd of Lord Dillon's tenants and their supporters gathered to await the arrival of the Process Server. A Plan of Campaign had been adopted by the tenants on Dillon's estate.[190] The day passed without incident and the Process Server did not appear. In the evening, Major Thomas Kent Neild RM, accompanied by three members of the RIC, drove into town. A cry was immediately raised that the Process Server had arrived. The crowd, thinking that Neild was the long awaited Process Server, immediately set upon him and the police were driven away. The horse was knocked to the ground and Neild was repeatedly beaten. It was only after the intervention of Father Loftus that the crowd stopped.[191] The Freemans Journal subsequently reported that no arrests had been made.[192]

Neild did not recover from the beating he received. He spent the next few months on sick leave and died of his injuries, aged 48, at 53 Lansdowne Road, Dublin on 24 April. The Connaught Telegraph reported that some of the men charged with affray were indicted at the Assizes of Castlebar. One was found guilty and in the case of the others the jury disagreed.[193] Neild had been a member of the 6th Royal Warwickshire Regiment and in July his wife Mary L. Neild was granted a pension of £100 as Neild had made no provision for her and she was now destitute.

Guardians of Castlebar Union & Harriet Gardiner: January 1887

Later that January the Guardians of the Castlebar Union went on the offensive and took six cases against Gardiner for evicting tenants without serving proper notice on them in accordance with the law. When the cases came up for hearing A.B. Kelly, Counsel for the Guardians, focused on the case of Thomas Dunne.[194] Thomas Dunne lived in Logaphuill and had land in Tully Beg (not Tully). The notice of eviction specified Tully as the townland where Dunne lived and it was therefore incorrect. Gardiner's lawyer John Garvey sought to have the case against his client dismissed because Gardiner had no tenant in Tully with that name so she could not be fined for evicting him without serving the proper notice. Kelly argued that the mistake as to the townland did not matter. The purpose of the law was to protect the destitute. Thomas Dunne was Gardiner's tenant and she had evicted him in September 1886 without serving the required notice on the Guardians. John Gordon RO gave evidence that in May 1885 the Guardians received notice of thirteen evictions on the Belcarra Estate but there was no notice given of the Eviction Order of August 1886 pursuant to which Dunne was evicted in September. Garvey argued that notice was not required on the second occasion as Dunne had been readmitted in 1885 as a *"caretaker"* and as such was an employee of Gardiner and not a tenant. Evidence was given by James Daly that:

…he was present at the eviction of Dunne in September last, and a cruel eviction it was, because Billy Cuffe her bailiff almost kicked the stomach out of Dunne's wife.

Garvey objected to this reference as a case was pending against Cuffe for the alleged assault. Garvey accused Daly of taking vindictive proceedings against Gardiner and suggested he held a grudge against her. Daly responded by stating that the case was taken in the interests of the rate payers that he represented and that he more pitied Gardiner than envied her.[195]

In the end the judge dismissed the case and did not impose a fine on Gardiner. This was not the end of the matter and Kelly and Garvey would get another opportunity to argue their cases before J.H. Richards QC., at the Ballina Quarter Sessions the following April.

Call for Public Meeting at Frenchill: January 1887

Police protection for Gardiner and Cuffe was provided in the form of an armed police unit consisting of five officers stationed in the Tully Hut located at the front of the Macken residence now occupied by Billy Cuffe. In January 1887 the Connaught Telegraph reported that a public meeting was to be held at Frenchill:

> ...the object of which is to call on the Government, by public memorial, that Miss Gardiner would be compelled to pay for the extra police force that aid her to carry out her barbarities on the Belcarra tenants.[196]

John Garvey (Long) & James Walsh in Court: February 1887

Following his release from prison in December 1886 John Garvey returned to Tully It would seem that he and his family had regained possession of their home as caretakers. At some point during February Billy Cuffe demanded that Garvey and his family leave and hand over the house. Garvey refused and Cuffe obtained an order for possession at Ballyglass Petty Sessions on 23 February. The Walsh family of Elmhall were also evicted on 2 October 1886 but they were not readmitted as caretakers. On 27 December 1886 Billy Cuffe found them back in the house. James and his wife Mary were both fined 5/- and had costs awarded against them at Ballyglass Petty Sessions on 23 February.

Notice of further Evictions & Acquittal of Cuffe: March 1887

On 19 March 1887 the Connaught Telegraph published a letter to the Editor from *"One of the Tenants"* highlighting the fact that the RO for the Belcarra District had been served with notice of Gardiner and Pringle's intention to evict 17 tenants including Rev. John Healy, CC., Belcarra.

According to the tenant:

> The pair of 'battered beauties,' as a certain respected gentleman called them, are accredited with boasting at their rent – office kennel, Castlebar, that they could do as they liked, that the Foreman Grand Juror with the shake in his head, backed up by a 'galaxy' of hungry land agents and a few bankrupt territorial owners from Tyrawly, was their friend; also that they felt gratified to Mr 'Standby' Crown prosecutor for not sending their Cousin Billy, before a Mayo petty jury in October last. Now, sir to be serious, those seventeen tenants about being evicted, under the eyes of our 'law and order' government, by a pair of disorderly wretches, were the most solvent on the Belcarra estate. They had the misfortune of holding, by lease, from the late Col Cuffe; but when the Gardiner hag became heiress she refused to take the rent from these tenants on the plea that she would 'smash their leases'. When three -and - a- half years rent accrued the pair of she tyrants thought it more advisable not to 'smash the leases,' they demanded rent. The tenants offered to pay two years rent. The offer was declined, and ejectment decrees were obtained. The County Court Judge, seeing the desire of the tenants to act justly, put a stay on execution. The time has expired. The tenants have offered still to pay two years rent down and two years rent before November next, or four years' rent in nine months. This offer has been rejected. The tenants must go, but the land will stand waste, as the cry will be raised, if the tenants be turned out, 'Death to anyone who takes the land from which tenants were evicted' In the face of this offer of the tenants, to pay four years' rent within one year, having been refused, they should be resolved, come what will, to resist the tyrannical oppression of those scourges on society.[197]

The letter highlighted the fact that, at that point in time, there were 20 empty holdings on the Belcarra Estate. Significantly the letter also highlights the fact that the Mayo Grand Jury had reversed a decision of an earlier Grand Jury against Billy Cuffe for his assault on Catherine Dunne. The letter is silent on the outcome of the case taken by Cuffe against Catherine Dunne.

Imprisonment of Patrick Connor & Thomas Dunne: March 1887

By the spring of 1887 Mary Connor and her infant child had been imprisoned four times for re-entering the Connor home. The Connor family must have had nowhere else to go and had no choice but to shelter the children in the house. Her husband Patrick had, up to that point, avoided imprisonment and was therefore able to continue to care for their other children and possibly keep some level of income coming in to the family. In March 1887 Patrick Connor and Thomas Dunne were each sentenced by Tomas Wilson Walshe at Ballyglass Petty Sessions to seven days imprisonment at Castlebar Prison for unlawful trespass on a house or resisting eviction. They were committed on Thursday 17 March and it was their first time in prison. The Castlebar Prison Records show that Patrick Connor was 30 years old, 5ft 6" in height, 10s 3lb, with brown hair, blue eyes and a fresh complexion. He could read but could not write. Thomas Dunne was 40 years old, 5ft 5", 10s 12lb, with black hair, brown eyes and a fresh complexion. He could also read but could not write. Following their release on Thursday 24 March they visited the office of the Connaught Telegraph. The paper reported:

> The description of the hospitality they received at the 'Queen's Hotel,' Castlebar, baffles all description. One of the victims- Thomas Dunne- states that he was compelled to pick oakum,[198] although it was not ordered by the court; and because he stuffed the holes in the window with a portion of the pickings, to keep out the hail, his suppers were stopped. Both he and Pat Connor got the plank bed, with leave to seek the

soft end of the board for a bolster, with a pair of old blankets and a faded rug.[199]

According to the article Catherine Dunne was in a poor state in bed after the kicking she had received from Cuffe six months earlier. Patrick Connor had made a pact with the Sergeant and agreed to go to jail peacefully on condition that his wife Mary (who also had a warrant against her), was allowed to remain with their children while he was locked up. After Patrick was taken away the Sergeant went back on his promise and went to Gordon RO to ask him to take custody of the five Connor children. The following day, Friday 18 March, Mary Connor and her infant child were taken to prison where they remained until Friday 25 March.[200] The report concluded that had Gordon not reported the matter to James Daly, the Sergeant and Billy Cuffe would have taken the remainder of the children to the Workhouse in Castlebar. Daly once again used the occasion to pass judgment on the workings of the Land League, the Belcarra branch and the perceived lack of support for the tenants:

> It is true there is a branch of the I N League in Belcarra dragging out a kind of miserable existence, and we believe its members have done all power by way of local aid and otherwise, to assist the victims of oppression, but, if we are credibly informed, they have got nothing for a very long time from headquarters. Those in office in O'Connell Street Dublin, and who wish to hear themselves called the Executive of the Irish National League, when applied to for funds to sustain the Belcarra tenants in their death struggle wrote to the local branch expressing their regret that they had not funds; while that very week, and at successive meetings, they had sent grants to a large extent to Munster Counties and to parties who did not need it one fifth as much as did the Gardiner – Pringle victims at Belcarra.

The Connaught Telegraph also reported that on the following Wednesday a further series of evictions and clearances would be carried out on the Estate, that the evictions would be resisted and the tenants had made an offer to pay two years rent but this was not accepted by Gardiner. Dublin Castle had instructed the police in the area to assist Gardiner and Pringle in their endeavours.

Relief for the Connor & Dunne Children: March 1887

The Castlebar Guardians met in late March after the eviction notices were served. A.C Larminie, P. Baynes and M. Flynn were present thought it was noted that owing to the Balla fair there was a small attendance of Guardians. On 26 March, the proceedings of the Guardians were reported in the Connaught Telegraph. The Guardians noted that those who Eviction Notices had been served on included a catholic clergyman[201] and the Vice Chairman of the Castlebar Guardians.[202] Larminie in jest asked the Chairman what would happen if he took one of the evicted farms for himself. The Chairman responded that if he did he should take out a life insurance policy but that he should not expect to have to pay too many instalments on the premium. The tenants had offered to pay four years rent but it was declined by Gardiner as she wanted her *"pound of flesh"*. The RO informed the meeting that he was called upon to relieve provisionally the children of two or three families whose parents had been imprisoned. The families in question included the children of Patrick and Mary Connor and Thomas and Catherine Dunne. An order was made asking the RO to relieve the Connor and Dunne children pending release of the parents from jail.

Court Fines Gardiner: April 1887

The case of the Castlebar Guardians against Harriet Gardiner for failing to serve the requisite forty eight hours notice on the Guardians prior to the eviction of Thomas Dunne and others came before J.H. Richards QC., at Ballina Quarter Sessions on Monday 11 April. On April 16 the Connaught Telegraph carried a full report of the proceedings.[203] Gardiner was represented by her lawyer John Garvey. A.B. Kelly representing the Guardians reminded the Court that Dunne held land in two townlands. He lived in Logaphuill but Tully was the townland given, both were separated by a small road. James Daly was called to give evidence of the eviction of Dunne and his family. He explained that he was present at the eviction by Gardiner, Pringle, Billy Cuffe and up to one hundred policemen. Garvey put forward the argument that Dunne was in the property as an employee of Gardiner, a caretaker for which he was paid a penny a week. Dunne had, according to Garvey, been admitted as a caretaker after the first eviction in 1885. Gardiner was evicting him as caretaker and not tenant. The law did not apply to a caretaker:

> The law applied the same as it would if a man were dismissing his coachman or servant, and turning him out of possession.

The Judge disagreed and Gardiner was fined £20 and ordered to pay costs. On appeal by Gardiner the decision was confirmed. A further appeal was initially sought by Gardiner but on reflection her counsel, Mr. Trench, did not proceed with the appeal and a cheque for £20 plus costs was sent to A.B. Kelly. It was reported by the Connaught Telegraph that there were six other cases concerning evictions on the Belcarra Estate awaiting the outcome of this case. The next mention of the case is in the 20 August Edition of the Connaught Telegraph. The Guardians had passed a resolution of thanks to A.B. Kelly on receiving a letter from him and a cheque for £20. The Guardians considered Kelly to be a very able lawyer having previously had a major victory for the Guardians in the case of the Castlebar Guardians versus Ellicott:

> By his construction of the Seeds (Ireland) Act, Mr. Kelly made the land, not the ratepayer, liable for seeds granted to defaulting tenants, so that now such amounts must be paid by the subsequent occupiers, and not from the rates of the Electoral Division. It is well for the Castlebar Guardians to have such an astute and able expounder of the law, as Mr. Kelly has proved himself to be – a Lawyer who leads them on all occasions to victory. Castlebar is an exception to the Boards of

Guardians in this respect – thanks to their legal adviser – as such bodies are generally unsuccessful at law.

The Constabulary & the Tully Hut: April 1887
The 16 April Edition of the Connaught Telegraph carried the following update on policing in the area including Tully:

> Constable Farrell Shannon, who, for the last year and a half, had been stationed in Castlebar (and for several years in this district) was transferred, during the past week, to the bleak but romantic region of Leenane, and is replaced here by Constable Patrick May, who, for over fourteen months, had been engaged at the not very enticing duty of guarding "filthy Billy Cuffe" the dirty doer of dirty work for dirty Harriet Gardiner. It is a pleasing exchange for the "Royal" May boy to get away from that nasty Tully Hut, and be able again to mingle in civilized society, apart from the odious contact of detestable brutes like the infamous woman kicker Billy! As to Constable Shannon, who was a most respectable high-minded man in his position, we may say that he carries with him the esteem and good wishes of all who knew him in Castlebar, and admired him for his sterling independence of character. Constable Hughes and Lydon have also to congratulate themselves on their felicitous removal from that detestable Gardiner –Cuffe Hut, at Tully, as the former has been transferred to the Guardianship of Sergeant Feely, at Balla, while the latter member of "Royalty" has fallen into comfortable quarters with our good natured friend, Sergeant Heneghan of Deergrove...

Cuffe gives Notice of a Rent Office: September 1887
In late September Billy Cuffe, assisted by the police, distributed warnings to tenants who had not paid their rent. On Saturday 1 October Gardiner held a Rent Office in Castlebar. The Connaught Telegraph reported:

Crowds of men might be seen in the vicinity of the local "Zoo" some engaging their time by reading the inscriptions on the pedestal of the General O' Malley Statue, while more of them were discussing the advisability of summoning up courage enough to serve notices on the feeble old Gardiner hag for having a fair rent fixed. Only three personages were found to pay rent, one of them being a loud spoken sample of that dangerous, unreliable and treacherous, class of village "patriots", whose nationality is hardly worth a naggin of the bad whiskey in which they talkatively deal. The Gardiner-Pringle hags, finding that there was no such thing as rent forthcoming, and that the only bills negotiable or likely to be on the side of the tenants, were documents called "originating notices", (a goodly number of which they had received on Saturday) took to flight early on Monday. [204]

Walter (Watty) Mc Nally & his Neighbours: October 1887

On 1 October the Connaught Telegraph reported that Walter Mc Nally of Frenchill had taken legal proceedings against his neighbours the Hopkins, Beirnes and Wards for allowing their cattle to trespass and for assaulting him and his wife Biddy. When the case came to be heard Mc Nally sought an adjournment because Biddy was unable to attend due to the fact that she could not leave her bed after the beating she received. At the point when the adjournment was about to be granted the Connaught Telegraph reported that Biddy arrived in Court to the amazement of her husband. The dispute, according to the report, centered on the evicted holding of Oliver Canton. Canton's neighbours allowed their animals to graze on his grass. Mc Nally had, according to the Correspondent, a *"claim to a monopoly of the "stolen fruits" of that waste soil, and feels indignant at the intrusion of others."* This may have been because Canton's wife was a McNally but this is not mentioned in the report. Evidence was given that Biddy Mc Nally had driven the animals from Canton's land on to her own potato crop and then accused her neighbours of trespass. The Magistrates found in favour of Mc Nally. Browne found that the neighbours were the wrong doers because they had their livestock on Gardiner's land without her consent or the consent of Billy Cuffe. On the assault charge Mc Nally gave evidence that Thomas Beirne had *"caught him and shoved him against the wall with his whole weight!"* Beirne was fined 10s and costs.

Castlebar Rent Office: December 1887
On Monday 5 December, as the year was coming to a close, Gardiner and Pringle held another Rent Office in Castlebar. Billy Cuffe had invited tenants to attend and pay their rent. The following Saturday the Connaught Telegraph, under the heading *"The Witches on The War-Path"* reported:

> On Monday last those graceful and beautiful beings, known to an admiring public (by whom they are affectionately endeared and respected!!) as Miss Harriet Gardiner and Miss Susan Pringle, visited Castlebar for the first time in some months. Their estimable and "nobly" descended gentleman of all operations and capacities the illustrious Billy Puck (or Cuffe) invited the tenants on the Belcarra estate to attend at the Zoological "office" and pay to the pair of old weather-beaten damsels their compliments in the shape of rent. A few snakes of the real serf type slunk in, and paid all that was demanded. They, however, were very few; but others, actuated with a little more pluck, demanded a reduction, to which they got the curt reply from the old Scotty dame that they would not get a farthing! With a mischievous grin and something that might be mistaken for a bow, they retired, but made not the smallest deposit, and are likely to continue so until the old Gardiner cup-tosser is brought to a sense of duty. She may threaten to evict, and carry out her threats; but she has reason to know that all the lands she now has, or is likely to take possession of, will remain as valueless to her as if they were situated in the Arctic regions, Miss Gardiner will likely have to give substantial reductions before she gets much rent from the

tenants on the Belcarra estate, notwithstanding all the snarling of her brace growlers – Pringle and Cuffe![205]

Other Evictions: 1885–1887

Not all of the evictions on the Belcarra Estate between 1885 and 1887 were reported in the press or were the subject of legal proceedings. Markings on the Cancellation Books highlight the possibility that there were others as the timing of changes to the entries on the books coincides with evictions elsewhere on the Estate. The tenement of Patrick Irwin of Barney is one such case. In 1885 his name was replaced on the Books by his unnamed representatives suggesting that he had died. This may have been John Irwin who occupied the adjacent tenement. In any case Gardiner became occupier in 1886 and by 1887 the house and buildings were recorded as *"down"*. In 1887 John Flanagan of Kilbrennan and Martin Skiffington of Deerpark Lower also had their names replaced on the valuation books by Gardiner.

BE JUST AND FEAR NOT- CROWBAR AND BAYONET RULE

While the baneful work of exterminating our people is heartlessly carried on by remorseless landlords, and while the youth of our famishing country find no resource left them but the emigrant ship and the bitter experience of law- enforced exile, it is painful to reflect on our hapless condition under a system of mis-government that, instead of protecting its subjects and fostering their interests, seems only to delight in treating them with brutality, and employing every devisable method for the extirpation from the cherished soil that bore them. That the territorial despots of Ireland –hereditary robbers of the people – are the favored pets of our so – called rulers, is an un deniable fact, and for the benefit of that cruel and always dishonest class of the community, British law, on this side of the channel, would seem to be solely instituted as it is, certainly, administered with shameful partiality, is plain to the most obtuse intellect; and thus it happens that Irishmen, in the land of their nativity, are treated with far less consideration than animals of the brute creation.[206]

Mass Evictions: Spring 1888

The heading *"Be Just & Fear Not-Crowbar and Bayonet Rule"* appeared in the April 14 1888 Edition of the Connaught Telegraph. Following a lull in evictions in early 1888, Gardiner and Pringle went back to work in late February and early March when up to 100 orders for eviction were served on the Belcarra Estate. Many tenants had offered to pay some rent but most were unable to pay. The Connaught Telegraph reported:

> In the majority of cases the tenants only owe one year's rent. In many instances they had offered the full rent due, and by some strange whim, or, as the Demon of Discord would move her, the Pringle old hag threw back the money in the faces of the tenants, and ordered the hapless serfs out of her sight. The greater number of those served with ejectments are unable to pay, and out they must go unless the County Courts Judge give an extension of time, or afford them the privilege

of paying by instalments. After years of rack-renting and persecution, most of them are unable to pay; but they must leave, having only one consolation and that is, that not one will be found to possess a single perch of the lands from which they are about being mercilessly driven.[207]

On Wednesday 21 March Gardiner obtained Magistrate's Orders at Ballyglass Petty Sessions against several Belcarra evicted tenants for re-entering their homes with their families. Under the headline *"Dirty Gardiner Still"* the Connaught Telegraph reported:

> That degraded monster of iniquity, Billy Puck (who calls himself Cuffe) acted in the dual capacity of summons server and prosecutor of the unfortunate serfs. We understand that summonses have been issued against another batch of the evicted on that tenant –persecuted estate, while over 100 ejectments are served for next sessions. [208]

Patrick and Mary Connor and Thomas and Catherine Dunne were each fined 10s and ordered to pay costs for trespassing on their homes in January. In default of payment they were to spend seven days in Castlebar Prison. A case against Mary Dunne, daughter of Catherine Dunne, was withdrawn due to her youth. Gardiner also obtained an order for possession against John Garvey (Long). The record shows that Garvey was in possession as a caretaker and refused to leave when requested to do so by Billy Cuffe.

Tully Hut: April 1888
On 14 April the Connaught Telegraph carried a lengthy article on landlordism, under the heading *"Be Just and Fear Not- Crowbar and Bayonet Rule."*

The extermination of the Irish people, emigration, English brutality, the mismanagement of Irish affairs and the *"the black coated police and the red- coated soldiery of the empire"* are all passionately dealt with. The article is however, of particular interest as it notes that twenty five percent of the tenants on the Belcarra Estate were under threat of eviction at that time. There is also a description of the manned police hut at Tully:

> Then this paragon of dissipated brutality, and nasty caricature of womanhood, has a police hut, manned by a sergeant and four other tunic-bearers, on her eviction- cursed property at Tully, for the purpose of guarding her ill-begotten relative, Billy Cuffe, who combines, in his abominable looking person, the various offices of bum-bailiff, rent warner, emergency man, special summons server, and any other filthy duty that may devolve on a conscience-lost tool of all dirty work, and this garrison is quartered on a peaceful locality, where there never was even the semblance of an "outrage" although the regular barrack of Belcarra, with its half-dozen of half-lazy occupants, is within less than an Irish mile of the Cuffe-Gardiner iron structure!

One of the men who served in the Tully Hut was Constable James Dignam. He was described in the Connaught Telegraph as a *"quiet inoffensive young fellow"* on the occasion of his transfer from Ballyhaunis to County Westmeath in 1893.[209] He had also served at Balla and Ballyglass.

The Case of Ann Staunton, Ballyshane: April 1888

On Wednesday 18 April the Castlebar Petty Sessions heard a case taken by Ann Staunton of Ballyshane against Pringle.[210] Staunton had gone to the rent office at Ellison Street, Castlebar to pay rent. After the visit Staunton alleged that Pringle had swindled her out of money over and above what was due. On Saturday 21 April, the Connaught Telegraph under the heading *"Pringle At Congenial Work!"* reported that Gardiner denied all knowledge of the affair in Court. Pringle also had difficulty recalling the events prompting Staunton's lawyer P.J. Kelly to raise the matter of Pringle's drinking:

Susan, however, was examined, but remembered very little of the transaction. "As far as my memory goes" was a favorite phrase with her, but Mr. P J Kelly (who appeared for Mrs. Staunton) told her to swear to facts and never mind her memory, which, he feared, is often very shaky. She could give no clear account of the transaction, but positively denied having charged the 10s 6d twice; and when nearly cornered by Mr. Kelly as to whether she had been dealing in something stronger than wine, she half-imploringly turned her pinched-up shriveled countenance towards the sympathising optic of the blooming J P, on the exalted place and exclaimed "that's not the way to treat a lady, I think!"

Pringle suggested that if she had the rent book she would be able to recall the events. The case was adjourned to allow Pringle to produce the rent book. There would appear to be no subsequent coverage of the outcome of the case.

Imprisonment of Mary Connor & Catherine Dunne: April 1888

Mary Connor was jailed for the final time on Saturday 28 April. W.T. Longbourne sentenced her to seven days imprisonment at Castlebar Prison for trespass. On the same day Longbourne also committed Thomas Dunne's wife Catherine for the same period and for the same offence. The Castlebar Prison Records show that Catherine was 46 years old, 5ft 6" tall, 9s. 9lb with sandy brown hair, blue eyes and a pale complexion. She was born in Lakehill, possibly near Knock.

Decisions in Rent Reduction Cases: May 1888

In May a number of applications for rent reduction were heard in Castlebar by the Land Sub-Commission No. 9 under the Chairmanship of J.H Edge. Reductions were granted in all cases taken by Belcarra tenants.[211]

Land Sub-Commission Decisions in respect of Tenants of Harriet Gardiner, Landlord.									
Tenant	Old Rent	£	S	D	New Rent	£	S	D
Pat Byrne		10	0	0		8	0	0
Mary Riley		4	10	0		3	10	0
Patrick Hopkins		5	10	0		4	5	0
John Walsh (Tom)		6	4	0		4	10	0
John Walsh (Pat)		5	13	5.5		4	0	0
Pat Connor Junr		5	10	0		4	5	0
Pat Fadden		5	18	8		5	0	0
Thomas & Owen Cooney		5	15	0		4	5	0
Pat Martin		7	0	0		6	0	0
Pat Walsh (Rd)		4	15	0		3	12	0
Pat Mc Donnell		4	12	6		3	5	0
Pat & Julia Walsh		9	0	0		5	12	6
Jane Malley		4	12	6		3	0	0
Pat Walsh (David)		5	12	6		4	5	0
Thomas & Luke Madden		9	5	0		5	15	0
Arthur Madden		4	12	6		3	2	6
Edward Rodgers		5	15	0		5	5	0
James Walsh		8	0	0		6	12	6
Pat Walsh (Pat)		8	15	0		8	15	0
Edward Lally		2	18	7		2	4	0
P. Connor, Senr., Rep. of O. Vahey		7	0	0		5	8	0
M. Mitchell, Rep. of M. Lally		8	0	0		6	10	0
Anne Staunton		17	10	0		10	10	0
Peter Kearns		15	2	0		12	0	0

The Case of Patrick Walsh of Logaphuill: July 1888
In July Patrick Walsh of Logaphuill was fined 1/- and ordered to pay costs by H.W. Jordan at Castlebar Petty Sessions for trespass by his mare and foal on 17 July. He had been summoned by Sergeant Charles Cox. Cox was, at that time, in charge of the Police Hut at Tully. The report contains a detailed description of the Tully Hut and Sergeant Cox.

> Tully Hut is an improvised structure got up by our landlord cherishing rulers for the advantage of dirty Billy Cuffe, the dirty bailiff, spy, and emergency tool of dirty whiskey -drinking Harriet Gardiner. There are four or five sable- coated "Royal" idlers quartered in this domicile, who have evidently nothing to do but look after their nasty protégé. But the regular barrack of Belcarra is little more than a mile away from them, and the usual constabulary duty need not give them much trouble; still, it would seem that-if only to show that they are policemen as well as Cuffe's men –they occasionally indulge in the luxury of a case in public court, and perform a slight touch of swearing exercise, just to keep themselves in practice and prevent the possibility of them getting rusty at the business!. Sergeant Charles Cox, who has command of this half-iron half-earthen fortification at Tully, is not, indeed a very fat, nor a very blooming, nor a very handsome individual; but he is, undoubtedly, a very honest, straightforward, and diligent displayer of yellow V's and one who will carefully attend to the duties of "Royal" calling. Very probably Pat Walsh of Logafoil would think him too good in this respect, as his harmless mare and her innocent foal were quietly walking along the road for themselves on the 17th inst, as was the custom there before ever a Cox, a Cuffe, or a hut came to Tully, and this prime boy of a sergeant summoned him for all that! [212]

John Garvey (Long) & Bridget Garvey: July- October 1888
By the summer of 1888 the situation must have been intolerable for the Garveys. On 11 July at Ballyglass Petty Sessions

a number of cases taken by Gardiner against Garvey and his wife Bridget were adjourned. Bridget Garvey stood accused of using forcible entry and taking possession of her home. John Garvey stood accused of using violence and intimidation towards Gardiner. Cuffe also had a case against John Garvey for using violence and intimidation against him. The cases arose out of the events of 3 April in that year when Cuffe had sought to prevent the Garveys re-entering the Garvey home. Later in July John Garvey was before Ballyglass Petty Sessions again and on this occasion he was imprisoned for one month for wrongfully taking possession of his house. He was released on Friday 24 August. The case taken by Billy Cuffe against Garvey for assault was withdrawn. The case against Bridget Garvey for wrongfully taking possession of her home was adjourned.

Trespass Cases: July 1888

At the same hearing a number of trespass cases taken by Gardiner against the tenants were listed for hearing. Two cases against John Connor for trespass by his cattle and sheep at Tully were adjourned. This was the beginning of a long line of similar cases against him. A case against Catherine Burke of Tully was also adjourned. Gardiner was however successful in another case against Catherine Burke for trespass of livestock and similarly against John Kelly, John Garvey Jnr., and Patrick Lavelle and fines were imposed in each case. In the case against Catherine Burke a number of the tenants appeared as witnesses against Gardiner including John Connor and his son Martin. On Saturday 11 August the Connaught Telegraph reported that Gardiner and Pringle were disappointed at the failure of a number of the trespass cases they had taken against the Tully tenants. Everything did not however go Gardiner and Pringle's way following the hearing at Ballyglass either as, according to the Connaught Telegraph:

> The pair of unfortunate old tenant-torturers came to grief on their return from Ballyglass to Castlebar, as the vehicle got a tumble, throwing the poor old creatures topsy-turvy. The

miserable frame of the Pringle hag was so light that she fared better than the old Gardiner bundle; and so the latter came to town with her head bandaged in old calico (a portion, it is said, if not all, of the unmentionables garment worn by her better half, Pringle) – a pair of bandages, a broken nose, and a half broken arm. A good many aver they were sober, and it was the old horse was drunk on the occasion.[213]

A few weeks later on 5 September the trespass cases taken by Gardiner against John Connor and Catherine Burke were adjourned again at Ballyglass Petty Sessions. The case against John Garvey's wife Bridget for wrongfully taking hold of a house was also adjourned.

Continued Persecution of John Garvey (Long): October 1888

On Wednesday 3 October the Garveys were back at Ballyglass Petty Sessions. John T. Dillon and Colonel W.B Longbourne sentenced John Garvey to three months imprisonment for wrongfully taking and holding his home on 13 September. Bridget Garvey was sentenced to one month for the offence of forcible possession of a house and land. This was the worst possible outcome. When Bridget Garvey was committed, the prison records show that she was accompanied by a female child. The remainder of the children were left to fend for themselves. Castlebar Prison Records show that when Bridget was committed she was 45 years old, 5ft 4", 124lb; with grey hair, blue eyes and a sallow complexion. Her place of birth is given as Prizon near Balla. Bridget Garvey was released on Friday 2 November 1888; John was released on Wednesday 2 January 1889. On 6 October the National League was again criticized by the Connaught Telegraph which highlighted the plight of the Garvey family:

> The visit of the pair of Scottish amazons to Ballyglass resulted in getting poor John Garvey and his wife, tenants on the Belcarra estate, terms of three and one month respectively,

for the crime of trying to hold the; "firm grip" on their old domicile in Tully, Garvey and his wife have suffered several terms of incarceration, varying from one week to one month, for a repetition of the same offence. The "Removables" are now improving their hand to see what virtue may result in giving this unfortunate man, Garvey, three months, though the poor persecuted creature has repeatedly offered a year's rent, which would not be accepted, because time for redemption has long since expired. Poor Garvey has been carrying on a heroic struggle, without the slightest aid from the National League, or any organization for the benefit of evicted tenants.

When the Castlebar Guardians met later that month James Daly chaired the meeting.[214] Forty five eviction notices had been served on the RO. Harriet Gardiner had served four of these. It was noted that John Garvey of Tully and his wife were serving three months and one month in prison respectively while their children were left on the wayside to starve.[215] On the same day that John and Bridget Garvey were imprisoned the previously adjourned trespass cases against Catherine Burke and John Connor were finally heard. Catherine Burke was ordered to pay compensation to Harriet Gardiner for trespass by a cow. The two cases against John Connor were dismissed.

Thomas Dunne Evicted Again: October 1888
A further case against Thomas Dunne came before J.H. Richards at Castlebar Land Sessions on Tuesday 30 October. Gardiner obtained a decree against Dunne and it was noted by Gardiner's lawyer Garvey that Dunne had been imprisoned numerous times for re-entering his home following eviction. Both Pringle and Gardiner were present at the hearing. According to the report in the Connaught Telegraph Pringle proved the case while Gardiner sat on a side bench with her arm in a sling.[216]

Part VII

The House of Gardiner, Pringle & Cuffe

Pringle At The Crowbar[217]

One of the most atrocious evictions witnessed in this part of the country for years took place here on Thursday last. Thomas Ward, of Frenchill, and his poor sick wife were cast on the roadside, and their once comfortable home levelled with the ground. The atrocity was carried out to satisfy the craze of the pair of heartless evictors, Gardiner and Pringle.[218]

Scandalous Exhibition of Debauchery: February 1889
In the spring of 1889 Gardiner and Pringle were engaged in surveying holdings on the Belcarra Estate. On Monday 18 February they arrived in Castlebar train station in a drunken state. The Connaught Telegraph reported that Gardiner was so drunk that she fell several times between Castlebar Train Station and the Mall.[219] She arrived at her destination covered in mud and blood from injuries to her mouth and nose. The pair took refuge in a property at the Mall guarded by the police while *"young urchins of the town"* were outside shouting and jeering. The Connaught Telegraph questioned whether Gardiner would be prosecuted for her scandalous exhibition of debauchery.

Gardiner & Pringle Rebuked: April 1889
On 27 March Gardiner served notice on the RO that she intended to evict seven families on the Belcarra Estate. Billy Cuffe assisted by police based at the Tully Hut travelled around the estate telling tenants to pay their rent or their houses would be levelled. The Connaught Telegraph reported that Gardiner and Pringle arrived in Castlebar during the week on a rickety old jaunting car.[220] Gardiner was in such a state of helplessness when she arrived that she had to be carried in to her house in Castlebar by two police men, Pringle and her bailiffs. Things did not go to plan on the legal front either and for the first time there is evidence that the authorities were losing patience with the pair. It was reported that Gardiner became very angry when she discovered that she had missed the legal deadline for eviction of the tenants on the Estate by a single day and as a consequence she would have to start the legal process over again from

the beginning. The fault in her mind lay with Pringle and Cuffe. The Connaught Telegraph reported:

> So disturbed was the poor half-mad, half-stupid and wholly "muddled" Harriet on that occasion, that she foamed, and raged, and bellowed in the nearly beastly style peculiar to her abandoned self; so that quarrels with Pringle, curses and personal abuse of unfortunate Billy Cuffe (whom she disdains to acknowledge any longer as a relative) and complete dissatisfaction with the world and everything in it, left the wretched old animal no other consolation than that usually derived from her favored companion of the Jameson production![221]

Things were no better when she attended eviction hearings at the Court in Castlebar on Thursday 4 April. The Connaught Telegraph Correspondent reported that Judge Richards:

> administered to both of them such a cutting rebuke as would be keenly felt by persons of benevolence…[222]

Richards accused the pair of causing a great deal of trouble and annoyance in his court and pointed out that if Gardiner had appointed a proper agent to manage her affairs, rents would be paid and the poor tenants would not be put to all the trouble and unnecessary expense that they had been put to. In the course of the hearing B. Whitney, Clerk of the Crown complained that his own office had been besieged by tenants from the Belcarra Estate seeking to lodge their rents with him before the time for redemption expired and thus avoid eviction. It was suggested that Gardiner and Pringle did not want to collect the rents before the deadline as this would enable the tenants to stay in their homes for another year. Whitney did not want his office used in this way. According to the Connaught Telegraph Correspondent, an application was made by Gardiner's lawyer John Garvey to Whitney's office to have the lodged rents released. Whitney refused because he had given receipts to the tenants who had lodged the rents and he could not release the money until he got the receipts back from the tenants. Tenants (including James Moran), used the opportunity in court to request an allowance of half the poor rates which the Judge accepted was their right.

Tully & Logaphuill Evictions and Demolitions: April 1889

Notwithstanding the setbacks and rebukes Gardiner and Pringle were back in action a few days later on Tuesday 9 April. Together with the Sheriff's representative John Jennings and a force of police they were back in Tully and Logaphuill on the business of eviction. Armed with locks, keys, hammers, nails and crowbars, Gardiner, and her crew, started the day at Frenchill at the home of Thomas Ward. Ward offered to pay one years' rent when they arrived at his house but it was refused and the crowbars were put to work. The Connaught Telegraph reported:

> When a portion of the furniture was rudely flung outside, it was discovered that Mrs. Ward, who is a feeble old woman, was unable to leave her bed. Against the brutal order of the "gentle" Susan Pringle, John Jennings, with creditable considerateness, openly refused to have the sick woman removed, without authority of a medical man, and so the matter fell through. A messenger was sent for a Castlebar doctor, who, however, felt better engaged at other duties than forming a portion of Gardiner's eviction crusade-particularly as the chances of professional remuneration from Susan or Harriet might look gloomy![223]

The Wards avoided eviction again but Cuffe was not finished with them. Gardiner then moved on to the house of Catherine Dunne and here Billy Cuffe got his revenge for the accusations that Catherine Dunne had made against him arising out of her eviction in September 1886. Catherine Dunne had initially succeeded in her action against Cuffe for assaulting her. On appeal however the case was not heard before a jury but instead came before a Grand Jury comprised of twenty three landlords and agents.[224] Cuffe was acquitted and once again he stood before the home of his accuser Catherine Dunne and her children. On this occasion Catherine Dunne was alone with the children. Thomas had gone to England to work there and earn money to redeem their holding. According to the Connaught Telegraph Correspondent Dunne had succeeded in getting work in England and had saved money but it was stolen by *"the son of an underling of Gardiner"* who borrowed it from the unsuspecting Dunne and fled to America with it. The impact on Dunne was catastrophic, he *"became a brain tortured maniac"* and was committed to a mental asylum in England.[225] Catherine Dunne and her children were thrown out and Cuffe had the house levelled. Thomas Dunne's name was finally replaced by Gardiner on the Cancellation Books for both Tully Beg and Logaphuill and the Dunne home is shown as demolished. The Cancellation Books also show that the home of Bridget Dunne in Tully Beg had been demolished by 1888 and her name similarly replaced. It had taken Cuffe four years to bring the Dunne occupation in Logaphuill to an end. The issue for Catherine Dunne now was where to take her children.

Following the destruction of the Dunne home, Cuffe, Gardiner and the others moved on to the Connor home at Tully and this house was also levelled. Patrick Connor's name was removed from the Cancellation Books in 1886; the house was removed in 1889. Patrick and Mary Connor had held on to their home for four years. In 1889 they left Tully with their family and emigrated never to return.

Eviction of Thomas & Mary-Ann Ward: May 1889
Just over one month later, Gardiner and Pringle concluded their persecution of Thomas and Mary-Ann Ward. The attempted eviction of a few weeks earlier had failed due to the Sheriff's unwillingness to put Mary-Ann out of the house before she was examined by a doctor. Gardiner, determined to finally evict the Wards and end their occupation at Frenchill, set about arrang-

ing for a doctor to make an unannounced call. Dr. Knott called on Mary-Ann on Wednesday 22 May and pronounced her fit to be removed. According to a letter published in the Connaught Telegraph the outcome was never in doubt as Dr. Knott was Gardiner's *"Greasy old friend and relative."*[226] The cost of the house call was paid for by Gardiner. The following day Gardiner arrived at Frenchill with a large police force to finally end the Ward occupation. A letter published in the Connaught Telegraph the following Saturday and signed *"Frenchill"* contains the following vivid description of the eviction:

> ...early the next day (Thursday) a large posse of police surrounded the Ward mansion, and, in a very short time, the nasty old fellow Billy Cuffe and an emergency man named Corcoran, who hails from somewhere about Farmhill with crowbars in hand, did the house levelling in real Balfourian fashion. Poor Ward's turf, potatoes and little furniture were strewn about the ditches, the rafters were cut and broken, the walls were pulled down, and the whole place left in total ruin, while the poor sick woman Mrs. Ward, was left stretchered under the wall in a downpour of rain!!

In 1887 Thomas Ward's name was replaced by Gardiner's on the Cancellation Books reflecting the earlier eviction. Following the demolition of the house and outbuildings the valuation was reduced.

Gardiner & Pringle build a New House in Tully: May 1889

The letter published in the Connaught Telegraph concerning the Ward eviction also highlights that on the day of the eviction a stone mason from Castlebar was working on a new house for Gardiner and Pringle in Tully. The mason and his men stopped work on the house to observe the eviction. According to the letter the mason was once an ardent nationalist and probably still considered himself to be. Work on the house resumed when the eviction was secured and the Ward house levelled. The mason's crew is described in the letter as a *"few groggy faced army pensioners, who hang out about the corners of the slums of Castlebar."* The stones of the evicted and levelled homes were employed in the construction of the new house. Though the precise location of the Deacy and Connor homes is unclear it is likely they were close to the construction site and it is the remains of these houses that are referred to in the letter. The old Macken house was retained and served as a caretaker's house for Billy Cuffe and his successors.

Front & side view of Gardiner & Pringle House, Tully, 2012. Porch to the front added during 20th Century. (Photograph by James O'Connor & Michael O'Connor with the kind permission of Mr. Bernard Gibbons, Tully).

The letter concludes with the following warning to Gardiner and Pringle:

> The people here look on and laugh at the whole performance, as it is generally believed that the pair of old tyrants will scarce be spared to see the interior of the new shanty discoloured

with smoke until they are called upon to cross the bourne over which travellers in this world of tears can never return. I can safely say that neither they nor those who are sustaining them in their dirty work can have the prayer or blessing of the dozens of evicted and half-famished serfs driven from their homesteads in Logafoil and Tully, after a most cruel and atrocious manner!

Trespass Cases: October 1889

The 12 October Edition of the Connaught Telegraph reported that Harriet Gardiner had taken forty seven cases against the tenants of Logaphuill for trespass. The cases were heard at Ballyglass Petty Sessions on 2 October though the records show that there were actually 23 cases before magistrates Lynch, Dunstervill[227] and Colonel Blake. Gardiner was absent and was represented by Pringle who had engaged John Garvey. P.J. Kelly represented the tenants. Kelly succeeded in having a number of the cases dismissed due to irregularities with signatures on the summonses. Gardiner had five cases against each of Patrick and Michael Lavelle of Logaphuill for trespass by a variety of livestock during the summer of 1889. Kelly succeeded in having the cases dismissed. There were also five cases against John Connor for trespass by livestock during that summer. Cuffe and Pringle gave evidence against Connor and in one of the cases he was ordered to pay compensation to Gardiner. Connor made no appearance for the remainder of the hearings. Patsy Cosgrave (alias Walsh), Logaphuill, was ordered to pay compensation to Gardiner for allowing his pigs on to Thomas Dunne's evicted lands. The report suggests that Patsy and his son William had made their services available to Billy Cuffe for drawing turf with their black mare. Thomas Walsh, Logaphuill was ordered to pay Gardiner compensation in one case and did not appear for two others. There were also cases for trespass against John Garvey (Long), his son John, and Logaphuill tenants, Thomas Conway, William Moran, Thomas Dunne, and Patt Stanton. The defendants did not make an appearance. An order for possession was granted against Bridget Madden of Elmhall. She had been evicted and allowed to re-enter as a caretaker. When Billy Cuffe demanded possession she refused. The court appointed Cuffe as Special Bailiff to take possession for Gardiner. A case taken by Billy Cuffe against Mary Walsh, Elmhall for assault on 28 August did not proceed as the defendant did not appear.

Attempted Shooting & Assault at Tully: December 1889

By December 1889 construction of Gardiner and Pringle's new house at Tully was complete. According to one source the house was built on the site of the Tully Police Hut.[228] As the house still stands today it is possible to pin point the location of the infamous Tully Hut. Patrick Macken's evicted house, at that point occupied by Billy Cuffe, stood a few yards away to the rear on the north side of the new house. Part of the limestone gable of that house still stands. We know from earlier correspondence published in the Connaught Telegraph that stones from evicted and levelled dwellings were used by the stone mason in building the new house.[229] The house had three rooms including a kitchen that was used as a Rent Office. Tenants entered by the back door on the north side of the building.[230] The house, which has now been vacant since the mid 1980s, is located at a cross roads in what would have been the heart of the old village. A long straight avenue runs from the main Castlebar road to the house.

It was to this house that Michael Cunniff of Barney, a small townland in the Parish of Breaghwy, went on Tuesday 3 and Wednesday 4 December to pay his rent. He had sold cattle at the market in Westport on the Monday and was in a position to make a payment to Gardiner. What happened next became what the Belfast Newsletter referred to as an *"Extraordinary action against Miss. Harriet Gardiner."*[231] Cunniff took legal proceedings against Gardiner accusing her of attempting to shoot him with her revolver and beating him with a stick. Gardiner, in turn, accused him of coming to Tully to rob her. According to a letter in the Connaught Telegraph a similar attempt was made by Gardiner on the life of the Widow Walsh later that day.[232]

Emergency Man looses an Eye: December 1889

The violence was to continue into December. On the evening of Saturday 14 December one of Gardiner's emergency men, a man named Londra, was on the road from Castlebar when he got into an argument with another man. Londra had a reputation as a fighting man and had his leg broken two years earlier in a fight. On this occasion he was reported to have left his cart on the road to go and beat another man. The man, in defending himself, hit Londra in the face, and as a consequence Londra lost an eye. In a letter to the Editor of the Connaught Telegraph the cases of Londra and Cunniff are used to illustrate the different approaches of the police. In the case of Cunniff no action is taken against his assailant. In the Londra case a posse of police is dispatched to find the perpetrator of the alleged offence. This is done according to the author of the letter to *"give an agrarian tinge to the drunken row, occasioned by the fighting proclivities of Londra."*[233]

Tully: December 1889

By the end of 1889, six years after the arrival of Gardiner, Tully was a very different place. Patrick Macken's house was now occupied by Billy Cuffe and his wife. The Mackens had left the village. Patrick's co-tenant John Macken and his wife had emigrated. The Deacy's had also left following the demolition of their house. Nearby were the ruins of Patrick Connor's house. Patrick and his family had emigrated. The stones of the Deacy and Connor houses now formed part of Gardiner's new abode next door to the Macken house. Both John Connor and Thomas Walsh had been evicted but both men had managed to redeem their holdings before the time for redemption had passed. Patrick Burke had either died or left the village though his house was still standing. Robert Cardy had also gone. Nearby his mother Bridget's house was also down. James Fallon had left and John Kelly had either died or left and his tenements were divided between Michael Lavelle, Patrick Lavelle and Thomas Garvey. The latter would appear to have succeeded to one of Kelly's houses. John Garvey (Long) was holding on to his house but only just. He had been evicted but had re-entered. James Garvey had died and was succeeded by John Garvey (James) one of the few men not to be evicted. Owen Vahey had died and his land passed to his relative by marriage Patrick Connor (not to be confused with Patrick Connor of Tully), who lived near the Daly residence at Coachfield. Patrick had also been evicted by Gardiner from the land he leased at Tully.

Part VIII

Gardiner in Decline & the Rise of Pringle

Gardiner in Decline

We learn that old Gardiner is about shaking off the mortal coil. She is laid up in the Tully hut, attended by old Pringle and Billy Cuffe. She has had medical advice and a visit from the parson. Apparently she is claiming her passport to cross the bourne from which sinners never return. Nil De Morituris! [234]

Trespass Cases: January 1890

On Wednesday 22 January 1890 Gardiner had 15 trespass cases before Dunstervill and Stewart at Ballyglass Petty Sessions and she did not succeed in getting a decision in any of them. Two cases against each of John Connor and Anthony Vahy and three against Thomas Garvey were adjourned. Cases against Lawrence Kearns, Belcarra and Patrick Lavelle, Logaphuill did not proceed as the defendants did not make an appearance. Three cases against Anne Corlis and her brother John both of Ballyfharna were also adjourned. A case against Bridget Madden for refusing to give up possession of her house at Elmhall was also adjourned. The reason for the adjournments is not clear but it may have related to Gardiner's ill health.

Gardiner on her Last Legs: February 1890

Though it is unlikely that many of the tenants on the Belcarra Estate had regular access to the press those that did read the 1 February Edition of the Connaught Telegraph must have felt a sense of relief at the news that their landlord and tormentor was on her death bed. The paper, in an article headed *"On Her Last Legs"* reported that Gardiner was laid up in her *"hut"* in Tully on her death bed attended to by Pringle and Billy Cuffe. The tenants would however have to wait another two years for Gardiner's death.

Trespass, Eviction & Boycott: February 1890

By mid February Gardiner would seem to have recovered though there is evidence that Pringle was taking more control of matters. On Wednesday 19 February Gardiner obtained a decree for possession at Ballyglass Petty Sessions against Bridget Madden of Elmhall and Billy Cuffe was appointed Special Bailiff by the court to take possession of the house. Susanna Pringle and James Cavanagh appeared as witnesses for Gardiner. Madden had held possession as a caretaker following an earlier eviction.

On the same day Blake and Dunsterville held that they had no jurisdiction to hear a case taken by Gardiner against Thomas Joyce of Newtown. According to Gardiner, Joyce had, on 6 February, agreed to supply six carts of turf to her but subsequently refused to deliver it. Joyce obviously had second thoughts about the bargain and may have been subjected to a warning of the consequences had he fulfilled the contract. Gardiner succeeded in an action against Patrick Lavelle for trespass and in two cases against John Connor. According to the Connaught Telegraph Correspondent there were, at that time, ten holdings in Tully and five of these were now evicted.[235] The report confirmed that farming practices in Tully had not changed since before the Famine. The land was still held as a rundale holding with little or no fences. Pringle, on Gardiner's behalf, sought to prosecute the remaining tenants by charging them with trespass for allowing their animals to walk on the waste and unfenced evicted holdings. In a case against John Connor, Billy Cuffe gave evidence of the trespass by Connor's horse and sheep. A defence that there were no fences was not accepted. Patrick Lavelle was also fined for trespass by his sheep.

Trespass Cases: March 1890
On Wednesday 19 March Gardiner had fifteen trespass cases listed for hearing at Ballyglass Petty Sessions before Colonel Blake. The cases included some of those adjourned at the 22 January sitting of the Court. There were five cases against John Connor, two against Anthony Vahy, four against Thomas Garvey, one against Catherine Burke and three against Anne and John Corlis. The defendants did not make an appearance.

Castlebar Quarter Sessions-Land Cases: April 1890

On Tuesday 1 April Pringle obtained a decree against Redmond Reilly for the payment of one year's rent in 14 days. Reilly had been willing to pay by instalments. Similarly Michael Cunniff had offered to pay his rent by instalments and the offer was accepted. The Connaught Telegraph reported:

> The blessed and holy Harriet had, altogether, no less than 39 ejectments at this sessions, against her Belcarra victims. 'Teetotaler' as she is, she does not deny that she is the "boy " to use a revolver properly![236]

The reference to the revolver was in the context of a case heard the day before at Castlebar Quarter Sessions.

Michael Cunniff & Harriet Gardiner: March – July 1890

Michael Cunniff and his brothers John and Patrick leased an eighty eight acre farm from Harriet Gardiner at Barney a short distance from Tully. Though the land was not split for valuation purposes the rates payable were. John and Patrick paid £10. 10/- each and Michael £11. 15/-. The higher valuation reflected the fact that Michael's share included a house.[237] The rent payable to Gardiner was likely to have been at least equal to the rateable valuation. This would have meant that the combined total for rates and rent was likely to have exceeded £60 per annum. In 1889 John Cunniff's name was struck from the Cancellation Books and replaced by Gardiner reflecting the fact that Gardiner had taken possession of the tenement. On Monday 2 December of that year, Michael Cunniff sold cattle at the market in Westport. The following day he made the short journey to Tully to pay his rent but there was nobody at Gardiner's house. Cunniff returned the following day. This time Gardiner, Pringle and Cuffe were at home. Cunniff went inside and the door was closed and locked by Pringle. Cuffe's wife was outside the house and nearby Anne Connor was putting washing out on a clothes line. Connor heard a commotion coming from the house and sometime after this she witnessed Cunniff emerging from the house.

The case taken by Michael Cunniff against Harriet Gardiner for assault, battery and threatening to shoot him while he was at her house in Tully on 4 December 1889 was heard on Monday 31 March 1890. As the police had not sought to prosecute Gardiner, Cunniff was left with no choice but to proceed by way of a civil action against her. Michael Cunniff was represented by P.J. Kelly who had instructed a counsel called O'Malley. As always Gardiner was represented by John Garvey. After the jury of M. Cawley, J. Gill, P. Corcoran, R.McAdam, P. Belgley and Thomas Mc Cormack was sworn in the facts were presented.

The facts of the Cunniff case were reminiscent of the unsuccessful case John Kelly had taken against Gardiner almost five years earlier. According to the press reports Cunniff had gone to Tully to pay his rent.[238] Gardiner threatened to shoot him and assaulted him. Gardiner had some time earlier obtained an order for the eviction of Cunniff and his two brothers but she had not succeeded in getting possession. When Cunniff arrived at Gardiner's house, Pringle complained that he was the first tenant to bring Gardiner to the Land Court and have his rent reduced from £14 to £10.[239] Gardiner accused him of coming to rob the office and went into another room returning with a revolver. She told Cunniff that he had not a moment to live. Pringle and Cuffe wrestled the gun away from her while Pringle encouraged Gardiner to take the stick and beat Cunniff which she did. Cunniff pleaded with them to let him out saying he would leave through the window if they did not. When he eventually escaped he went to the police but they took no action.

In his evidence Michael Cunniff explained that Gardiner emerged from a room with a revolver, put out her tongue, accused him of coming to the office to rob it and told him that he had not a moment to live. Pringle intervened and stopped her saying that if they shot him they were done and encouraged Gardiner to beat him with a stick which she did for five minutes. He went to the police and spoke to Sergeant Potter who told him to take this case. Cunniff explained that when Gardiner became aware of the case against her she took an action for ejectment against him.

Across the road from Gardiner's house was the home of John and Anne Connor. The distance between the houses would have been no more than one hundred meters. Anne Connor, and her daughter Anne, gave evidence in support of Michael Cunniff. According to Cunniff, old Anne Connor had witnessed what had happened to him and told everyone about it. Anne Connor's daughter Anne told the Court:

> I live near Miss Gardiners office; heard great noise in it; saw Cuffe's wife looking in on the window; saw Cunniff after he came into our house; he was terrified looking; he said he was badly beaten in the side. To Mr. Garvey – I was spreading out clothes; heard great noise and kicks at the door.

Gardiner, Pringle and Cuffe each gave evidence that contradicted the Cunniff and Connor version of events. Pringle explained that Cunniff had told her that he was going to get the money for the rent from John Connor and went off to do so. An odd statement as Cunniff had gone to the house to pay the rent. Gardiner said that she had a revolver and used it for shooting birds at Farmhill. She had a stick but did not use it on Cunniff. She was using the stick to walk as she was not well. She had not been drinking and did not threaten Mrs. Walsh. The evidence of Cuffe and Pringle generally supported Gardiner but was inconsistent in a number of respects. John Garvey, Gardiner's lawyer summed up:

> ...the plaintiff [Cunniff] was there uncorroborated, why wasn't the sergeant brought forward to prove that the man received an injury. If he received the wounds there was not one there to corroborate him; did they believe he got one blow, one wound, or received one injury on the day in question. He told the jury to look at the case as if they were to exchange

the positions of people, and deal with the case as if they were of different stations in life. They all know that feeble lady on the table. She was much worse then than now. Although she is much recovered, he would ask them, as honest men, could that feeble lady inflict those wounds that were sworn to. All they heard about the revolver was mere romance, to excite the passions of the jury. He never knew a more honest and honorable body than the R.I.C, they do not go too far to carry out a conviction, but do not fail to do their duty to secure a conviction, as they would have done in this case if they thought a grievous assault had been committed. [240]

In reply O'Malley for Cunniff stated that the:

...jury were asked to propound one of the most monstrous propositions ever he heard. They were asked to disbelieve every word sworn by his client as if they were palpable perjury and a fabrication. That unpracticed man against whom they could throw nothing to mar his antecedents or past character went to the police and stated his case. Miss Gardiner denied ever hearing a word of it from the police. That was the evidence they were asked to believe. He did not show his marks, and because not they should disbelieve him. The evidence of Miss Connor was uncontradicted. She described his frightened appearance. We were censured for not having the sergeant. The sergeant could not prove to the assault? But why had not Miss Gardiner the sergeant to contradict Cunniff if he had not the money to pay. Presenting a pistol at that shattered old man from toil was able to shatter his nerves! For what was he detained for 20 minutes? What made him say he would break the window? What was he impounded for? Truth was on the plaintiff's side. Perjury of the Grosse kind. When Gardiner denied that the police came there Pringle admitted it. They deny the imprisonment, while Cuffe admits it. The assault took place on December 4[th,] and the sessions came off on the 2nd of January, which shows the reason why he did not take action at once. Cuffe said Miss Gardiner held the stick perfectly quiet. Miss Gardiner admits she thumped the ground with it to quiet the man. That shows the credence they could give the affidavit of the women of bread acres and ample fortune. He would ask them to give ample damages against one who, were it not that she was hindered, would be the means of sending his client to eternity, and have them on their trial for his life. [241]

The judge then summed up:

...the issue was a narrow one. Cunniff swore he was assaulted, and the defendant and two others swore he was not assaulted. The judge said if they did not consider the evidence on the other side stronger they were bound to dismiss the case. He did not believe there was a revolver there. The man may imagine there was, she having the reputation of carrying one. He could not see the motive Miss Gardiner had in attacking him at all. He was paying his rent and Miss Pringle making out the docket. What reason they had in locking the door he could not say, but it was a strange proceeding. The kicking of the door might cause the excitement Miss Connor deposed to. He did not think a feeble woman could do him much harm. There were discrepancies in the evidence that might occur in any case.

It took the jury thirty minutes to find in favour of Cunniff and award him £10. The case was appealed by Gardiner and it came before the Mayo Assizes on Monday 15 July.[242] Gardiner succeeded in the appeal. The judge took the view that three people (Cuffe, Pringle and Gardiner), had stated on oath that Cunniff was not beaten. Against this there was only the evidence of Cunniff given on oath that he was beaten. The door had been locked by Pringle and not Gardiner. Had Cunniff taken proceedings against Pringle and not Gardiner, the outcome might have been different. The evidence in the appeal focused on Gardiner's health (it was suggested that she was very ill when the alleged assault happened), her use of stimulants, her ownership and use of a revolver and whether she used her stick on Cunniff. She told the Court that she had been shot in 1869 and that she kept a revolver. She was in her own words *"a great shot"*. At one point in her evidence she stated that Billy Cuffe was not worth anything and should not be believed and that she had found him doing a good many things wrong. The court found that Gardiner had not assaulted Cunniff.

Eviction of John Garvey (Long) & Bridget Garvey: May 1890

Up to May 1890 all attempts to finally evict John and Bridget Garvey were unsuccessful. The Garveys had repeatedly re-entered after they were evicted and both had been imprisoned but they still held on to their home in defiance of Gardiner and the authorities. In 1887 John Garvey owed Gardiner one and a half year's rent. A year's rent was offered but Gardiner refused to accept it. Each year following a year's rent was again offered but this was also refused. In 1889 John Garvey had planted a crop on the land and was jailed for doing so. The crop was lost while he was in prison. Pringle was determined to conclude the matter. An earlier attempt to evict the Garveys failed as Bridget Garvey was confined to bed due to poor health. On Tuesday 5 May Pringle arranged for Dr. Jordan senior to call on Bridget Garvey. He did so and duly certified that she was fit. Early the following morning the Sheriff's bailiff Jennings, accompanied by Billy Cuffe and a large number of police descended on Tully armed with guns and crowbars. The events of the morning are recorded in a letter dated 8 May and sent by Watty Cox of Frenchill to the Editor of the Connaught Telegraph.[243]

According to Cox, the Garvey house was one of the most comfortable on the Belcarra Estate. Bridget Garvey had lived there for twenty five years and had brought a *"large fortune"* with her when she arrived in Tully. Cuffe and Jennings accompanied by two other men hired for the task entered the house and taking the four corners of the bed carried Bridget Garvey outside and left her alongside a wall a short distance from the house. The demolition of the house proved difficult but Cuffe and his assistants eventually succeeded in removing the roof and pulling down the walls. Later Rev. A. Waters CC., assisted by Charles Daly, who lived close by in Coachfield, and other neighbours took the bed and Bridget Garvey to the shelter of a barn of a neighbour. The neighbour is not identified but it was subsequently reported that he received a letter from a Ballina Solicitor (most likely Gardiner's long standing lawyer John Garvey), threatening legal proceedings against him if he gave shelter to John Garvey (Long) or his wife.[244]

Following the eviction John Garvey (Long) received a summons to Ballyglass Petty Sessions on a charge of attempting to assault Billy Cuffe and for re-entering the site of his ruined home. Cuffe found Garvey on the property two days after the eviction and a scuffle ensued. On 14 May Garvey was fined 10/- and ordered to pay costs for assaulting Billy Cuffe. In default of payment he was to be committed to Castlebar Prison for seven days. Cuffe and Captain James Potter gave evidence against Garvey. A case taken by Garvey against Cuffe for assault on the same date was dismissed. James Garvey also had a case against Cuffe but Cuffe made no appearance. Arising out of the same events, Cuffe also took a case against William Garvey, John Garvey (Long)'s son, but the boy was not in court. It would seem that both James and William Garvey came to the aid of John. Based on the 1901 Census Records, William would have been about 13 years old in 1890.

Westport Quarter Sessions: June 1890
When Westport Quarter Sessions opened on Monday 9 June before County Court Judge J.H. Richards, the proceedings were dominated by actions taken by Gardiner against her tenants for nonpayment of rent.[245] It would seem that while the actions were taken in the name of Gardiner as landlord, Pringle had taken charge of the interaction with tenants and represented Gardiner in proving the cases. Decrees were granted against Michael Gannon, R. Flanagan, Pat Byrne, W. Hynes and P.

Staunton. A case against John Walsh, represented by P.J. Kelly, was dismissed. A decree was also granted against James Daly. Daly argued that Gardiner had turned the court into a rent office and that she had not demanded the rent as she was required to do. The judge agreed that there was evidence of sharp practice on the part of Gardiner who did not have a proper agent to conduct her business. Nevertheless he granted the decree against Daly. A case against John Blowick was settled whilst a case against Pat Biggins brought to light more sharp practice on the part of Pringle in drawing up receipts and issuing them. Biggins paid what was demanded in full as he did not want his wife prosecuted while he was in England.

An Alcohol Fuelled Dispute: June 1890

The following week Gardiner and Pringle were back in Castlebar. On Wednesday 18 June after a day of drinking they left Castlebar on the back of an old dray cart bound for their residence at Tully. They were accompanied by Billy Cuffe, their coachman, referred to in a report in the Connaught Telegraph as *"big Mick"* and a police escort comprising two policemen from Belcarra. In the back of the cart there was a cargo of alcohol including two bottles of *"Old Malt"*. What happened next is best summarized in the Connaught Telegraph:

> As soon as the precious cargo got clear of Castlebar...the brace of "gentle" inebriates began to dispute between themselves till sharp words were followed by a regular scraping and hair teasing match! Were it not for the timely intervention of the police the battle of the Kilkenny cats would, we are told be nothing compared to what the Gardiner-Pringle scratching contest would come to! While the battle was raging the valet is accredited with having a "swig" out of one of the bottles which caused another great fight after they arrived at Tully hut, as each of the "Ladies" of course charged the other, with stealing a march on the Whiskey.[246]

The police took their names when they arrived at Tully but the Connaught Telegraph questioned whether they would be prosecuted like other public transgressors concluding that the law and justice would, in their case, turn a blind eye. The Connaught Telegraph was however wrong on this occasion and Gardiner was fined 10/- for drunkenness.[247]

Relief for Tenants at Fairhill, Belcarra: November 1890

In November the Connaught Telegraph reported that General Cox had instructed his agent, Charles Daly, to reduce rents by twenty per cent on Cox's property at Fairhill near Belcarra. In response to this gesture up to half of the tenants paid one full years rent. The Connaught Telegraph called on other landlords to follow this example in a year of exceptional distress.[248]

THE DEMISE OF BILLY CUFFE & THE ARRIVAL OF JAMES HARTE

The tenants of the Belcarra estate are for the present relieved from one of the greatest pests and scourges that ever desecrated their land. Owing to the internal broils and scuffles in the house of Gardiner, Pringle, and Cuffe, the latter got his exit from her (SATANIC) majesty, Pringle.[249]

A Noted Evictor Evicted: February 1891
Things were not going well between Billy Cuffe and his masters. During the Cunniff litigation in July 1890 aspects of the evidence given by Cuffe contradicted the evidence given by Gardiner and he had made a number of unhelpful admissions.[250] It is also likely that Gardiner and Pringle held Cuffe responsible for the failure to clear the remainder of the tenants at Tully and elsewhere on the Estate. It is therefore not surprising that on Tuesday 24 February Gardiner and Pringle brought their arrangement with Billy Cuffe to an abrupt end. It was just over five years since he had arrived in Tully. There is no evidence that any of Cuffe's children were living with him and his wife at Tully. Gardiner and Pringle had arranged for a group of men from Ballina under the command of a man named Joynt to remove Cuffe from the house at Tully. Cuffe initially refused to leave but ultimately agreed to go peacefully in return for *"some trifle."*[251] He was then driven away by the men. A letter published in the Connaught Telegraph under the heading *"A NOTED EVICTOR EVICTED"* informed the Editor that:

> For some months past the unfortunate old man of the dirty work was kept between the hammer and the anvil, and, as a reward for his fidelity and bravery, as a heartless evictor and grinder of the poor, he got run out of office on Tuesday last in dishonour with his landladies, and his memory will be execrated and cursed by many a poor victim to eviction on the estate; for those who knew him best say that, he never looked in better form or wore a grin of satisfaction on his counte-

nance, save when he was wielding, the crowbar or prowling in ambush to catch some poor victim in the act of revisiting the ruin of his once happy home.

According to the letter Gardiner and Pringle had already lined up Cuffe's replacement:

> It is reported that some other waif or stray, having not one less than ten youngsters, is coming to take the place of old Billy Cuffe. If he does not act similarly to his predecessor walker will be his name. It is, however, certain that stray donkeys have a gala time of it on the waste holdings, or in other words, they are doing a roaring trade among the thistles which grow luxuriantly, and will grow there, while old Pringle is this side of the styx.

The man referred to in the letter was James Harte.

James Harte Assaulted: May 1891

James Harte arrived in Tully in the spring of 1891. By the time summer arrived he had well and truly settled in and even had his own case before Castlebar Petty Sessions on Wednesday 22 July. The case was a prosecution for assault taken against a young man by the name of John Feeney from Ballyhean. Feeney had been summoned by DI Mac Dermott for an alleged assault on Harte. It would appear that neither Gardiner nor Harte wanted to prosecute Feeney but Mac Dermott took the initiative in the matter. When the case came before Colonel Stewart RM, and H. W. Jordan, Feeney was represented by P.J. Kelly. The case was reported in the Connaught Telegraph the following Saturday.[252] Several witnesses gave evidence and using this it is possible to build up a picture of what happened to Harte.

Harte had been drinking ale at a public house in Castlebar with Henry Gallagher from Logaphuill. In the evening they left Castlebar in the direction of Belcarra. There were a number of people on the road that evening making their way out of

Castlebar and it would appear that many of them were from Tully and Logaphuill. At Saleen just outside Castlebar, Harte was struck from behind with a stick and his arm was dislocated. Harte did not know who hit him but thought it was Feeney. Dominic Byrne testified that he had seen Harte knocked down but did not see who hit him though Feeney was nearby. Mary Dunbar, an employee of Gardiner, went to Harte and with the assistance of a policeman picked him up. Dunbar explained that she was making her way to Belcarra in Dominic Byrne's cart. She stressed that there was no ill feeling towards her as a consequence of her working for Gardiner. She testified that Harte was a Herd.[253] Tim Gannon gave evidence that Harte was whistling and appeared to be drunk. Feeney, a quiet boy from Ballyhean, came up behind Harte and struck him lightly on the arm. Henry Gallagher explained that on the railway bridge at Saleen Harte came from behind and struck Gallagher's ass causing Gallagher to fall off. Gallagher had heard that Harte was assaulted but did not see Feeney hit Harte. Gallagher's daughter was married to Feeney's brother. Feeney was fined 20/- and ordered to pay costs or in default he was to spend 14 days in prison.

Gardiner Drunk & Disorderly: June 1891

The next reported event of any consequence also took place on the road out of Castlebar to Belcarra and again alcohol played its part. On the afternoon of Saturday 13 June Constables Hartigan and McGovern were tasked with providing an escort for Gardiner and Pringle on their journey between Castlebar Railway Station and Tully. The pair travelled in a cart belonging to Martin Tonra who went to the Railway Station to collect them. Gardiner was very drunk and Hartigan charged her. At the subsequent hearing Gardiner did not appear and was not represented. Constable Hartigan informed the court that:

> She was shouting, cursing, and attempting to hit Miss Pringle with a stick. Martin Tonra came with his cart to meet them at the Railway Station and I and Constable Mc Govern had

to escort them for miles along the road, her conduct was so violent.

Gardiner was fined £1 and ordered to pay costs. In default she was to spend 14 days in Castlebar Prison. There is no evidence that she went to jail so it is assumed that the fine was paid. The case marks a turning point in Gardiner's relationship with the authorities. Gardiner had been fined before for drunkenness and indeed for assault but it is evident from the testimony that the police had run out of patience. Her absence from court also suggests that the fighting spirit she had shown in the past was waning. The Connaught Telegraph viewed the outcome as a victory for law and justice:

> Too long had the public scandals of these dissipated wretches been not only connived at, but actually shielded by the "police protection"; and it is consoling to find men like Constable Hartigan who will not flinch from the straightforward line of duty, whether the delinquent be "lady" Gardiner, the famous evictor and house –leveller, or any other drunken vagabond that makes himself a nuisance to society! Such honest and independent performance of duty displayed by this honest Constable and the properly inevitable decision of Colonel Stewart, will gain more respect for the impartial administration of the law than twenty cases against twenty drunken "tramps" of the ordinary class could effect.[254]

DEATH OF HARRIET GARDINER

Miss Harriet Gardiner, a notable figure in the history of the land agitation in the west of Ireland, passed away at her residence, Belcarra, yesterday, after a lingering illness. Her strained relations with her tenantry were frequently the subject of considerable litigation and newspaper comment; and Mr. G A Moore in his book, "Parnell and His Island" refers, under a nom-de-plume, to her eccentric habits and peculiar attire while parading the streets of Castlebar with a constabulary escort, as she was always under police protection. She was almost continually engaged in a land war with her tenantry, and her eviction campaigns are matters of history.[255]

The Death of Harriet Gardiner: July 1892

Harriet Gardiner died at her house in Tully on Monday 25 July 1892, four days after her seventy first birthday. Her remains were removed from the house under cover of darkness for burial at Killala. The Connaught Telegraph had the following to say about her death and life:

> A weird and grotesque figure, and a baneful one, has passed away from this mortal stage, in the person of her who was known as Miss Harriet Gardiner, of Belcarra, in this County. Such a being, if pictured by the pen of the imaginative novelist, would have been wondered at as the creation of a disordered fancy: but the fact of her actual existence for so many years, under the full glare of notoriety, proves the truth of the ancient aphorism that "the truth is strange – stranger than fiction". She will long be remembered in the County of Mayo, not alone for her semi-masculine attire and her repulsively eccentric ways, but for the Pharaoh –like and utterly unfeminine hardness of heart which she exhibited for years towards a most miserable and poverty- stricken tenantry. Had she been a mere private individual, charity would compel the drawing of a veil over her misdeeds, in the somber presence of Death; but it would be a failure of duty were not the solemn lesson of a sordid heartless life and a miserable end to be pointed from the story of this un feminine oppressor of the poor, who strove

to drown the upbraidings of an evil conscience in the maddening oblivion of intemperance. The dismal tragedy of her life and the Nemesis of its close ought never to be forgotten. She occupies a unique niche, even in the temple of that dark pantheon which is filled with the ghosts of Irish landlordism.[256]

In assessing the life and impact of Gardiner the Connaught Telegraph provides some excellent insights into why Gardiner had such a difficult and ultimately catastrophic relationship with her tenants. Gardiner came into her inheritance, a large property, at a young age with no restrictions as to the management of the property. She possessed an *"Elizabethan"* temper and an uncompromising will. As a consequence she soon found herself embroiled on all fronts:

> When the land troubles came, Miss Gardiner set her face against any concession and played the part of Helen Mac Gregor[257] strutting about the country with pistols in her belt and moss trooper boots and shortened skirt, posting up eviction notices with her own hand and looking on callously at eviction scenes which often melted the hearts even of the policemen, soldiers, and legal functionaries For years she waged a relentless war against the peasantry in this horrible Dahomey Amazon[258] fashion; and during all this time there was only one attempt on the part of the maddened peasantry to molest her….There is no figure in Irish History comparable to that of Harriet Gardiner….Miss Harriet Gardiner stood alone and unique.[259]

Following the death of Gardiner, Pringle succeeded to her Belcarra Estate including the house at Tully where they had both lived. The companion and agent had become the landlord.

The Morley Commission: November 1892
In November 1892 the events of the spring of 1885 at Tully and Logaphuill were revisited by the Connaught Telegraph which identified the cases as ones especially deserving of in-

vestigation by the Evicted Tenants Commission or the Morley Commission.²⁶⁰ The tenants (to the extent they were still alive and had not emigrated), were encouraged to tell their version of the events to a Connaught Telegraph reporter. The reporter interviewed a number of them including Thomas Ward and John Garvey (Long) and the findings are summarized in the 12 November Edition of the paper.

Thomas Ward gave a detailed account of his own struggle against Gardiner and then Pringle. For him problems began in the spring of 1884 when he was struck down by a fever. Following his recovery another member of his family became ill. Medical expenses and the general economic depression took their toll on his ability to pay rent and he fell into arrears. Eviction and imprisonment for him and his wife followed and his house was finally levelled in 1889. Pringle had on one occasion visited his home and accused him of being head of the Land League in the district but this was not true. Ward confirmed that Oliver Canton had died in the Castlebar Workhouse. Records show that he died a pauper at the age of 80 in December 1887. After their eviction Patrick and Mary Connor and their family went to England. A number of the Deacy family had also left Ireland following their eviction and others lived near Castlebar. James Walsh of Elmhall was living in a hut near his ruined home. Catherine Dunne went to America. Patrick Macken and Bridget Cardy had died and John and Mary Macken had emigrated.

Death Certificate, Oliver Canton, December 1887.

Nationalist Demonstration at Belcarra: November 1892
On Sunday 28 November over two thousand people attended a nationalist gathering in Belcarra convened for the purpose of discussing the approach to be adopted by tenants in response to impending evictions.²⁶¹ Those present included Daniel Crilly

MP.[262] A letter of apology was received from William O'Brien MP.[263] He could not attend as he wished to be present at the evictions that were scheduled to take place on the estate of Lord Sligo the following morning. A telegram was received from John Deasy MP stating that he was unable to attend due to the illness of his mother. Rev. Colleran CC, Balla, was elected chairperson of the meeting while Fr. Greany and Charles Daly were appointed secretaries.

Colleran delivered a lengthy speech outlining the history of evictions on the Belcarra Estate.[264] Pringle had essentially taken up where Gardiner had left off and was now demanding rents that could not be paid. She had threatened legal proceedings against any who failed to pay. According to Colleran, George Cuffe had been a charitable, reasonable and humane man who treated tenants fairly and had granted abatements from time to time as the circumstances required. Gardiner and now Pringle had turned out tenants but had not benefited. No *"grabbers"* had appeared so the land lay vacant. Colleran had heard that a *"grabber"* had arrived in the Frenchill district. He was not of the catholic faith and Colleran suggested that he should be boycotted but he did not use the word:

> As he did not belong to their creed he did not wish to say anything hard of him, but he would say he ought to consult the feeling of his catholic neighbours. They should treat the land-grabber as pious man. Pass him by believing that he was absorbed in prayer. Don't disturb him in his meditation.[265]

John Mc Ellin then proposed and Edward Cannon seconded three resolutions as follows:

> That we request the Congested Districts Board to purchase either voluntarily or by compulsion the interests of the landlords in the large grass farms in this neighborhood and migrate to them the over-crowded tenants from the cut away bogs and worn-out patches of mountain lands.

> That we call upon the landlords in this district to recognize the great depression of the times by granting substantial abatements in the current year's rent, and by abolishing arrears to a substantial extent help the tenants to tide over the coming winter.
>
> That considering the cruel treatment which we the tenants on the Gardiner –Pringle estate, have received at the hands of the landlord for the last nine years, we are satisfied now as we always have been to leave our case to the arbitration, one to be selected by Miss Pringle and one us, - a course which, we, believe will lead to full justice being done to the tenants.[266]

Daniel Crilly MP., delivered a lengthy speech focusing on the *"merciless landlords of Mayo."* Gardiner and Pringle had turned out nine families but had gained no advantage in doing so. They received no rent and had to pay the rates which otherwise would have been payable by the tenants in occupation leading to the conclusion that:

> We have to-day each one of us a serious duty to perform. We are fighting for nationhood, and this action that has been taken by the landlords of Mayo is not merely taken for the purpose of recovering their rents, but it is a part and parcel of a vile and foul conspiracy to rob Ireland of self –government.[267]

Rev. Colleran Seeks Rent Abatement: December 1892

On Wednesday 7 December 1892 Rev. Colleran, representing 140 of the tenants on Pringle's Belcarra Estate, went to Pringle's house at Tully, accompanied by a number of the tenants to request a 25 per cent abatement of their rent in light of the economic circumstances or failing that a referral of the matter to arbitration. Pringle's response was clear and uncompromising, full payment of rent and legal costs without any reduction. The meeting was reported in the Connaught Telegraph the following Saturday which noted that the tenants left without paying anything.[268] According to the Correspondent, Pringle would do well to have regard to the statements of Henry Chaplin MP and James Lowther MP made at the Agricultural Show in London where they declared that rents were excessive and that landlords must come forward and give generous reductions.[269] Failing that, Parliament should intervene and link the value of the land to the price of agricultural produce. Later that month the Freemans Journal published a lengthy letter from Rev. Colleran detailing his engagement with Pringle.[270]

James Harte assaults Constable Quigley: December 1892

On 17 December James Harte assaulted Constable Bernard Quigley of Belcarra with an ash plant. The circumstances that gave rise to the assault are not reported but the RIC came out in force in support of their colleague when the case came before Colonel Blake and Tomas Wilson Walsh at the 18 January sitting of Ballyglass Petty Sessions. Several officers gave evidence in support of Quigley and Harte was fined for the offence.

Problems with Service of Writs: April 1893

The service of Writs on tenants at Belcarra was proving to be increasingly difficult and dangerous. In 1887 Thomas Kent Neild RM had died from the beating he received at Charlestown when a crowd of tenants mistook him for a Process Server. On the Belcarra Estate Process Servers feared for their safety so Pringle, through her lawyer John Garvey, applied to court to dispense with personal service of Writs on tenants. According to an affidavit of one of the Process Servers, when he tried to serve Writs on tenants he was attacked by a mob, knocked down, beaten and pelted with mud. Eight Writs were taken from him by force and he was told not to return. He could not serve further Writs without putting his life in danger.[271] Vice Chancellor Henry Richards ordered that the Writs could be served by registered post and by posting copies in the local police barracks.[272]

Trespass Cases: April - October 1893

On 12 April 1893 at Ballyglass Petty Sessions, Pringle had nine cases for trespass by livestock at various times during the spring of that year against John Connor. She was successful in all but two of the cases and Connor was ordered to pay damages and costs. There were also several trespass cases against Michael and Pat Lavelle, John Burke, John Garvey (Long), Thomas Garvey and Thomas Walsh. It would seem that John Garvey (Long) was at this point back in possession of his home possibly as a caretaker because his name remained absent from the Cancellation Books or he may have been renting a house from Patrick Lavelle (See Appendix I). Damages and costs were awarded against the tenants in most cases. John Connor succeeded in two cases for trespass against James Harte but Harte succeeded in a trespass case against Connor a few months later in August. The trespass war between Connor and Pringle continued into the autumn and at Ballyglass Petty Sessions on 25 October Pringle had nine new cases against him for trespass by livestock during August and September. He was ordered to pay damages and costs and both parties were ordered to make up their fences. Pringle was also successful in several cases against Anthony Vahy, Michael Lavelle and John Garvey. A case against Patrick Cunniff of Cloonlynchacun was dismissed. John Connor and his son Martin had three cases against James Harte for trespass and an attack by Harte's dog on Martin Connor's livestock. Harte was ordered to pay damages and costs in one of the trespass cases. The other cases were dismissed.

Trespass Cases: October - November: 1894

Twelve months later, on 3 October 1894, at Ballyglass Petty Sessions there was a long list of trespass cases scheduled for hearing against Logaphuill tenants including John Burke, Michael Lavelle, Henry Gallagher, Richard Ward, Owen Dunne, Patt Walsh, Augustus Staunton, Luke Londra and John (William) Walsh. Pringle however had no success as the tenants did not turn up for the hearings. A few weeks later on 14 November John Connor was back at Ballyglass Petty Sessions. Pringle had eight trespass cases against him and she succeeded in getting an order for damages and costs in four. There were also cases against Michael and Patrick Lavelle but the defendants made no appearance. At Ballyglass on 12 December John Connor was again ordered to pay damages and costs in another action taken by Pringle against him for trespass.

Trespass Cases: February 1895
Another series of trespass cases were scheduled for hearing at Ballyglass Petty Sessions on 13 February but the tenants, John Connor, Catherine Burke, Michael Cunniffe and Patt Mannion did not turn up for the hearings. The case against John Connor was the last taken by Susanna Pringle against him and it is thought that he died later that year.

Eviction of James Harte & Death of John Connor: May 1895
Before John Connor died he would have witnessed the eviction of his neighbour and nemesis James Harte. On 11 May 1895 the Connaught Telegraph published the proceedings of a meeting of the Castlebar Guardians. F. Vahy RO brought before the Board the case of James Harte who had been evicted at Tully on 2 May. Harte arrived in Tully in the spring of 1891 following the dismissal of Billy Cuffe as Gardiner's Bailiff. In May 1891 he had been assaulted at Saleen outside Castlebar by John Feeney from Ballyhean. In December 1892 Harte himself had been convicted of assault. Now four years after she brought him to Tully Pringle had dispensed with him and he and his wife had been evicted. Vahy was seeking to recover five shillings that he had paid out in connection with the eviction. James Daly took serious issue with the Board reimbursing the amount at the expense of the people of the district. According to Daly, Harte was a stranger brought into Tully as a caretaker manager by Pringle and she should have supported him instead of evicting him. The Guardians should not accommodate any landlord or evictor. Vahy had arranged for a car to come from Castlebar to assist with the eviction as Harte's wife was ill. Daly argued that

the Union should not pay for this and questioned if the woman was from Tully. She was not and there is no doubt that Daly knew the answer to the question when he asked it arguing that it was reprehensible that a car would be brought out to accommodate Pringle in the eviction of a tenant. Daly accused Vahy of being an emergency man for Pringle. Other Board Members took issue with an Officer being labelled an emergency man. After a heated debate the matter was not settled and was referred to the Local Government Board for resolution. With the eviction of Harte and death of John Connor the trespass war between the Connors and Pringle came to an end. A new bailiff, William Kearns, arrived in Tully and moved into the vacated Caretaker's House with his family. It would seem that Kearns brought a new management style. He avoided confrontation and the courts and the trespass cases ended.

Sale of Hay from Evicted Tully Holdings: October 1895

In the autumn of that year Pringle advertised for sale the meadows growing on the evicted lands at Tully. It did not take long for the matter to be brought to the attention of the Connaught Telegraph Correspondent who reported that Pat Surdival had attended the sale and had offered to buy a large rick of hay that had been cut on the holdings for the past three or four years.[273]

Part IX

Nationalism on the Belcarra Estate

Controversy Over Funds

After a residence amongst us of more than three years, a period the most dangerous and trying which ever occurred in this country, it is truly painful to us to bid you farewell... but we cannot, under any circumstances, forbear to express our gratitude, and declare our respect for such men. It will ever be a pleasing reflection to us that, when the unhappy disturbances which lately disgraced this kingdom required the exertions of the military, our town had the good fortune, in a great measure, to fall under your protection. From your vigilance and discipline in garrison, and from your activity and gallant conduct in the field, we have reaped most important advantages and feel ourselves called upon to declare that you have eminently contributed to the security which we now enjoy. Permit us then to express our sincere concern and regret at parting with you; and rest assured that, however widely separated we may be, the warm affections and good wishes of the inhabitants of Castlebar shall ever await each individual of the Roxburgh and Selkirk dragoons.[274]

The Races of Castlebar: August 1798

The above address was published in the Caledonian Mercury two years after the English forces suffered a humiliating defeat at the hands of General Humbert at Castlebar. The address concluded with the words;

> Signed by the unanimous desire of the inhabitants of Castlebar.

On the road that runs between Castlebar and Belcarra at a point a short distance from the village of Tully there is a small bridge that crosses a narrow, slow moving river just at the bottom of Frenchill. The river runs through low bog lands in the townland of Logaphuill almost parallel to what today is known as the Cottage Road. On one side of the river is the hill known as Frenchill, on the other, a continuous hill or *"tulaigh"* which gives the townland of Tully its name. The river flows into a small, deep and somewhat inaccessible lake a few hundred yards from the bridge. In August 1798 four or five French Dragoons under the command of Bartholomew Teeling were killed at or near this bridge by the retreating English forces under the command of Lord Roden. There are a number of versions of the detail of the engagement on that day.[275] In one, a group of Lord Roden's foxhunters, seeing they were being pursued by a small number of French turned and lay in wait beneath the bridge. They shot Teeling's escort and a number of Grenadiers. Teeling was captured. In another version Teeling approached the English under a flag of truce to offer terms but was fired on. The dead French were buried at Frenchill and in 1876 a monument was erected there in their honour.

Monument at Frenchill overlooking Tully & Logaphuill- From the Lawrence Collection of Photographs 1870-1910 (Courtesy of the National Library of Ireland).

Daly & Nally decide to Build a Monument at Frenchill: 1875

In 1875 James Daly and Fenian leader Patrick W. Nally from nearby Balla decided to build a monument to honour the French soldiers killed in the engagement with the English forces at Frenchill in 1798. A collection was organised by Daly in 1875 for the works, a fact that later gave rise to controversy. The unveiling of the monument in December 1877 was attended by Charles Stuart Parnell as well as Daly himself and John

O'Connor Power. The remains of a number of French soldiers, uniforms and French Francs dated 1798 were apparently discovered during the construction works for the Monument. The inscription on the Monument reads:

> In grateful remembrance of the gallant French soldiers who died fighting for the freedom of Ireland on the 26th August 1798. They shall be remembered for ever may they rest in peace.

Controversy over Funds: 1880

Daly had, by the late 1870s, become one of the most influential men in Mayo.[276] As time passed however a rift developed between him and the Land League. Daly accused the League Executive of providing insufficient assistance to evicted tenants and suggested that the officers of the League were profiting from League funds while at the same time pursuing radical policies that would not bring immediate assistance to the farmers in Mayo. According to Jordan, Daly had by 1880 become convinced that the League and Michael Davitt had set out to discredit him and had tried to take over the Connaught Telegraph.[277] In the Police Biography of Daly, Sergeant Clark reported that the cause of the quarrel between the League and James Daly was that Daly held Land League funds that he refused to account for or give up and that it was generally believed that Daly closed on a large portion of the funds he collected in 1875 and 1876 for the Frenchill Monument.[278] Daly responded to these allegations in the Connaught Telegraph in his usual robust style:

> The parties used to circulate the reports are some low, dissipated fellows, who never lost a shilling by anything that would benefit Ireland- parties who appear very often in the law courts, not for any honourable cause, but for wife beating (groans for them). I am not here in the pay of the Land League, nor in the pay of the Government. I am under no obligation to the latter. So far as the Land League is concerned, they owe me £5 to the 1s I owe them.[279]

Maude Gonne visits Frenchill: 1896

By 1896 the controversy was forgotten and thoughts turned to the centenary of 1798. On Monday 25 May 1896 Maude Gonne arrived in Castlebar and together with James Daly they made their way to Frenchill to view the monument. Daly gave Maude Gonne a five franc piece found in the grave of one of the French soldiers during the building of the monument together with a bullet discovered embedded in the front of a fort close to where the encounter took place.[280] Afterwards Maude Gonne made her way to Sion Hill on the outskirts of Castlebar where more French soldiers were buried. The Connaught Telegraph reported that Maude Gonne would deliver a lecture later that summer in Castlebar to raise funds to renovate the Frenchill Monument.

CENTENARY CELEBRATIONS AT FRENCHILL: 1898

If General Humbert arrived a few months earlier, before the revolution of the Irish in the South had been crushed out in blood, he would have succeeded in delivering the country from the hated yolk of England, and they would not now in Ireland have to mourn the loss of nearly half their population, and the ruin and destruction of their beautiful land. They would not have famine and evictions, and the starvation of the people under English rule, and she would not witness the spectacle which she had seen this year of people starving in their homes. If the English Government had not helped the landlords, there would have been no evictions. The English Government had organised famines in order to drive the people out of the land. It was responsible for all the miseries of the country, for the congestion of the population, and for the frequently recurring starvation. She hoped that no Irishman would join the English army, and she asked all to make a vow to follow the example, and abide by the principles of the heroes who died in 1798 in the cause of liberty and in the holy effort to make Ireland free.[281]

Centenary Celebrations: August 1898

Maude Gonne was back in Frenchill two years later for the 1798 centenary celebrations. On Sunday 29 August 1898 a large meeting was held in Castlebar to celebrate the French and Irish victory over English at Castlebar. Notwithstanding that there was a storm and heavy showers the Freemans Journal reported that people thronged into the town from miles around.[282] Crowds began to gather on Sion Hill at 11am. The Islandeady contingent of the UIL, with their 98 *banner* was the first to arrive followed closely by the Ballina 98 Club accompanied by a band and banner. At midday a wagon displaying the tricolour arrived with the French delegation that had travelled to Ireland for the occasion. The band played the French national anthem and loud cheers came from the crowd at the mention of the names of General Humbert, General Hoche and Wolf Tone. Commandant Du Chateau of the French delegation placed wreaths from the Societe de la Jeune Irlande, Paris, and the Societe du Souvenir Francaise upon the graves of the French soldiers at Sion Hill. Following this solemn moment when heads were bared, the bands started to play *"Who fears to speak of 98"* and *"The Marseillaise"* alternately. A procession was then formed and it made its way out of Castlebar passing along Staball in the direction of Frenchill. The town was decorated with French, American and green flags together with the colours of the United Irishmen of 98, orange, green and white. When they arrived at Frenchill wreaths were placed upon the graves of the French soldiers and a large bronze wreath was placed at the monument. On the return trip to Castlebar, the procession passed a group of fifty policemen armed with rifles and batons. At Castlebar a meeting was held on the Mall. The Freemans Journal reported that:

> The meeting in the Castlebar green was one of the largest ever held there. Fifteen bands were present, and the large array of banners, some on wagonettes, some of them really fine canvasses representing scenes of the progress of Humber's battle band through Mayo in 1798, lent a picturesque glow of colour to the scene.[283]

When the meeting started Dr Jordan of Castlebar proposed that James Daly take the chair. The motion was seconded by John McHale, President of the UIL. The Freemans Journal reported:

> Mr. Jas Daly, who was loudly applauded on taking the chair, said that he felt highly honoured at being asked to take the chair at so large and influential a meeting. Their object was three-fold. In the first place they were met to celebrate the memory of the dead, and in the second instance to bid a hearty welcome to the French and American delegates who came to join them in this celebration this day. Their third object was to declare their determination to abide by the principles of the men of '98 until their country was free again and took its place amongst the nations of the earth.

William Doris then proposed, and John Mc Govern of Newport, seconded, the following resolutions:-

> Resolved – that we congratulate ourselves and all concerned in the great success we have achieved in this befitting grand celebration of the centenary of the heroes of the famous "Castlebar Races."
>
> Second –That we thank the gallant sons of France, and gratefully acknowledge their kind co-operation in this celebration, also for the beautiful wreaths and trophies they have presented us with to decorate the Frenchill monument.
>
> Third –That we pledge ourselves here today that our efforts will be unceasing, and that we will, by every constitutional and physical means, follow in the footsteps of the gallant men of 1798, until Ireland shakes off the bonds of slavery, and her sons make her a nation.
>
> Fourth –That we ask those of our American brethren here to-day to be the bearers of a message to our exiled friends in the Great Republic, that they will use every means to prevent an unholy alliance with England, the pirate of the world, who are responsible for all the wrongs and sufferings of Ireland, and we ask those who in the name of justice have brought liberty to Cuba to consider the case of Ireland, who is suffering from even greater wrongs and tyranny under the alien rule of England.
>
> That whereas the British Government have by perpetual coercion and disarmament, by their ill treatment of political prisoners and by refusal of amnesty, by their withholding of relief to the distressed districts, by their enormous over taxation, by their denial of the rights of self –government to the Irish people, have proved the incapacity of the English Parliament to govern Ireland upon constitutional principles and according to civilized usage, we hereby resolve that every opportunity

should be taken to educate public opinion abroad upon Irish misgovernment, and that copies of this resolution be sent to the president of the American Republic, the president of the French Republic, the president of the South African Republic, The Czar of Russia, and the Emperor of Germany.

Maud Gonne then delivered a speech about the heroic French and Irish soldiers who under the leadership of General Humbert so nearly succeeded in freeing Ireland. Cipriani delivered a speech in French and reminded those present of the example of the countries which had fought for and won the freedom of their native lands. Mr. Cox, of Boston called for Irish people to unite in their opposition and bring an end to factions concluding that:

> If the movement was not likely to obtain them freedom let them organise a movement that would.

Unity was also the central message of Commandant Du Chateau who called on, and advised the Irish people to organise and unite. Speeches were then delivered by John Dillon, MP., William M. Field MP.,[284] and William O'Brien. William Rooney addressed the meeting and urged the crowd to support the movement for the revival of the Irish language. [285]

Huge credit must be given to Daly and those who organized such a large international gathering and secured attendees form the United States, England and France.

Une Cérémonie Français en Irelande,
Le Petit Parisien, Supplément Littéraire
Illustre, August 1898.

Part X

Grabbers & Graziers

Daly Versus Everyone

The reason I assign for troubling is my desire to inform the readers of the Connaught Telegraph as to the course I intend pursuing with regard to the series of attacks made upon my character in the last issue of your paper, which recently appears to have been a willing medium for encouraging and circulating libellous attacks on me. [286]

James Daly: Grabber, Grazier or Bailiff

James Daly sold the Connaught Telegraph to T.H Gillespie in 1888 and thereafter focussed on farming and local politics. With the passage of time and the ever shifting sands of local and national politics, Daly's motives and position as a large land holder were questioned by some. At political meetings around Mayo and in letters written to, and published by, the Connaught Telegraph, Daly was accused of being a grabber, a grazier, and a bailiff. These allegations need however to be examined in the context in which they were made and more importantly by whom they were made because much of what was said and written was said and committed to paper in the context of fiercely fought local political campaigns involving Daly and his political adversaries. At this point in time the focus was also moving somewhat away from the landlords who were gradually being consigned to history as tenants began to acquire the ownership of their holdings through the various land purchase schemes. From its foundation by William O' Brien at Westport in 1898, the UIL targeted large land holders and graziers and called for a redistribution of land amongst small tenants. The UIL was very active on the Belcarra Estate in the early part of the 20th Century. The UIL did not confine itself to targeting landlords, it also called for the redistribution of large holdings of land held by tenants such as James and Charles Daly.

Harriet Gardiner's Bailiff

Dealing with each of the allegations in turn, was Daly at one time Gardiner's bailiff? According to Feingold he was. Feingold references an article in the 30 May 1908 Edition of the Connaught

Telegraph as the source for this conclusion. Feingold relates that according to oral tradition Daly fell out with Gardiner probably sometime before 1869 following a disagreement over the eviction of a tenant from one of her estates and Daly was either dismissed or resigned as a consequence and the episode motivated Daly to pursue radical politics.[287] Our research has not revealed any reference to James Daly having acted as Gardiner's bailiff other than a reference in a letter written to the *"Electors and Ratepayers of the Castlebar County Electoral Division"* by Thomas J. Loftus, Vice Chairman of Castlebar District Council and President of the Castlebar branch of the UIL. Loftus wrote:

> You know how, to the delight of every enemy of the aspirations of the people and of the National organisation, Mr. James Daly, at the head of a porter brigade, tried to smash the Nationalist Demonstration recently held in Castlebar and with his own hands flung the sink of the streets at Mr. Gwynn MP., how he was condemned by the speakers as a "faction politician," the leader of a rowdy mob, who was "a defunct grazier," "an exploded political bladder who commenced his career as a bum bailiff for Miss Gardiner"; and how he was afterwards condemned by the Castlebar District Council.[288]

If Daly was Gardiner's bailiff (and there is little evidence that he was), it is highly unlikely that he was employed by her at Belcarra because her interest in the Estate only materialised in 1883 when George Cuffe died. At that time Daly was already engaged in his anti- Gardiner campaign in the pages of the Connaught Telegraph. The allegation in the Loftus letter was not made by Loftus himself, he was referring to speeches made by others at political rallies. The letter written by Loftus was expressly written for the purpose of seeking support for himself in the forthcoming County Council election. Daly was his opponent. In the same letter Loftus wrote that Daly had been disqualified from sitting on the District and County Councils as he had made a composition with his creditors offering them 2/6 in the £1. The Connaught Telegraph Correspondent wrote:

In Castlebar division Mr. Daly and Mr. T.J. Loftus are pursuing a more active canvass; and each of them has addressed numerous meetings through the division.

On balance therefore it would seem certain that Daly did not act as Gardiner's bailiff on the Belcarra Estate and possibly not at all.

Grabber & Grazier

There are numerous references in this period to Daly being both a *"grabber"* and a *" grazier"* but the two require separate consideration. The former was a label given to those who took the evicted holdings of tenants once they had been cleared by a landlord. The latter was a term used to describe landlords or latterly tenants with large holdings whose approach to farming was to establish large cattle grazing farms. To achieve this landlords cleared their estates of tenants and replaced them with livestock. With the landlord class in decline and the breakup of the large farms underway it was natural for the land movement to turn to the next obstacle standing in the way of the multitude of small tenant farmers in their quest to gain ownership of land. Tenants with large farms were considered graziers. Daly had an interest in a number of farms including a 79 acre holding at Ballyshane on the Belcarra Estate. Tenants with large holdings sought to purchase directly from landlords and in doing so avoided having their holdings divided amongst small tenants. In March 1899 a Breaghwy voter, in a letter to the Connaught Telegraph wrote:

> James is not a grabber, of course, and would not grab a farm for the world, moryagh! The large grazing tracts he holds at present, and Foy's nice little piece of land at Kilkenny, only came into his care by accident. O! quite by accident. He would not grab, not he! Is it the leader of the League and the heart and soul of patriotism to be a grabber? why perish the thought it is impossible! How could he be a grazier and grabber and be denouncing, in all the moods and tenses both grazing and grabbing.[289]

In another politically motivated letter the author, *"LK"*, wrote of Daly:

> What is the country coming to, that the people cannot see the hypocrisy of these ambitious political leeches, that are bloodsucking the country? who grasp and grab at everything, from political representative situations of honour, to every nice piece of grass land that becomes untenanted, and who laugh, and roar with laughter, at the poor country fools who believe in their sincerity, and vote them into positions of trust and influence.[290]

In an earlier letter published by the Connaught Telegraph under the heading *"Daly v. Everybody"* LK wrote:

> From the bailiff that went barth-hunting in his "sugaun" leggins to the patriot that became treasurer to every petty political movement in the country I have known James and I have never known him yet to treat an opponent fairly. Look back at the files of your paper- The Telegraph- get back to the journalistic days of our subject and you will find that under the "able" editorship of Mr. Daly, it became a weekly issue of personal animus against all who were not of his opinions. [291]

Maurice Moore, Daly's political opponent at that time, in a letter to the Connaught Telegraph wrote:

> Unlike Mr. James Daly, I have no farms to divide and do not seek to cover my own misdoings by virulent abuse of everyone else.[292]

Daly's brother Charles had similar allegations made against him. Charles Daly had a large farm on the Belcarra Estate at Coachfield and he went on the offensive when it was suggested that he was a grabber and grazier. A meeting of the UIL was planned for 19 February 1899 to deal with the issue of *"grabbers"* and *"blacklegs"*. The Connaught Telegraph reported that

Charles Daly announced at Belcarra two days before the meeting that he intended to attend the gathering:

> and proclaimed to all and sundry that he would perform tracheotomy on the man who would call him a "grabber" [293]

There is no evidence that James Daly grabbed any land on the Belcarra Estate. As to the suggestion that he was a grazier, he clearly was, but not perhaps in the sense that that term was originally conceived. Daly did not clear the land he rented from Cuffe and then Gardiner to make way for livestock. Daly was, through his own means, in a position to hold several large holdings of land and he was a farmer as well as an agitator and politician. It was not surprising that the land movement with its overriding objective of returning the land to the people regarded Daly and other large land holders as an obstacle. This conflicted position that Daly found himself in provided his political opponents with plenty of ammunition to use against him at the political rallies around Mayo and in the pages of the paper he once owned and edited.

The Tully Grabber

When a man takes a farm from which another has been evicted you must shun him on the roadside when you meet him, you must shun him in the streets of the town, you must shun him in the shop, you must shun him in the fairgreen and in the marketplace, and even in the place of worship, by leaving him alone, by putting him in a moral Coventry, by isolating him from the rest of his country as if he were the leper of old, you must show your detestation of the crime he has committed.[294]

Imprisonment of Conor O'Kelly M.P., January 1902

On 16 January 1902 the Speaker of the House of Commons informed the House that he had received a letter from Robert F. Starkie RM informing him that Conor O'Kelly, MP for the Constituency of North Mayo, was convicted on 18 December 1901, before a Court of Summary Jurisdiction at Castlebar, formed under the provisions of the Criminal Law and Procedure (Ireland) Act, 1887, on the charge of having taken part in an unlawful assembly at Tully. Starkie had sentenced O'Kelly to two months imprisonment without hard labour. O'Kelly was born in Claremorris in 1873 the son of William O'Kelly, a draper.[295] In addition to being an MP, O'Kelly was also Chairman of Mayo County Council and a Justice of the Peace.

Tully Evicted Holdings: 1901

By 1901 the lands of the evicted tenants at Tully had been vacant for fifteen years. Using the Cancellation Books and the 1901 Census Records it is possible to build up a picture of who was living in the village at that time and which holdings lay vacant.[296] According to the records there were now nine houses in the village and seven of these were occupied. William Kearns, his wife Kate and three children were living in the caretaker's house that was originally Patrick Macken's house. Kearns was appointed Pringle's bailiff following the departure of James Harte. Pringle's house lay vacant next door. Martin Connor and his sister Ann lived nearby. Their parents John and Ann had died during the 1890s. The Cancellation Books show that

Martin Connor leased a second tenement from Pringle. This was the house previously occupied by Patrick and Catherine Burke and it was now vacant. Thomas and Margaret Walsh and their daughter Ann lived a short distance away.

The 1901 Census Records show that John Garvey (Long), his wife Bridget and four of their children were living in a house in the village on the night the census was taken. His name is not however shown on the Cancellation Books indicating that he was still in occupation as a mere caretaker or perhaps the house was not actually his own. The Cancellation Books for the Townland of Logaphuill show that from 1891 he was leasing a house from Patrick Lavelle. The entries in the Cancellation books show Pringle in occupation of the tenement that was previously John Garvey's.

Cancellation Books: Townland of Tully; Parish of Drum; Union of Castlebar 1901					
Names			Area: Rundale Holding: Total 118a., 3r., 35p	Rateable Annual Valuation		
Occupier	Immediate Lessor	Description		Land	Buildings	Total
S. Pringle	In Fee	House, Office Caretakers House		£6, 13s	£1, 7s	£8
S. Pringle	In Fee	Land		£2, 12s		£2, 12s
Thomas Walsh	S. Pringle	House, Land		£2, 15s	5s	£3
Martin Connor	S. Pringle	House, Office, Land		£5, 7s	8s	£5, 15s
S. Pringle	In Fee	Land		£4, 3s		£4, 3s
John Garvey Jnr.	S. Pringle	House, Office, Land		£5, 2s	13s	£5, 15s
S. Pringle	In Fee	House, Office, Land		£5, 2s		£5, 2s
Martin Connor	S. Pringle	House, Land		£2, 13s	7s	£3
S. Pringle	In Fee	Land		£2, 14s		£2, 14s
Patrick Lavelle	S. Pringle	Land		£4, 7		£4, 7s
Thomas Garvey	S. Pringle	House, Land		£4, 2s	8s	£4, 10s
S. Pringle	In Fee	Land		£3, 10s		£3, 10s
Michael Lavelle	S. Pringle	House, Office, Garden	1r., 8p	3s		3s
Total			119 a., 1 r., 3p.	£49, 3s	£3.8	£52, 11

John Garvey (James), his wife Delia and elderly mother Alice lived nearby as did John Garvey (Laheen), his wife Maggie and mother Bridget. This is the tenement of Thomas Garvey shown in the table above. The Cancellation Books show that Patrick Lavelle had land in the village and Michael Lavelle had a house and small garden. Pringle is shown to be in occupation of six vacant holdings.

Coercion at Tully: December 1901

In August 1901 John Garvey (James), entered into an arrangement with Bailiff William Kearns to lease an area of bog about half a mile from his house in Tully. He was still in occupation of the bog in December. Garvey was one of three related men in the village with a first name of John. To distinguish him from the others he was known as John Garvey (James). The others were known as John Garvey (Laheen) and John Garvey (Long). John Garvey (Long) and his family had endured a fifteen year struggle to hold on to their home and land at Tully. They had suffered eviction and imprisonment. All three men lived in the village within a few hundred meters of each other and William Kearns.

There are two principal sources for the events of Sunday 1 December 1901. In the subsequent court hearings a number of the police present on the day gave a detailed account of what happened in support of the prosecution's case. Their evidence was supported by their note books, allegedly completed on the day as events unfolded. The other source for the events is the press reports that followed the event. In broad terms the different accounts do not differ significantly. O'Kelly and the four other accused elected not to give the court their own account of the events. The following account is based principally on the police evidence. Material differences with what was subsequently reported are highlighted.

Sergeant Fitzgerald was on duty at Ballyhean together with Constables Lally, Joseph Bolger and Pat Munnelly, when a crowd of people started to gather after last Mass at 12.15pm. At about

12.30pm a band appeared. Michael Horan, Martin Staunton and John Garvey (Long) were in the crowd. At 1.30pm Conor O'Kelly arrived and a large meeting was then held in the chapel yard chaired by Martin Staunton, Vice-Chairman, Castlebar Board of Guardians. The meeting was addressed by Patrick Higgins, Conor O'Kelly, MP., and Michael Horan. The purpose of the meeting was reported in the Connaught Telegraph the following week:

> Mr John Garvey[297] will rank high from this forward in the ranks of grabberdom. He has beaten all records by grabbing no fewer than four evicted holdings. Miss Gardiner, of evil memory, "cleared" these places many years ago and ever since they remained derelict. But Garvey grabbed them all the other day –including one belonging to his uncle and namesake, a poor, bent old man of seventy years, who had held on bravely in the hope that he might come to his own, although he might have long ago joined his family in America. He suffered want in Ireland for this. The other victims of the heartless Garvey are Mrs Macken, Mrs Deasy, and John Connor…[298]

After the meeting Conor O'Kelly went to Henry Higgins's Public House. At 2.15 pm O'Kelly set off in the direction of Tully. The band and the crowd followed together with the police. The crowd halted at Frenchill to give the band time to catch up. The Ballyhean crowd was made up of between 60 and 70 people. Others joined at the Frenchill crossing. The group moved on down the hill, across the small bridge in the direction of Tully and when they reached the crossroads they turned left and made their way down into the village. At this point the crowd had swelled to between 160 and 170 in number.

Sergeant John Mc Carthy and Constable John Flynn both stationed at Belcarra were on duty in Tully together with three other policemen when, at about 3pm, the crowd accompanied by the fife and drum band arrived. According to the Mc Carthy account, the crowd and band turned left off the main Castlebar road at Tully and made their way up the lane. The police made a stand, Mc Carthy raised his hand and the band stopped. In Court McCarthy gave evidence that a good many of the crowd were armed with sticks but violence was not used. The subsequent account in the Connaught Telegraph paints a somewhat different picture of the encounter:

> The police tried to stop the people, until Messrs O'Kelly, Staunton, and Higgins arrived. Things began to look lively. Mr. O'Kelly MP, called upon the people to resist ruffianisim, and with the fearless young leader at their head they pressed on, flung themselves on the police, pushed them back, and walked straight on. In a minute the immense crowd of cheering Mayomen had gathered right in front of the grabber's house. Viva Mayo! A long table was commandeered as a platform. When Mr Staunton arose as Chairman Sergeant Fitzgerald and two policemen caught hold of him. The people came to Mr Staunton's rescue and the police were thrust back.[299]

According to McCarthy the band was accompanied by Conor O'Kelly, John Garvey (Laheen), John Garvey (Long), Staunton and Horan. O'Kelly challenged Mc Carthy's authority to stop them on a public road. Mc Carthy stated that he had received orders from his superiors to prevent any meeting in the place. Horan questioned whether McCarthy could hold any such orders as the meeting had only been called the previous evening. Horan explained that they were all members of the UIL and had come to Tully to form a branch of the League. Following further exchanges between the parties the police continued to block their passage. O'Kelly and Horan then said that they had been invited to visit the house of John Garvey (Laheen) and were allowed to go through accompanied by Mc Carthy himself and Sergeant Fitzgerald. Three constables were left on the road to hold back the crowd and band. At that point however the crowd crossed the fence into Pringle's land and flanked the police on the road. At John Garvey (Laheen)'s house a table and chair was taken into the garden. Mc Carthy attempted to prevent a meeting taking place while O'Kelly questioned his authority on private land. There were about 150 people in Garvey's yard when Martin Staunton was selected to chair the meeting. McCarthy's evidence continued:

> John Garvey (Long) then struck the table with a stick and said that they would allow no one to touch Mr O'Kelly; Mr O'Kelly said they would hold their meeting and went towards the chair telling me not to pull him down like I did at Dunamoona;[300] he got on the chair and Sergeant Fitzgerald and myself pulled him down twice; the crowd then became excited and threatened and crushed in on us, part of the crowd gathering between us and Mr O'Kelly, who then slipped to the other side and got on the table; I was afraid to use any more force, Mr O'Kelly then began to address the crowd, about 160 or 170; there was great cheering, and Mr Horan and Mr Staunton called for order; The table was placed about 30 yards from the house of John Garvey (James); the other defendants were present when Mr O'Kelly was making his speech and I was three or four yards from him; he spoke for about 15 minutes. [301]

Mc Carthy had taken a note of O'Kelly's speech and this was later read in court:

> A grabber is the greatest menace to the peace of the district… Wherever there is a grabber he means crime. It is necessary that you must put down the grabber with a strong hand, that the grabber Garvey may be made to unloose his hold from the widow's land… We are resolved that no grabber will be allowed to grab the home of another farmer. Fellow Nationalists, what right has Garvey to grab another's land. The land is vacant for the last twenty years. Mr Garvey went to the agent and got this land and consigned poor creatures to America. All charity must have dried up in his heart. It seems there is no pang in his heart for the poor widow, and he will have to put up with a strong inclination of the people of Ballyhean if you went back without making Garvey feel that

he could be victimised if you acted men... Shun Garvey, leave his crops to rot in the field; shun him at mass – everywhere. It would take but a short time to deal with the Landlords if we had not the grabber to deal with. Mr Wyndham's land bill will be prepared to make Garvey's holding firm in his hands. When you make Garvey and Garvey's class feel that they cannot go against the wishes of the people... let the Constabulary show that they came here to-day to denounce Garvey, the grabber, to make an example of him, to tell the people that he is dangerous, to avoid him...

After the speech O'Kelly spent some time in the house of John Garvey (Laheen). He then departed taking the crowd with him.

Complaint against the Tully Five: December 1901
Following the meeting a complaint was made by DI Thomas Dowling, Castlebar against Conor O'Kelly, Michael Horan, Bridge Street, Castlebar; Martin Staunton, RDC Killadeer; John Garvey (Long); and John Garvey (Laheen). Dowling alleged that they took part in an unlawful assembly at Tully causing:

> terror and alarm to his Majesty's quiet and peaceable subjects, and particularly to John Garvey, and while so assembled did speak and utter language calculated to intimidate the said John Garvey, and to incite others to intimidate the said John Garvey.

Summonses were served on all five men on Saturday 7 December.[302]

Alleged Assault & Abusive Behaviour: December 1901
When the crowds and band left Tully they did not take with them the feelings of anger and resentment that had built up in the village and it would appear that matters came to a head between the Garveys and William Kearns later that week. Save for the Ballyglass Petty Sessions Records there is no detailed account of what actually happened in the village the following Wednesday 4 December. What the records do show however is that arising

out of the events of that day John Garvey accused William Kearns of using threatening and abusive language towards him. William Kearns made a similar allegation against Garvey. William Kearns' son (also known as William), accused Margaret and Maria Garvey of assaulting him and the women in turn accused him of assaulting them. John Garvey also accused James Lavelle of maliciously assaulting him. James Lavelle for his part accused Edward Garvey of assaulting him and Norah Garvey of using threatening and abusive language towards him.

At Ballyglass, on the morning of Wednesday 11 December, Conor O'Kelly MP., in his capacity as a Justice of the Peace, sat on the bench beside Robert F. Starkie RM., Alan Bell RM., and Thomas Heraghty JP., for the hearing of the Garvey, Kearns and Lavelle assault and abusive language cases that followed the events at Tully a week earlier. With the exception of the two cases against James Lavelle (no appearance), the other cases were all dismissed. Conor O'Kelly then left the bench and joined his four co-accused for the hearing of the case against them.

Tully Five Hearings Commence: December 1901
The case against the five men was heard by Robert F. Starkie RM., and Alan Bell RM.[303] Horan, Staunton and the Garvey's were represented by Mr. Kirwan, Solicitor. Conor O'Kelly represented himself. E. Murphy instructed by Malachy Kelly, Crown Solicitor appeared for the prosecution.[304] The defence sought an adjournment to enable them to prepare their case and summon the necessary witnesses. Starkie adjourned until Monday 16 December. The five men were jailed pending the next hearing as they refused to give the necessary guarantees to secure bail.

UIL Meeting: December 1901
That evening a special meeting of the Castlebar branch of the UIL was held to show support for the men.[305] Joseph Gilmartin proposed the following resolution, which was seconded by P.A Horkan and unanimously passed:

Resolved – That we congratulate Messrs Conor O'Kelly MP., Michael Horan, our worthy President; Martin Staunton, John Garvey (Long), and John Garvey (Laheen), on their courageous, determined and united action in refusing to give a guarantee to the Crown pending a motion made in their favour at the King's bench. It plainly shows the stuff these gentlemen are made of. We hope that the cause for which they are to-night placed in a prison cell will produce many such men. We promise the enemies of the United Irish League that even though they have deprived us of their services for a time that the fight against English misrule and Irish Landlordism will go on until the objects of the United Irish League are attained.[306]

Hearing Resumes: December 1901

On Monday 16 December the defendants were back in Court, this time in Castlebar, before Starkie and Bell. Kirwan immediately sought another adjournment arguing that he had been unable to secure the services of leading Kings Counsel Mr. Cherry, in the short time available since the last adjournment. The prosecution resisted the application but it was granted by Starkie on the understanding that Cherry would be available the following day. The Connaught Telegraph reported that Conor O'Kelly was subjected to serious and continued intimidation by the police and that a crowd headed by a fife and drum band that had arrived from Crimlin was broken up by the police.[307] The hearing resumed at 12pm the following day. Before matters got underway Cherry asked the court to remove two police men sitting behind him as they were interfering with communications between him and his clients. Starkie agreed.

The Case for the Prosecution

Crown Prosecutor Murphy opened the case for the prosecution. According to Murphy:

> That meeting was, so far as he could make out, organized by the defendants, and upon that occasion speeches were made by Mr Conor O'Kelly which exceeded in violence and impro-

priety anything that counsel ever heard or read. Mr O'Kelly denounced the man in the most violent language, and advised that the man should be subjected to the most rigorous system of boycotting, and in fact that his life should be made a burden to him. One of the accused men, Garvey, did occupy this land some fifteen years ago, but he had no more right to interfere with John Garvey (James) than he (counsel) had, and any such interference by a combination of persons was a crime.[308]

The other defendants had not made speeches but:

they were assenting and assisting, and enforcing everything Mr O'Kelly said…

Before calling witnesses Murphy concluded that:

Mr O'Kelly was a member of Parliament for one of the divisions of the county. That was an honourable position; he was also Chairman of the County Council and he was a magistrate for the county, and therefore charged with the peace of the county, but so far as he counsel could make out, Mr O'Kelly's conception of his duty was not as a legislator to make laws, or as a magistrate to administer laws, but on every occasion to break the law. Mr Horan was, counsel believed, a very respectable trader in Castlebar, and possibly having no other occupation on Sunday, he was anxious to get a little notoriety by embarking upon projects of this kind. Neither he or Mr O'Kelly had as much land in Mayo as would sod a lark. Staunton was a farmer and District Councillor and the Garveys lived in the immediate neighbourhood of Tully.[309]

Sergeant John Mc Carthy, Belcarra; Sergeant Fitzgerald, Ballyhean; and Constable Pat Munnelly, Ballyhean then gave evidence for the prosecution followed by John Garvey (James). The latter accepted that he had taken a portion of Mrs Macken's evicted holding. John Garvey (Long) was his uncle. He was not on speaking terms with John Garvey (Long) or John Garvey (Laheen). His house was 30 or 40 yards from John Garvey (Long)'s house. On the day of the meeting he did not go outside but could hear the name *"Garvey"* being called out. Notwithstanding that he had leased the grazing rights on the land up to March 1902; he had told the bailiff on 1 December that he no longer required it. Under cross examination by Cherry he continued:

> I know John Garvey (Long) well; he is my uncle; I was on good terms with his son; I knew about his eviction; I knew that he was evicted; there is about one rood of cut away bog on the portions I held for 2 years at £ 7, 10s a year; I knew his son went to America and came back; I know he brought some money back with him; I didn't know that the landlady was offered her full rent if she would take back old John Garvey; The land I took last August was owned partly by five people; I did not know that all these people had offered to pay their rents; I was to pay £3 15s for the land; I had already paid £1, and all the grass that was on it was eaten. I have lost nothing by giving it up; I had intended to take my cattle off it and feed them at home.[310]

The prosecution case concluded on Tuesday afternoon and the hearing was adjourned.

The Case for the Defence: December 1901
The next morning Cherry informed the Court that he would not be calling any witnesses for the defence. Instead he focussed his defence on a number of legal arguments. In his view the Court had now to decide one of the most important cases decided in Ireland for some time. According to Cherry:

> Mr Murphy had appealed to him to avoid political discussion. It was rather difficult to avoid that, especially after Mr Murphy's speech, because it now became plain that the object of the Crown in this prosecution was not the punishment of what they regarded as crime at all, but was an attempt on the part of the Executive to interfere with a political party,

and to seek to alter the conduct of members of Parliament in relation to political matters in their own constituencies. If that were the object of the prosecution, and if it were brought in that way before a Bench constituted under a special Penal Act passed in a time of great disturbance and allowed to remain in abeyance for a number of years, and if the present was the first of a series of attempts to prosecute members of Parliament and other leading men – If that was the reason and if that was the way in which it was to be done it would be extremely difficult to avoid treating the matter as a political matter. If it was treated as a political matter, and not as a matter of law, it was the Executive of the country and the persons they sent down to represent them at these prosecutions that were responsible for that being done. He should avoid as far as possible treating the matter as a political matter. If the object of the Crown was not to punish the five defendants, there was no justification for the prosecution. The object of the prosecution was to stop the movement.[311]

Cherry then questioned the impartiality and jurisdiction of the Court:

>...it was a very unfortunate matter that charges of such an important nature, involving high constitutional questions, involving the right of public meeting, and the right to assemble together and to walk in procession, play bands, and listen to speeches – that charges, which involved those questions should be brought before a tribunal especially selected by the Executive for the occasion. The same authority which sent Mr Murphy to prosecute in the case sent down the magistrates to hear it. They should be very careful that they did not go beyond the special jurisdiction which they possessed under the Crimes Act. A charge of unlawful assembly was the only one which they could determine. If they dealt with any other indictable offence they should send the case on for trial in the ordinary way. The whole of the evidence given in the present case tended to show that it was one of boycotting. That was not the charge on which the Crown proceeded. They knew

that if they proceeded on a charge of boycotting and conspiracy the magistrates would have to send the case for trial they would not be able to get a jury to convict in the county Mayo.[312]

By using the Criminal Law and Procedure (Ireland) Act, 1887 the authorities avoided a trial by jury. A jury selected in Mayo would not deliver the desired convictions. The Resident Magistrates were more reliable. Cherry concluded that as there was no violence on the day there could be no question of unlawful assembly and that what happened was no different to an Orange meeting in Belfast on 12 July or a Trade Union meeting in England.

The Decision of the Magistrates: December 1901
The decision of the Magistrates was delivered by Starkie who stated:

> We are of opinion that the meeting at Tully on the 1st December was an unlawful assembly as charged. We consider that the evidence shows that the leaders with a number of other persons came to Tully that day to intimidate John Garvey (James), or, in other words, to frighten him into giving up these lands; and also to intimidate other persons who had taken land under similar circumstances. We quite agree with Mr Cherry that a distinction should be drawn between the five defendants. We therefore convict the defendants of the unlawful assembly charged, and the court orders that Conor O'Kelly, Member of Parliament, should be imprisoned for two months without hard labour, and that Michael Horan be also imprisoned for one month without hard labour; Martin Staunton to be imprisoned for one calendar month without hard labour, and John Garvey (Long) and John Garvey (Laheen) be imprisoned for fourteen days each without hard labour, the imprisonment in each case to be in his Majesty's prison at Castlebar.[313]

Case for Appeal: December 1901
Cherry did not wish to appeal as to do so would have amounted to an acceptance that the court had jurisdiction. He asked how-

ever for a stay on the imprisonment of the defendants pending a review by the superior courts of the jurisdiction issue. O'Kelly was willing to give an undertaking to make no further speeches (except in the House of Commons), pending the review. Horan was unwilling to give any undertaking. The prosecution resisted the request stating that O'Kelly had already made public speeches since the events at Tully and the granting of the application might give the impression that he had the right to continue to do so. Starkie refused the request and the men were taken into custody.

The Connaught Telegraph reported:

> There was a delay of over three hours before the warrants for their committal were made out, during which time the crowds of Nationalists who came in to witness the proceedings indulged in leave taking, and the prisoners were kept busy shaking hands etc. When the warrants were finally signed by the magistrates, the prisoners were taken out in single file between two constables. When they emerged from the Courthouse they were greeted with a ringing cheer from a large crowd that assembled outside. Mr Conor O'Kelly M.P, who was in the lead took off his hat and shouted "God save Ireland" which was responded to by another ringing cheer. Mr Michael Horan called for a cheer for the United Irish League, which was enthusiastically responded to. To prevent further remarks from the prisoners, all – with the exception of Mr Conor O'Kelly, MP – were taken hold of by the police and linked along at a very quick pace, surrounded by at least 50 constables, the crowd following and cheering wildly for each of the prisoners. On church hill the crowd was prevented from escorting the prisoners further by a large force of police which were lined across the road under the command of County Inspector Milling and District Inspector Lownes; but history repeated itself very graphically, as a great portion of the crowd took to the fields and succeeded in going forward and giving a farewell cheer as the prisoners entered the jail.[314]

Nationalist interest in Tully Case: December 1901

During the three days of the hearing there was a large police presence in Castlebar. The case attracted significant interest from nationalists who came from near and far to attend the hearings.[315] The Connaught Telegraph Correspondent questioned the need for a large police presence in the town. According to his report much of their time was spent seeking to thwart the efforts of the Ballyhean and Park fife and drum bands. The latter led by Giles Barrett circumvented the police by crossing fields and managed to march down Staball reminiscent of the *"races of Castlebar"* when the French came to town just over one hundred years earlier.

Mayo County Council Meeting: December 1901

James Daly presided at a meeting of Mayo County Council on Friday 20 December when Thomas Callaghan proposed and William Doris seconded the following resolution:

> That we condemn the action of the Crown of preventing the right of free speech in the County. Our worthy chairman and other Nationalists in our county have been sent under Wyndham's policy to spend Christmas in the dungeons of a lonely prison because their motto is "Live and let live." We congratulate them on their honourable defence and the able stand they have made for the cause we all have at heart, and trust they will return to liberty full of health, strength and vigour, and that a few more such prosecutions will have the effect of putting down land –grabbing more effectually than all the speeches that can be made.[316]

Daly questioned why they did not prosecute T.W. Russell in the North as he spoke more strongly than they do in the West. Melvin hoped they would send them all to jail as they always fill the jails before they legislate in Ireland. It is an old trick of theirs he said and suggested that they would now give a land bill or something. The resolution was passed.

Release of the Garveys: January 1902

At 7.40 am on Tuesday 7 January John Garvey (Long) and John Garvey (Laheen) were released from prison. The police anticipating trouble had a large force of constabulary stationed around the prison and on the roads leading to it. The two men were met at the prison gate by a delegation appointed by the Castlebar branch of the UIL and were taken to P. J. Mc Lynskey's Main Street, where they were, according to a report in the Connaught Telegraph, hospitably entertained. A sergeant and two constables stationed themselves outside Mc Lynskey's and the men were shadowed all day. At 3pm, a specially convened meeting of the Castlebar branch of the UIL was held. James Gavin UDC presided. The secretary, Joseph Gilmartin read the following:

> Address to Messrs John Garvey (Long), and John Garvey junr, of Tully, on their release from Castlebar Jail, after suffering 14 days imprisonment under the Coercion Act and the police of degenerate Geraldine.
>
> Dear Sirs – We the members of the Castlebar Branch United Irish League, wish to offer you our sincere congratulations on your release from prison after serving your country's cause against the policy of English misrule and Irish landlordism. We cannot forget the great sacrifices you have made by going into jail on the eve of Xmas. We confidently hope and pray that you may live long to enjoy the respect and esteem of your patriotic countrymen who are proud of recognizing in you true soldiers of the National cause.
>
> We remain dear sirs, on behalf of the Committee,
>
> Yours faithfully
>
> John McHale, President of the West Mayo Executive, Michael Lavelle, Vice Pres. Castlebar Branch, Joseph Gilmartin, Sec., Castlebar Branch.[317]

John Garvey (Long) thanked the people for their kind address. He said that this was not his first time in jail and he would not fear imprisonment again in the same cause.

On the release of the Garveys the Castlebar Board of Guardians requested Pringle to receive a deputation from the Board to make arrangements for the reinstatement of John Garvey (Long) to his evicted holding at Tully on reasonable terms.[318]

Prison Treatment of Conor O'Kelly MP: February 1902
Whilst the Garveys had been released O'Kelly was still in prison. On 10 February Patrick McHugh, MP for North Leitrim raised the issue of the treatment of Conor O'Kelly at Castlebar Prison.[319] The response from George Wyndham MP.,[320] contains an excellent description of what life was like in Castlebar Prison for an MP and educated person.[321]

Release of Conor O'Kelly: February 1902
The release of Conor O'Kelly was widely reported. In a defiant speech at Claremorris he was reported to have said that:

> ...his views in regard to grabbing and grabbers were unchanged, and described the resident Magistrates as "Punch and Judy Justices." Some of his friends, he remarked, objected to going to prison because of their association with a certain class of people in jail. He sympathised with this feeling but he did not share it. Any man, who had spent six months in the House of Commons with gentlemen who had figured in the divorce courts of New Zealand and in meat and Austrian horse scandals was absolutely unconcerned with whatever brand of human nature he came into contact.[322]

John Garvey (Long) gets his Land back: December 1902
On 13 December the Connaught Telegraph celebrated the return of John Garvey to his land one year after the gathering at Tully that led to his arrest and imprisonment.

Assault on a Sunday: June 1903
John Garvey (James) removed himself from the evicted land of John Garvey (Long) and sought to distance himself from the affair but the bargain he had struck with William Kearns was not forgotten by his neighbours and he was branded a grabber. It is reasonable to assume that there was a considerable amount of resentment towards him in the village. On Sunday morning 28 June 1903 he set out for Mass at Belcarra. To get to the public road he needed to cross the land of Edward Garvey, son of John Garvey (Long). When he reached the public road he was confronted by a number of men and women including Edward Garvey, John Garvey and John Garvey's wife. The reports do not specify whether it was John Garvey (Long) or John Garvey (Laheen) but it is reasonable to assume it was the former. John Garvey (James) was surrounded and the crowd began to cough and hiss. According to his account of events John Garvey tore his hat and caught him by the breast of the coat. He was assaulted by the women and knocked unconscious by a blow to the back of the head with a stone. Two men by the name of Lavelle gave evidence that the assault occurred. James Lavelle gave evidence that he had seen John Garvey raise his hand as if to strike John Garvey (James). Sergeant Green from Belcarra deposed to having seen a pool of blood on the road and Dr. Hopkins gave his opinion that the wound on the victim's head was consistent with having been struck by a stone. John Garvey was sentenced to one month in prison but this was reduced on appeal to a fine of £10 and an order to pay costs.[323] Later that year on 19 November at Ballyglass Petty Sessions, Alan Bell sentenced a seventeen year old Edward Garvey to one month's imprisonment at Castlebar for assaulting John Garvey (James).

The Ballyhean (Tully) Grabber: 1906
In July 1906 the House of Lords, in the context of a debate concerning the Justices of the Peace Bill, discussed the appropriateness of certain Irish Magistrates acting as Justices of the Peace. Lord Muskerry brought the attention of the House to:

...the disloyal and violent speeches of certain magistrates in Ireland, and to the manner in which they had incited the people to commit illegal and criminal acts; and also to the fact that certain of those magistrates were members of disloyal organisations, and had attended meetings of these bodies, where not only disloyal but also illegal and criminal proceedings were advocated; [324]

In support of his argument Lord Muskerry made reference to a speech of Conor O'Kelly MP:

On May 27th last, Mr. Conor O'Kelly, J.P., addressed a meeting at Callow, near Swinford, County Mayo, held for the purpose of intimidating a local bailiff named Thomas Durkin, popularly known as "Tom Watt." And this is what Mr. O'Kelly said— There are many grabbers in Mayo, but what did we do with the grabber of Ballyhean? And what did we do with Padden down in Erris? They prosecuted us for that also, but it failed. They will have to prosecute us again if this wretched creature does not give up the land he should never have touched. If you mean business, let no man in this parish be contemptible enough to have any dealings or any intercourse with Tom Watt. The immediate result following this speech was that on June 4th; Thomas Durkin found his mare dead, mutilated in the most shocking manner, apparently with a knife.[325]

Five years after the events at Tully, Conor O'Kelly was using the boycotting of John Garvey (James) of Tully as an example of how *"land grabbers"* should be dealt with. His time in Castlebar Prison had not dampened his enthusiasm for the cause.

Conclusion

Truly is the dawn of freedom appearing - truly the emancipation of the tenant farmers of Ireland. The south is awakening, slowly but surely.[326]

UIL Meeting at Belcarra: October 1907

On Sunday 19 October 1907 a meeting was held at Belcarra after Mass to re-organise the local branch of the UIL. The meeting was chaired by D. Mullen DC., and there was a large crowd in attendance including a government note taker.[327] A lengthy speech was delivered by C.W.P Cogan and the following resolutions were adopted by the meeting:

> That we the Nationalists of Belcarra, pledge our support to the United Irish League, and we call upon all Nationalists of this district to come forward and join its ranks.
>
> That we pledge our support to the Irish Parliamentary Party, under the able leadership of Mr. John E. Redmond.
>
> That we condemn the grazing system and we call upon the owners of eleven months and non residential grazing ranches to give them up to the Congested Districts Board or Estate commissioners for the purpose of having them split up and distributed amongst the small landholders and landless people.
>
> That we pledge our support to the Gaelic movement, the labourers' and town tenants' movements, Home Rule, a catholic University, and the development of our home industries.

In the course of his lengthy speech Cogan said that:

> it was the duty of the people to see that every grazing ranch in that district was cleared of its bullocks and sheep and that in their place should be planted the young men and young women who at present were forced to look for homes in the land of the stranger in some foreign clime.

Cogan's speech was followed by a speech by T.S Moclair of Castlebar. The Connaught Telegraph correspondent reported:

> Dealing with the proposed sale of estates in the district, the speaker criticised the attitude of the tenants on large holdings on the Pringle estate who sought to purchase direct from the landlord, and thereby do a great injustice to smaller tenants, who would have their holdings properly striped and divided if the estate was purchased either by the Congested Districts Board or the Estate Commissioners.

The Connaught Telegraph reported that over seventy persons handed in their names and subscriptions to the new UIL branch. D. Mullen was elected President, L. Kearns, Secretary and Mr. Flannery, Treasurer.

Susanna Pringle: Final Years

When Harriet Gardiner died in 1892 she left Farmhill and her Belcarra Estate to Susanna Pringle. Quinn relates that after the death of Gardiner there was a significant change in Pringle. Her dress improved, she stopped smoking in public and reduced the amount of alcohol she consumed.[328]

Quinn attributed the change to a Mrs. Lindsay of Killala with whom Pringle lived. Quinn may have been referring to Sarah Lindsay, wife of Henry Lindsay, Church of Ireland Sexton in Killala or it may have been Ellen Lindsay, a Publican and Post Mistress in the town. Quinn does not specify a date but what is certain is that she was living at Farmhill with her domestic staff in 1901 as the Census Records show. By 1906 she was living at Ballinglen Cottage, a Knox property in the Parish of Doonfeeny.[329] She became active in public life as a member of Killala District Council and Chairman of the Board of Guardians.

Pringle did not however alter her approach in her dealings with her tenants at Belcarra. The evicted holdings at Tully and elsewhere on the Belcarra Estate remained vacant up until she died in 1910. After her death Farmhill became a parochial house until it was demolished in the 1950s.

Surname	Forename	Age	Sex	Relation to head	Religion	Birthplace	Occupation	Literacy	Irish Language	Marital Status
Pringle	Susanna	74	F	Head of Family	Presbyterian	East Indies	-	Read & write	-	Not Married
Granaghan	Michael	53	M	Servant	RC	Mayo	Farm Labourer	Read & write	Irish & English	Married
Kerney	Anne	20	F	Servant	RC	Mayo	Domestic Servant Cook	Cannot read	Irish & English	Not Married
Barrett	Michael	31	M	Servant	RC	Mayo	Farm Labourer	Read & write	Irish & English	Married

National Archives of Ireland: Census of 1901: House 1 in Farmhill (Killala, Mayo).

James Daly

James Daly played an active role in local politics up until his death in 1911. The 1901 Census Records show Daly at home with his family and staff at Spencer Street, Castlebar.

Surname	Forename	Age	Sex	Relation to head	Religion	Birthplace	Occupation	Literacy	Irish Language	Marital Status
Daly	James	60	M	Head of Family	RC	Mayo	Farmer	Read & write	Irish & English	Married
Daly	H J	50	F	Wife	RC	Mayo	House Keeper	Read & write	Irish & English	Married
Daly	James	15	M	Son	RC	Mayo	Scholar	Read & write	English	Not Married
Daly	Anne	13	F	Daughter	RC	Mayo	Scholar	Read and write	English	Not Married
Daly	Nellie	11	F	Daughter	RC	Mayo	Scholar	Read & write	English	Not Married
Daly	Nora	4	F	Daughter	RC	Mayo	Scholar	Cannot read	English	Not Married
MacHale	E	52	F	Visitor	RC	Mayo	House Keeping	Read & write	Irish & English	Married
Hagerty	Cathin	26	F	Servant	RC	Mayo	Domestic Servant-General	Read & write	Irish & English	Not Married

National Archives of Ireland: Census of 1901: House 58, Spencer Street.

James Daly died in 1911. He is buried in Castlebar Cemetery. On 22 March 2011, the centenary of his death was commemorated in Castlebar. The Editor of the Connaught Telegraph wrote:

Daly has been all but airbrushed out of Irish history and his achievements in the fight for the rights of tenant farmers and his role in founding the Land League along with Michael Davitt should not be forgotten. He used his pen and the pages of the Connaught Telegraph to tackle and eventually break the grip of largely absentee landlords on land banks in Ireland.[330]

James Daly's major contribution to bringing landlordism to an end in Mayo and the role he played in highlighting the plight of the tenants undoubtedly deserves further detailed consideration and recognition. On the Belcarra Estate he led from the front in the campaign against two of Ireland's most notorious landlords endeavouring at all times to secure the position and rights of the tenants and their families.

The Tenants

While the stand against the Tully Grabber was celebrated by the land movement and made its way into the popular speeches of members of parliament, little changed on the ground following the departure of the large crowds and marching bands. Tenants continued to pursue rent reductions all the time operating under the constant threat of eviction by Pringle.[331] By 1901 Thomas Ward was back in possession of his home at Frenchill where he lived alone as his wife Mary-Ann had died.[332] In April 1902 his death was reported in the Connaught Telegraph. He was 73. In 1905 James and Mary Hopkins took up residence in Tully and Patrick Connor of Logaphuill regained his land at Tully in that year also. In 1901 he married Anne Connor, daughter of John Connor and they had two children but Anne died in 1908. In 1901 Ann's brother Martin Connor married Margaret Malley from Tawnylaheen and they had eight children. In the spring of 1906, almost twenty years after Gardiner had driven the Deacy family from Tully, John Deacy attempted to sell his leasehold interest in the long vacant Deacy holding at Tully and Clogherowan. It would seem that the sale did not proceed immediately as Pringle served an eviction notice on him in respect of the lands in June 1908.[333] Sometime after that he disposed of his interest to John Gibbons. In January of that year Edward Lally engaged Charles Daly to dispose of his leasehold interest at Cloonaghduff near Belcarra.

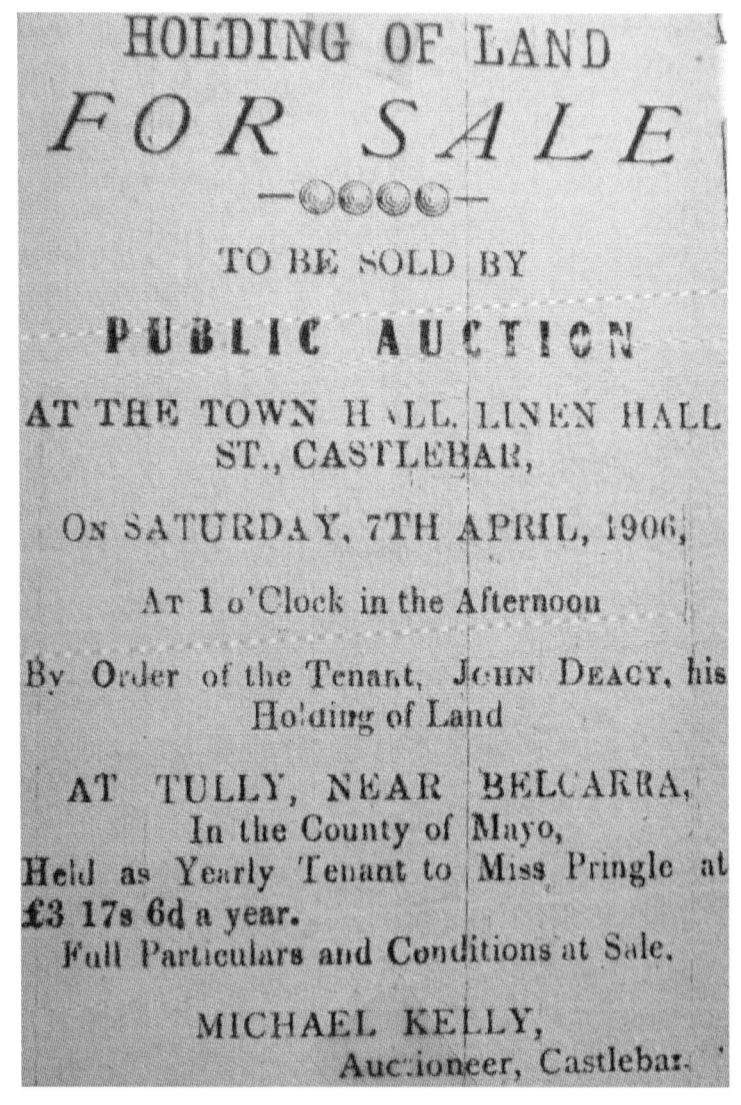

> **HOLDING OF LAND**
> **FOR SALE**
> —◦◦◦◦—
> TO BE SOLD BY
> **PUBLIC AUCTION**
> AT THE TOWN HALL, LINEN HALL ST., CASTLEBAR,
> On SATURDAY, 7TH APRIL, 1906,
> At 1 o'Clock in the Afternoon
> By Order of the Tenant, JOHN DEACY, his Holding of Land
> AT TULLY, NEAR BELCARRA,
> In the County of Mayo,
> Held as Yearly Tenant to Miss Pringle at £3 17s 6d a year.
> Full Particulars and Conditions at Sale.
> MICHAEL KELLY,
> Auctioneer, Castlebar.

Notice of Auction 1906: Deacy holding, Tully.

As Pringle lay on her death bed Edward Garvey, son of John Garvey (Long), was attending a sitting of the Land Sub-Commission in Castlebar seeking to have the rent he paid to Pringle reduced. His lawyer Mr. Verdon commented that:

> I regret to say that at this present moment Miss Pringle may not be alive.

By 1911 William Kearns, the last bailiff in Tully, had died and his wife Catherine had become head of the Kearns household though the designation on the Cancellation Books remained *Caretaker's House* and the Kearns name is not recorded. In the 1911 Census Records the house is shown as occupied by Catherine Kearns and three of her children. Sometime after that the family left Tully and returned to Killala. After the death of Pringle, the CDB took control of the tenement before the freehold was acquired by John and Sarah Gibbons. The holding was amalgamated with the adjacent Deacy holding that John Gibbons had acquired a few years earlier from John Deacy. The Gibbons family have lived there ever since.

Following her death in 1910 the CDB took control of Pringle's lands at Belcarra and managed the transition of the freehold from Pringle's estate to the tenants. The tenants purchased the lands with funds provided by the Board. The monies were repayable by the new freeholders to the Board over a period of years. In Tully and Clogherowan the land was divided up among the remaining tenants and other new comers from the wider community. In November 1918 our great grandfather Martin Connor purchased the freehold to the house and land where he was born 67 years earlier in 1851. By 1920 the task of transferring the freeholds was broadly complete and Harriet Gardiner and Susanna Pringle were consigned to history and quickly forgotten.

Bibliography & Works Consulted

Bibliography

1. Armstrong, Rev., Thomas., *"My Life in Connaught: with Sketches of Mission Work in the West"* Elliot Stock, London, 1906.

2. Becker, Bernard H., *"Disturbed Ireland: Being the Letters Written During the Winter of 1880-81"* Macmillan & Co. London, 1881.

3. Burke, Bernard., *"A genealogical heraldic history of the landed gentry of Great Britain & Ireland"*, Vol. II, 8th. Ed., Harrison & Sons, London, 1894.

4. Caird, James., *"The Plantation Scheme; or, The West of Ireland as a Field for Investment"* William Blackwood & Sons, Edinburgh and London, 1850.

5. Campbell, Fergus., *"Land and Revolution, Nationalist Politics in the West of Ireland 1891-1921"* Oxford University Press, Oxford, 2005.

6. Curtis, L. Perry., *"The Depiction of Eviction in Ireland"* University College Dublin Press, Dublin, 2011.

7. Dublin Mansion Relief Committee., *"The Irish Crisis of 1879-80"* Brown & Nolan, Nassau-Street, Dublin, 1881.

8. Feingold, William L., *"The Revolt of the Tenantry, The Transformation of Local Government in Ireland 1872-1886"* Northeastern University Press, Boston, 1984.

9. Hickey, D. J. & Doherty, J. E., *"A new Dictionary of Irish History from 1800, Land Acts"* Gill & MacMillan, 2003.

10. Jordan, Donald E., Jr., *"Land and Popular Politics in Ireland, County Mayo from the Plantation to the Land War"* Cambridge University Press, 1994.

11. Lavelle, Frank., *"Pringle & Gardiner Landlords"* Balla/Belcarra/Manulla Magazine, Christmas, 1997.

12. Moore, George., *"Parnell and His Island"* Swan, Sonnenschein, Lowrey & Co., London, 1887.

13. Quinn, J.F., *"History of Mayo"* Vol. I, Brendan Quinn, Ballina, 1993.

14. Quinn, J.F., *"History of Mayo"* Vol. IV, Brendan Quinn, Ballina, 2000.

15. Samuel Lewis., *"Topographical Dictionary of Ireland"* (1st Ed., 1837, 3 Vols.).

Other Works Consulted

1. Flanagan, Thomas., *"The Year of the French"* Henry Holt & Company, New York, 1979.

2. Freyer, Grattan., *"Bishop Stock's Narrative of the Year of the French 1798"* Irish Humanities Centre, Ballina, 1982.

3. Grenham, John., *"Tracing Your Irish Ancestors"* 3rd Ed., Gill & Macmillan, Dublin, 2006.

4. Hamrock, Ivor., *"The Famine in Mayo"* Mayo County Council, 2004.

5. Herity, Michael., *"Ordnance Survey Letters Mayo"* Four Masters Press, Dublin, 2009.

6. King, Carla and McNamara, Conor., *"The West of Ireland: New Perspectives on the Nineteenth Century"* The History Press Ireland, 2011.

7. Lavelle, Frank., *"My Own Place"* Balla/Belcarra/Manulla Magazine, Special Millennium Edition, 2000.

8. Lawless, Emily., *"The Races of Castlebar"* J. Murray, London, 1913.

9. Marlow, Joyce., *"Captain Boycott & The Irish"* The History Book Club, London, 1973.

10. Moore, George., *"Parnell and His Island"*, edited by King, Carla., University College Dublin Press, Dublin, 2004.

11. Moran, Gerard., *"The Mayo Evictions of 1860"* Nonsuch Publishing, Dublin, 1986.

12. Nelson, Ivan, F., *"The Irish Militia 1793-1802 Ireland's Forgotten Army"* Four Courts Press Limited, Dublin, 2007.

13. Ni Cheanainn, Aine., *"The Heritage of Mayo"*, Western People Ltd., Ballina, 1988.

14. O'Hara, Bernard., *"Davitt"* Mayo County Council, Westport, 2006.

15. Smith, Brian., *"Tracing your Mayo Ancestors"* 2nd. Ed., Flyleaf Press, Dublin, 2010.

16. Stanford, Jane., *"That Irishman"* The History Press Ireland, Dublin, 2011.

17. Statistical Survey of County Mayo, 1802.

18. The Mayo News., *"Mayo in the Twentieth Century"* Westport, December 1999.

19. The Connaught Telegraph., *"Commemorative Issue"* Castlebar, April 1996.

Web Sites Consulted

1. www.ancestry.com

2. www.findmypast.ie

3. www. freepages.genealogy.roots.com/

4. www.landedestates.ie

5. www.leitrim-roscommon.com/1901census/

6. www.mayoancestors.com

7. www. mayolibrary.ie

8. www.museumsofmayo.com/belcarra.htm

9. www.nationalarchives.ie

Newspapers Consulted

1. Aberdeen Journal

2. Birmingham Daily Post

3. Caledonian Mercury

4. Connaught Telegraph (CT)

5. Freemans Journal & Daily Commercial Advertiser (FJ)

6. Liverpool Mercury

7. Newcastle Courant

8. Pall Mall Gazette

9. Reynolds Newspaper, (London England)

10. The Belfast Newsletter

11. The Bristol Mercury & Daily Post

12. The Glasgow Herald

13. The Irish Canadian

14. The New York Times

15. The Preston Guardian

16. The Morning Chronicle (London England)

17. Williamsport Pennsylvania Daily Gazette and Bulletin, (Evening Edition)

APPENDIX I

TOWNLANDS & SELECTED TENANTS

Townlands in the Belcarra Estate

Parish of Ballyhean: Logaphuill, Ballyhean.

Parish of Breaghwy: Ballyshane and Barney.

Parish of Drum: Ballaghfarna; Cloonagh; Clogherowan; Cloonaghduff; Cloonlynchagaun; Cuillare; Curanny; Deerpark Lower; Derreen; Elmhall; Ballycarra (Village of Ballycarra); Deerpark Upper; Glebe; Gortaruaun; Kilbrenan; Kilnageer; Knocknaveagh; Lissaniska; Logaphuill, Drum; Tully; and Tully Beg.

Selected Tenants

Gortaruaun: Tenants 1883-1893

Owen Vahey (House, Buildings & Land) » 1886 » Patrick Connor

Charles Daly (Land)

Michael Lally (House & Land) »1886 »Michael Mitchell

Barney: Tenants 1883-1893

Patrick Irwin (House, Buildings & Land) »1885»Harriet Gardiner»1893»Susanna Pringle

Anne Staunton (House, Buildings & Land)

Patrick Hynes (House, Buildings & Land)

William Hynes (House, Buildings & Land)

John Moran (House, Buildings & Land)

John Duffy (House, Buildings & Land)

Patrick Duffy (House, Buildings & Land)

John Cunniff (Land)

Patrick Cunniff (Land)

Michael Cunniff (House, Buildings & Land) » 1889» Harriet Gardiner»1893»Susanna Pringle

Ballyshane: Tenants 1883-1893

James Daly (Land)

James Gavin (House, Buildings & Land)

Michael Roache (House, Buildings & Land) »1887»William Roache

Thomas Heneghan (House, Buildings & Land)

Anne Staunton (Land)

Patrick Irwin (Land) » 1885»Harriet Gardiner» 1885»Reps of Pat Irwin»1886»Harriet Gardiner»1895»Susanna Pringle. Note: See also Barney

John Irwin & Anne Staunton (Land) Note: See also Barney

Patrick Hynes & William Hynes (Land). Note: See also Barney

Patrick Staunton (Land)

Elmhall: Tenants 1883-1893

James Walsh (House, Buildings & Land) »1887»Harriet Gardiner»1891»Susanna Pringle

Bridget Madden (House, Buildings & Land)

Thomas Madden (House, Buildings & Land)

David Burke (House, Buildings & Land)

Patrick Daly (House, Buildings & Land) »1891»Note on Cancellation Book: Daly evicted from house but not land. House has become a "Herd's House"

Catherine Dea (House, Buildings & Land) »1887»William Faddian

Tully Beg: Tenants 1883-1893

Bridget Dunne (House & Land) »1887»Harriet Gardiner»1893»Susanna Pringle

Thomas Dunne (Land) »1887» Harriet Gardiner»1893» Susanna Pringle

John Gallagher (of Errew) (Land) »1886»Harriet Gardiner» 1893» Susanna Pringle

Austin Staunton (Land)

Patrick Walsh (**William**) (Land)

John Walsh (**William**) (Land)

John Burke (Also Logaphuill) (Land)

Sarah Londra/Richard Londra (Land)

Logaphuill (Parish of Ballyhean): Tenants 1883-1893

Walter Mc Nally (House & Land)

Patrick Beirne (House, Buildings & Land)

Patrick Hopkins (House, Buildings & Land)

Oliver Canton (House & Land) »1887 »Harriet Gardiner »1893 »Susanna Pringle

Thomas Ward (House, Buildings & Land) »1889 »Harriet Gardiner »1893 »Susanna Pringle

John Ward (House, Buildings & Land)

Julia Walsh (House, Buildings & Land)

Robert Nesbitt Mc Adams (House, Buildings & Land)

Michael Reilly (House, Buildings & Land) »1884 »Mary Reilly

Logaphuill (Parish of Drum): Tenants 1883-1893

Bridget Walsh (House, Buildings & Land) »1884 »Patrick Lavelle »1887 »Michael Lavelle

Owen Vahey (House, Buildings & Land) »1886 »Patrick Connor

John Garvey (House) Note: This house appears for the first time in 1891-Landlord is Patrick Lavelle. Head Landlord is Harriet Gardiner

Charles Daly (House, Buildings & Land)

Patrick Walsh (Wm) (House, Buildings & Land). Note: Also has land in Tully Beg

John Walsh (Wm) (House, Buildings & Land). Note: Also has land in Tully Beg

Michael Lavelle (House, Buildings & Land)

John Burke (House, Buildings & Land). Note: Also has land in Tully Beg.

Thomas Dunne (House, Buildings & Land) »1887 »Harriet Gardiner »1893 »Susanna Pringle

Patrick Heneghan (House, Buildings & Land)

Thomas Walsh (Phil) (House, Buildings & Land)

John Walsh (Phil) (House, Buildings & Land)

Michael Mitchell (House, Buildings & Land) »1885 »Thomas Mitchell »1887 »Patrick Mitchell

John Finn (House, Buildings & Land) »1885 »Martin Cunnane

Patrick Staunton (House, Buildings & Land)

Austin Staunton (House, Buildings & Land). Note: See also Tully Beg

Thomas Walsh (Phil) (House, Buildings & Land)

John Walsh (Phil) (House, Buildings & Land)

William Moran (House, Buildings & Land) »1893 » Winifred Moran

Richard Londra/Sarah Londra (House, Buildings & Land) »1889 »Thomas Londra

Thomas Mitchell (House, Buildings & Land)

Thomas Mitchell (House, Buildings & Land). Note: Amalgamated with previous holding 1887

Michael Mitchell (Tom) (House, Buildings & Land): Note see also Gortaruaun.

Patrick Burke (Jun) (House, Buildings & Land) »1887 »Margaret Beirne

John Kelly (Land) »1895 »Michael Lavelle. Note: Seems to have been incorporated into **Michael Lavelle** tenement from 1895 (see above)

James Fallon (House, Buildings & Land). Note see also Tully. House is listed as a Freehold. Gardiner is not the Landlord/Owner

Charles Cardy (Garden). Immediate Lessor is Patrick Walsh. Tenement ceases to exist 1887

Charles Cardy (House, Buildings & Land) »1887 »Harriet Gardiner »1893 »Susanna Pringle. Note: House recorded as a ruin in 1895

APPENDIX II
NATIONALIST DEMONSTRATION AT BELCARRA 28 NOVEMBER 1892: ATTENDEES[334]

Balla: Rev. M. Colleran, CC, Balla; Rev. Father Greany, CC, Balla; John Mc Ellin; P. Conway; Thomas Reilly; Thomas Gannon; Thomas Conway; Michael Goulding; -Kenny; M. Jennings; and Thomas Brennan.

Ballyhean: Edward Dea; Thomas Winterscale; Thos Mc Hale; John M Donnell; Pat Higgins; Pat Fadden; John Ryan; and Jas Ryan.

Belcarra: Thomas Daly; John Blowick; P. Kerins; L. Kerins; John Tuffy; Patrick Staunton; - Cooney; Thomas Irwin; P. Surdiville; John Brennan; Darby Moran; and Charles Daly.

Castlebar: Rev. P. O'Flaherty, CC, Castlebar; Rev. J. O'Malley, CC, Castlebar; A. Cunningham; Denis Flanagan; D. Dunne; P. Flannelly; P. J. Feeney; M. Walker; Malachy Thornton; and John Ainsworth.

Others: Daniel Crilly M.P; Edward Cannon, Knockmore; William Brennan, Clogher; Michael Gallagher, Ballynulty; Jas Egan, A. Mc Evilly, Ballyglass; T. Reilly, - Tuohy , - Mc Nicholas, - Higgins, - Conroy, - Griffin, – Egan, - Moran, - Brennan, PLG, James Burke, Lightford; and Martin Conroy, Ballyshane.

APPENDIX III

FRENCHILL 1898 CENTENARY MEETING: ATTENDEES[335]

Dignitaries: John Dillon, M.P; William O'Brien; M. Commandant DU Chateau; William Field M.P; Miss Maud Gonne; James Daly, Castlebar; Dr Jordan, Senior, Castlebar; Dr Jordan, Junior, Castlebar; William Rooney, President, Celtic Literary Society, Dublin; Captain Kilroy, Buffalo; M. H. Cox, Boston; and T. J. O'Beirne, London.

French: M. Steigler, Madame Steigler; M. Commandant M. Chateau, member of the "Societe de la jeune Irlande", Paris; M. Marin; M. Ducroid; Signor Cipriani; M. Meriadier; and Professor Monis.

Aughagower: Pat Carney; E. Henry; M. Sheridan; J. Gibbons; M. Sheridan; P. Malone; P. Duffy; Jas. Holland; T. Geraty; Thos. Gibbons; Myles Kerrigan; Michael Staunton; Tom Basquill; John Greevey; John Jennings; Pat King; Pat Mc Donagh; and Michael Sheirdan.

Balla: T. Conway, P L G; T. Walsh; T. Reilly; M. Murphy; Thomas Murphy; Jas. R. Malley; John T.Kelly; J. McEllin; T. Higgins; Ml. Heneghan; J. Stenson; Thos Keville; B. O'Donnell; M. Mc Entyre; Anthony Dempsey; Ml. Golden; Mc Ellin; F. Conway; F. Revell; and M. McCabe.

Ballinrobe: Ml. Feenick; Martin Feenick; Frank Fahy; M. J. Swords; L. Lydon; M. Sannon; T. Swift; W. Regan; N. Fox; D.

Lydon; P. Connolly; T. Flannery; J. Meenahan; M. H. Feenick; F. Preston; J. Morris; and P. O'Connor.

Breaffy: T. Levelle; M. Conry; J. Callaghan; F. Horan; T. Callaghan; W. Cummins; B. Bourke; P. Callaghan; T. Mc Tigue; O. Callaghan; T. Loftus; J. Conway; W. Lavelle; P. Hynes; W. Conry; M. Mooney; J. Conway; J. Corcoran; P. Corcoran; T. Jordan; M. Ferris; T. Cummins; J. Mc Donnell; T. Lyons; P. Golden; J. Walsh; P. Mannion; A. Cannon; P. Staunton; T. Dardey; P. Molloy; P. Barrett; T. Heneghan; A. Fox; J. Ward; P. Callaghan; P. Gordon; W. Callaghan; and D. Callaghan.

Claremorris: Miss. Bebe Nally; Thomas Brett; Mr. Cleary; Mr. O'Beirne; T. H. Kean; D. Muldoon; Martin Griffiths; and Thomas Kennedy.

Islandeady: Peter Tuohy; Thomas O'Boyle; T Mullarkey; M Flynn; John Walsh; M. Rice; J. O'Brien PLG; Anthony Clarke; P Clarke; Jas Chambers; Anthony Cawley; R. Greavey; P. Greavey; M. Gibbons; P. Mylott; P Malley; Anthony Corcoran; John Tuohy; John Collins; Martin Mullarkey; James Lannon; Martin Lannon; Henry Staunton; John Tuohy; Edward Mc Hale; P. Mc Hugh; John Durkan; M Swanton; and F. Jennings.

Glenisland: M. Cawley; Walter Garry; Ed. Salmon; Martin Reilly; John Kean; P. McAndrew; D. McGarry; J. Ginnelly; P. Clarke; M. Jeffers; M. Hyland; Peter Mc Cormack; and J. Healy.

Keelogues: P. Vahey, CPLG; Martin Mc Hale; Michael Dempsey; Edward Mc Donnell; Michael Logan; Dan Farrell; John Carney; Edward Walsh; and Pat Malley.

Belcarra: C. Daly and L. Kerins.

Mayo Abbey: P. Stephens.

London: G. Lavelle and F. J. O'Beirne.

Manchester: J. Barrett and J. Dillon.

Keelogues: Patk Vahy; James Mullaney; M. Mc Hale; Michael Lynch; W. Bourke; John Molloy; M. Mc Hale; Pat Mc Nicholas; E. Mc Donnell; M. Lehan; P. Mc Donnell; D. Farrell; J. Carney; James Mc Gowan; John Joyce; John Walsh; Martin Hyland; Pat Hyland; John Joyce; Edward Joyce; John Gannon; James Hyland; Michael Mc Intyre; Pat Rielly; Hugh Corley; Michael Murphy; James Duffy; Thomas Ward; Bartley Hyland; Pat Clynes; Thos. Durkan; Pat Boyle; John Walsh; James Walsh; Thos Hyland; Pat Malley; James Ryan; John Bourke; and James Mc loughlin.

Knock UIL: Martin M'Loughlin; Patrick Beasty; Patrick Bierne, Junior; Ambrose Laven; and Patrick Beirne, Senior.

Neale: E. Jennings; M. J. Sears; Pat Jennings; T. Conroy; John Conroy; M. Conroy; Pat Casey; Pat Malley; P. Farraher; Pat Conroy; T. Connor; and Jas Burke.

Ballintubber: M. O'Malley PLG; J. Prendergast; M Gibbons; Peter Flynn; Michael Phibbin; Anthony Cannon; Thomas Tuohy; P. Tuohy; Thos Corley; and Martin Corley.

Others: John Mc Govern, Newport; John McHale; President of the UIL, William Doris; and Mr. E. Barry, Solicitor.

APPENDIX IV

PRISON TREATMENT OF CONOR O'KELLY, MP: EXTRACT FROM HOUSE OF COMMONS DEBATE[336]

MR. M'HUGH (*Leitrim, N.*) I beg to ask the Chief Secretary to the Lord Lieutenant of Ireland, whether he can explain why Mr. Conor O'Kelly, M.P. for South Mayo, now a prisoner in Castlebar Gaol, has been obliged to sleep on a plank, and was confined to his cell for 22 hours out of 24 each day: What is the diet supplied to him; in what way does his prison treatment differ, in regard to reading and writing materials and visits, from that of an ordinary convict in the same gaol; and is he allowed to write to his friends and to receive letters from them.

MR. WYNDHAM Mr. Conor O'Kelly, who was committed to Castlebar Prison on December 18th 1901, under sentence of two calendar months imprisonment for unlawful assembly, was liable under Rule 24 of Local Prison Rules for the first month of his sentence to sleep on a plank bed. He slept, however, on the plank bed for only three nights after his committal, being then supplied with a mattress by order of the medical officer. He has been confined in his cell for 22 hours out of the 24, getting the usual period of two hours exercise in the open air as required by subsection 9, section 109, of 7 Geo. IV., cap. 74. The medical officer has not ordered him any further period of exercise on the ground of health. The diet prescribed by rule for prisoners sentenced to imprisonment without hard labour for two months is class 2 (b) diet for one month and class 3 (b) diet for the remainder of the sentence. These approved dietaries are prescribed under the General Prisons (Ireland) Act, 1877. The medical officer during the first month of Mr. O'Kelly's sentence made the following changes of diet:—Tea in lieu of cocoa for breakfast, 8oz. of bread in lieu of potatoes for dinner, and 8oz. of bread extra daily. During the second month of his sentence the medical officer directed that the class 2 diet should be continued instead of class 3, and that the extras already mentioned should be continued with the addition of one pint of milk extra daily. The governor reports that when Mr. O'Kelly became entitled to third-class diet he requested the medical officer to allow him to continue on second-class diet with the extras, as he said that diet agreed with him, and his request was granted. There are no "convicts"—i.e., prisoners sentenced to penal servitude—in Castlebar Prison. Mr. O'Kelly is subject to the same rules in respect of reading and writing materials, visits, and letters, as other local prisoners. He is entitled to the use of books from the prison library and a slate, but not to newspapers, nor is he entitled to visits or letters during the term of his imprisonment. He has, however, by permission of Government, received one visit from a solicitor on the 6th instant. The governor further reports that, had the prisoner desired to write a letter on business or family affairs of an urgent nature, he would (under the authority vested in him in such cases) have allowed the prisoner to do so, but that the prisoner did not express any such desire. Mr. O'Kelly, a few days after his committal, applied to the Prisons Board for permission to procure certain educational works not in the Castlebar Prison Library, with a view of continuing his University studies. The Board, in order that educated prisoners should not be at a disadvantage by being in a small prison with a limited library, directed that a supply of educational works (mathematics and classics), containing several of the books applied for, should be sent from a larger prison to Castlebar Prison. Mr. O'Kelly has been exempted from the obligation of wearing prison clothing, having been permitted under Rule 28 of the prison rules to wear his own clothing. Mr. O'Kelly, having availed himself of the provisions of section 16 of the Act 19 and 20 Vict., cap. 68, was exempted from labour. Had the prisoner not chosen to avail himself of this exemption he would have been employed five or six hours daily at out-door labour. Mr. O'Kelly, while being treated as the law requires, has applied for and has been accorded every concession allowed by the law.

APPENDIX V

TO THE EDITOR FREEMAN AND NATIONAL PRESS[337]

Balla, Mayo, December 14th, '92.

Dear Sir- At the request of the tenants (to the number of 140) on the Gardiner –Pringle estate at Belcarra, I interviewed Miss Pringle at her rent office, Tully, on Wednesday, the 7th inst, to ascertain what terms she was willing to give them. They authorized me to convey to her that they would pay her a year's rent with an abatement of 25 percent. To end the trouble and secure peace this holy season of Christmastide they would pay with a reduction of even 20 per cent. Should those terms not satisfy her they would leave the matter to arbitration. But no, she would make no concession whatever. She must have the very last penny which the law allows her. She insists upon the payment of all law costs, all arrears of rent without any abatement. Because they cannot in those trying times comply with those unreasonable demands they are, forsooth, to be harassed, persecuted, and ultimately evicted by this amiable Scotch lady, who publicly avowed that she would never rest till she "desolated the whole property". To my mind she has adopted the most effectual means to accomplish that end by the manner in which she has treated the tenants for the last decade of years. As agent of the late Miss Gardiner she allowed the rents to accumulate for three and a half years, at the end of which she processed them for three and a half years' rent. By extraordinary efforts the better-to-do class of tenants managed to put together the three and a half years' rent, with heavy law costs, and thus for the time being succeeded in retaining their homesteads, while the poorer class were hurled from their homes; some of them to emigrate to a foreign land, some to take shelter with their friends, and some to die in the workhouse or asylum of Castlebar. Miss Pringle, in six months time, processed the tenants in possession for a bare half year's rent, which they were obliged to pay with the costs. In two years after she processed them a third time. After they were served she intimated to them through her bailiff, that should any of them forward to her by bank draft the amount of rent and costs any time before the day on which the decrees were to be granted she would stop any further proceedings against them. Well, what happened as a matter of fact, some tenants did send her a bank-draft for the amount of rent and costs, and though she had deposited the cash to her credit, yet she went into the courthouse of Westport, and got decrees against those very tenants. Now, I come to the last proceedings. For a period of a year and a half before last May she never held an office to collect rent, nor did she call for any rent. All of a sudden on last July, through her solicitor, the tenants received notice that unless they paid down on the nail a year and a half's rent proceedings would be forthwith taken against them. They offered to pay a year's rent, as much as they could do for the present owing to the unfavourable year. Their offer was rejected with scorn, writs issued against them, but before the writs could be served the proprietress, Miss Gardiner, passed to her account, and yet Miss Pringle, her successor for the time being at least, insists on the payment of £2 for each of those writs which have never been served, and also upon the payment of all rents due which accumulated through her fault. Had she called for a year's rent this time last year it would have been paid. That would not suit her policy. Comment on the above facts is unnecessary. I question if there are to be found within the four shores of Ireland any tenantry so cruelly, so unjustly treated as the Pringle tenantry.

I have to apologies for the length of this letter; but in justice to those persecuted tenants it is only fair that their crying grievances should be ventilated through the columns of your widely-circulating journal and the sympathy of the public elicited in their favour.

Thanking you in anticipation for publishing the above remain yours, J. Colleran, CC.

APPENDIX VI
SUMMONS SERVED ON TULLY FIVE

The King at the prosecution of District Inspector Thomas Dowling, R. I. C. Castlebar, complainant.

Conor O'Kelly, MP; Michael Horan, Bridge Street, Castlebar; Martin Staunton, R D C Killadeer; John Garvey (Long) Tully or Logaphuill; John Garvey, Tully; defendants.

Whereas, a complaint has been made to me that you, the defendants, on Sunday, the 21st day[338] of December, 1901, at Tully, Belcarra, in the county aforesaid, took part in an unlawful assembly, to wit, that you, the said defendants, with other persons to the number of 20 and more, whose names are unknown, unlawfully and tumultuously did assemble together to the disturbance of the public peace, and while so assembled did cause terror and alarm to his Majesty's quiet and peaceable subjects, and particularly to John Garvey, and while so assembled did speak and utter language calculated to intimidate the said John Garvey, and to incite others to intimidate the said John Garvey.

This is to command you, and each of you to appear as a defendant on the hearing of the said complaint at Ballyglass Petty Sessions on Wednesday, the 11th day of December, 1901, at 12 O' clock, noon, before such justices as shall be there in pursuance of said Act.

(Signed),

Alan Bell, R. M. Justice of said County.
This 7th day of December, 1901.

APPENDIX VII
LIST OF ATTENDEES AT COURT APPEARANCES OF TULLY FIVE[339]

Killawalla: Martin Walsh; Martin Kirby; Anthony Kirby; Anthony Walsh; Michael Murphy; Walter Mac Evilly, D.C; Pat Walsh; John Conway; John Kerrigan; Patt Kerrigan; Thomas Kirby; John Walsh; Michael Walsh; Thomas Tunny, Michael Baynes; Michael Ludden; Edward Chambers; Pat Gibbons; Michael O Day; Pat Moran; Denis Moran; and John Walsh.

Parke: John Clarke; Pat Mac Glynskey; M. Devanny; Giles Barrett; N. Duffy; M. Kerins; L. Mc Hale; Martin Mc Hale, D. C; J Kelly; John Mc Hugh; L. Devanney; M. Conway; T. Hopkins, E. Barrett; T. Flynn; and John Murphy.

Present in Court when the Prisoners were being removed: Rev. M. O'Connell, PP, Carnacon; Rev. J O'Malley, Castlebar; Rev. P O'Flaherty CC; P. J. Tuohy, Co. C; J. Gilboy UDC, Westport; Wm Doris, MCC; Pat Higgins, MCC; Patrick Timlin, UDC; James Gavin, UDC; H. Hopkins, RDC; T. J. Loftus, UDC; Giles Barrett, RDC; J. Keane, RDC; M. Cawley, RDC; Jos Gilmartin; T.H. Gillespie; Thos Durkan; A. Hynes; B. Moran; John Hynes; Charles Daly, RDC; John Clarke, Sec. Co, Council; G. B. Virtue; T. J. Walsh; P. Browne; John Clarke (Parke); Joseph Conroy; Master of Workhouse; P. Grimes, RDC; T. Hopkins RDC; Patrick Doyle; J. J. Collins; Peter Corcoran; T. A. Wynne; M. J. Sheirdan; J. T. Lyons, Claremorris; T Conway, RDC, Balla; R. A. Gillespie; H. Fadden, Ballyhean; P. Joyce; P. Walsh; P. Richardson; Patrick May; and Michael Mitchell.

APPENDIX VIII
UIL MEETING AT BELCARRA 19 OCTOBER 1907:[340] ATTENDEES

C.W.P Cogan (UIL Organiser); T.S. Molclair, Castlebar; Lawrence Kearns, Belcarra; D. Mullen, D.C. Walshpool (Chairman of the meeting); P. Staunton, D.C. Drum; P. Brennan; - Huges; T. Reilly, Jun; P. Corley; P. McEntyre; P. Biggins; James Moran; E. Rodgers; T. Londra; Michael Londra; T. Bourke; Pat Walsh; John Prendergast; T. Cunningham; R. Flanagan; Wm. Cooney; P. Moore; John May; M. Roache; P. Cunningham; John Blowick; James Carney; John Brennan; J. Surdival; John Hopkins; R Bodkin; T.P. Daly; M. Cooney; P. Flanagan; John Hughes; Thomas Hughes; F. Leonard; J. Bourke; T. Mullen; Michael Loftus; P. Mullaney; P. Tuffy; John Bourke; P. Durkan; John Conroy; P. Heaney; John Prendergast; M. Joyce; Wm. Flannery; Edward Walsh; John Naughton; J. Walsh; Pat Murray; W. McCann; P. Cunnane; John Cunniffe; John Walsh; M. Devaney; J. Staunton; Michael Hughes; A O'Grady; J. Armstrong; P. Daly; T. Flaherty; John Gavin; John Nally; P. Rooney; P. McKeon; John Surdival; P. Mullen; P. Kelly; M. Roper; P. Murphy; M. Fahy; P. Mooney; John Kerrigan; Patrick Connor; M. Garvey; T. Foy; P. Moylett; M. Connolly; John Mulee; A. Kenny; and John Gibbons.

APPENDIX IX
1901 CENSUS TULLY[341]

House 1: Tully[342]

Surname	Forename	Age	Sex	Relation to head	Religion	Birthplace	Occupation	Literacy	Irish Language	Marital Status
Garvey	John	58	Male	Head of Family	RC	Co Mayo	Retired Farmer	Cannot read	Irish & English	Married
Garvey	Bridget	55	Female	Wife	RC	Co Mayo	-	Cannot read	Irish & English	Married
Garvey	Nora	27	Female	Daughter	RC	Co Mayo	-	Read & write	-	Not Married
Garvey	William	24	Male	Son	RC	Co Mayo	Farm Labourer	Read & write	-	Not Married
Garvey	Edward	17	Male	Son	RC	Co Mayo	Farm Labourer	Read & write	-	Not Married
Garvey	Anne	14	Female	Daughter	RC	Co Mayo	Scholar	Read & write	-	Not Married

House 2: Tully

Surname	Forename	Age	Sex	Relation to head	Religion	Birthplace	Occupation	Literacy	Irish Language	Marital Status
Kearns	William	57	Male	Head of Family	RC	Co Mayo	Caretaker	Read & write	Irish & English	Married
Kearns	Kate	48	Female	Wife	RC	Co Mayo	-	Read & write	Irish & English	Married
Kearns	Kate	18	Female	Daughter	RC	Co Mayo	-	Read & write	-	Not Married
Kearns	Martin	15	Male	Son	RC	Co Mayo	Scholar	Read & write	-	Not Married
Kearns	Bridget	12	Female	Daughter	RC	Co Mayo	Scholar	Read & write	-	Not Married

House 3: Tully

[Vacant]

House 4: Tully

Surname	Forename	Age	Sex	Relation to head	Religion	Birthplace	Occupation	Literacy	Irish Language	Marital Status
Connor	Martin	37	Male	Head of Family	RC	In Mayo	Farmer	Read & write	Irish & English	Not Married
Connor	Ann	30	Female	Sister	RC	In Mayo	Farm Assistant	Read & write	Irish & English	Not Married
Deverin	Pakey	15	Male	Cousin	RC	In Mayo	Servant	Read & write	English	Not Married

House 5: Tully

Surname	Forename	Age	Sex	Relation to head	Religion	Birthplace	Occupation	Literacy	Irish Language	Marital Status
Garvey	John	42	Male	Head of Family	RC	Co Mayo	Farmer	Read & write	English	Married
Garvey	Delia	38	Female	Wife	RC	Co Mayo	-	Read & write	English	Married
Garvey	Alice	72	Female	Mother	RC	Co Mayo	-	Read	Irish & English	Widow

House 6: Tully

Surname	Forename	Age	Sex	Relation to head	Religion	Birthplace	Occupation	Literacy	Irish Language	Marital Status
Garvey	John	30	Male	Head of Family	RC	Co Mayo	Farmer	Read	-	Married
Garvey	Maggie	26	Female	Wife	RC	Co Mayo	-	Read & write	-	Married
Garvey	Bridget	60	Female	Mother	RC	Co Mayo	-	Cannot read	Irish & English	Widow

House 7: Tully

Surname	Forename	Age	Sex	Relation to head	Religion	Birthplace	Occupation	Literacy	Irish Language	Marital Status
Walsh	Thomas	55	Male	Head of Family	RC	Co Mayo	Farmer	Cannot read	Irish & English	Married
Walsh	Marget	54	Female	Wife	RC	Co Mayo	-	Cannot read	Irish & English	Married
Walsh	Anne	22	Female	Daughter	RC	Co Mayo	Farmer's Daughter	Read & write	-	Not Married

About the Authors

Michael M. O'Connor, LL.B., LL.M (Cantab.)
Michael M. O'Connor is a native of Tully, Belcarra, County Mayo. He attended Belcarra N.S and St. Gerald's De La Salle College, Castlebar. In 1990 he graduated from Trinity College Dublin with a first class honours degree in Law. In 1991 he was awarded the title of scholar by Sidney Sussex College, University of Cambridge and graduated with a Masters in Law, first class honours. He is a solicitor of the Supreme Court of England & Wales (1992) and the High Court of Ireland (2000). He is a partner in one of Ireland's leading law firms. His interests include social history, genealogy, archaeology and folklore. He lives in Oristown, Kells, County Meath and Murrisk, Westport, County Mayo with his wife Caroline and three daughters Ciara, Katie and Helena.

James R. O'Connor, BA.,
James R. O'Connor is a native of Tully Belcarra, County Mayo. He attended Belcarra N.S and St. Gerald's De La Salle College, Castlebar. In 1991 he graduated from Trinity College Dublin with an honours degree in English Language and Literature. In 1998 he graduated from Galway –Mayo institute of Technology with a National Diploma in Business Studies (Marketing & Enterprise Skills). His interests include local history, photography and archaeology. He lives in Ballyshane, Breaghwy, County Mayo with his wife Susan and three sons Callum, Evan and Daniel.

Endnotes

1. The Morning Chronicle (London England), 29 December, 1832. According to the 29 December 1832, Edition of the FJ, Michael Hughes was killed, Thomas Rodgers & Owen Gallagher were dangerously wounded, four others were slightly wounded and four were missing presumed killed or wounded.
2. CT, 18 April, 1885.
3. CT, 9 October, 1886.
4. www.landedestates.ie
5. Quinn, (2000), Vol. IV, 200.
6. Becker (1881), 57.
7. Quinn (1993), Vol. I, 187.
8. Moore, (1887), 192-193.
9. The Irish Canadian, 19 May, 1887.
10. See: www.landedestates.ie
11. List of Land Owners of Ireland, 1876.
12. Moore, (1887), 196.
13. Newcastle Courant, 31 December, 1869.
14. Aberdeen Journal, 5 January, 1870.
15. See Quinn, (2000), Vol. IV, 200-201 where a lengthy report on the attack from the Tyrawley Herald is reproduced.
16. For details of the Court proceedings and press coverage see Quinn, (2000), Vol. IV., 201-202.
17. FJ, 3 November, 1880.
18. FJ, 3 November, 1880.
19. FJ, 11 January, 1883. The Goulden family received aid from the Mansion House Evicted Tenants Fund.
20. Birmingham Daily Post, 9 December, 1880.
21. Liverpool Mercury, 9 October, 1880.
22. Williamsport Pennsylvania Daily Gazette & Bulletin, (Evening Edition), 9 December, 1880.
23. The Glasgow Herald, 25 January, 1881.

24   Pall Mall Gazette, 5 January, 1881.
25   The Bristol Mercury & Daily Post, 25 January, 1881.
26   Becker, (1881), 53-55.
27   Moore, (1887), 193-194.
28   The poet Robert Burns used this expression to refer to Scotland.
29   CT, 27 October, 1883.
30   Burke, (1894), Vol. II, 1659.
31   East India Register, Bengal. The Bengal Presidency was a British Colonial region in South Asia. It included areas that are now within modern day Bangladesh, and the Indian States of West Bengal, Assam, Bihar, Meghalaya, Orissa and Tripura together with Penang and Singapore.
32   Burke, (1894), Vol. II, 1659.
33   CT, 3 November, 1883.
34   The Irish Canadian, 19 May, 1887.
35   History of the Congregations of the Presbyterian Church in Ireland, 1886, Belfast: James Cleeland. Edinburgh: James Gemmell, 246-247.
36   Armstrong, (1906).
37   The letters of *"Norah"* on her Tour through Ireland, Being a Series of Letters to the Montreal *"Witness"* as Special Correspondent to Ireland, 1882, Mc Dougall, Margaret Dixon, Montreal: published by public subscription as a token of respect by the Irishmen of Canada.
38   CT, 31 March, 1883.
39   See: www.landedestates.ie
40   CT, 31 March, 1883. See also CT, 7 April, 1883.
41   Davis, J., The Royal Military Chronicle or British Officers Monthly Register, Chronicle & Military Mentor, Volume II, London, 1 January, 1811, 284.
42   List of Landowners in Ireland, 1876.
43   FJ, 17 November, 1885.
44   Pall Mall Gazette, 28 November, 1881.
45   FJ, 17 November, 1885.

46 Dublin Mansion Relief Committee, *"The Irish Crisis of 1879-80"* Brown & Nolan, Nassau-Street, Dublin, 1881, 107.
47 CT, 12 October 1883.
48 The Ordinance Survey Books 1837 lists the name *"Tulaigh"* as an alternative name for Tully.
49 House Books, Field Books and Tenure Books were the original notebooks of the surveyors who compiled the Valuation of Ireland that became known as Griffiths Valuation.
50 Castlebar Prison Records, 8 September 1886.
51 Church Marriage Record, Balla RC Parish.
52 Birth Record, Balla RC Parish.
53 Cancellation Books; County Mayo, Barony of Carra, Parish of Drum, Townland of Tully.
54 Griffiths Valuation 1856-1857.
55 Marriage Record, Balla RC Parish.
56 Church Marriage Record, Balla RC Parish.
57 Cancellation Books; Barony of Carra; Parish of Drum; and Townland of Tully.
58 See also Lavelle (1997), Balla/Belcarra/Manulla Christmas Magazine, 13.
59 George Bingham, 3rd Earl of Lucan (1800-1880), was responsible for mass evictions and land clearances in Mayo during the time of the Great Famine. The land was cleared to create extensive grazing farms. See Caird, (1850), 22-25.
60 There are a number of different spellings of *"Logaphuill"* used in the records and other sources including *"Lugaphuill"* and *"Logafoil"*.
61 Cancellation Books; County Mayo, Barony of Carra, Parish of Ballyhean, Townland of Lugaphuill.
62 Cancellation Books; County Mayo, Barony of Carra, Parish of Drum, Townland of Lugaphuill.
63 Letter dated 12 October, 1881 from Patrick W. Nally (Fenian and sports man from Balla, County Mayo), to the Executive of the Land League, cited Jordan, (1994), 280.
64 James Daly evidence to the Bessborough Commission.

65 Feingold (1984), 95.
66 Hearing of fair rent appeals at Castlebar Courthouse, 7 November, 1905. See CT, 18 November, 1905.
67 See Moran (1994) 189-207 for an excellent summary of Daly's political rise.
68 Dublin Mansion Relief Committee, *"The Irish Crisis of 1879-80"* Brown & Nolan, Nassau-Street, Dublin, 1881, 5.
69 CT, 22 March, 1879.
70 Dublin Mansion Relief Committee, *"The Irish Crisis of 1879-80"* Brown & Nolan, Nassau-Street, Dublin, 1881, 8.
71 Feingold (1984), 96-97.
72 CT, 26 April, 1879.
73 Moran (1994), 195.
74 CT, 18 March, 1882. See also Feingold (1984), 146.
75 CT, 22 March, 1879.
76 The 31 January Edition of the FJ reported that the attendees included: Major A.G. Wyse, RM (48th Regiment, a veteran of the Crimea and the Indian Mutiny); J.W Pepper S.I; James Daly; J.B. Walsh; C. Daly; J. Ellicott; P. Kearns; J. Daly; J. Barrett; J. Carney; and T. Reilly.
77 FJ, 31 January, 1881.
78 The Preston Guardian, 29 January, 1881.
79 CT, 27 October, 1883.
80 CT, 2 June, 1883.
81 CT, 2 June, 1883.
82 CT, 12 October 1883.
83 CT, 7 July, 1883.
84 FJ, 21 January, 1843.
85 CT, 7 July, 1883.
86 CT, 12 October, 1883.
87 CT, 12 October, 1883.
88 CT, 3 November, 1883.
89 CT, 20 December, 1884.
90 CT, 3 November, 1883.
91 CT, 10 November, 1883.

92 CT, 29 December, 1883.
93 The heading *"An Angel of darkness"* appeared in the 17 October 1885 Edition of the CT.
94 CT, 4 April, 1885.
95 CT, 12 November, 1892.
96 Castlebar Workhouse was opened in 1842 to accommodate up to 700 inmates. The Sacred Heart Home is now on the site.
97 CT, 27 December, 1884.
98 CT, 27 December, 1884.
99 CT, 17 January, 1885.
100 CT, 4 April 1885.
101 CT, 4 April, 1885.
102 CT, 4 April, 1885.
103 CT, 12 November, 1892.
104 CT, 4 April, 1885.
105 CT, 16 May, 1885.
106 CT, 21 June, 1885.
107 Letter dated 24 June, 1885, published in the CT, 27 June, 1885.
108 Letter published in the CT, 4 July, 1885.
109 CT, 18 July, 1885.
110 CT, 1 August 1885.
111 The suggestion was that the land was in Tully and this was correct.
112 CT, 22 August, 1885.
113 CT, 29 August, 1885.
114 CT, 5 September, 1885.
115 The letter is actually dated 10 August, 1885 so the sequence of events or letter writing is not entirely clear.
116 CT, 19 September, 1885.
117 CT, 29 August 1885. On 17 September 1864 Thomas Garvey of Tully married Bridget Leheen. They had at least three children; John (b.1866); Maria (b.1868); and Thomas (b.1872). The report suggests that Laheen was Garvey's second wife.
118 CT, 17 October 1885.

119 CT, 17 October, 1885.
120 CT, 17 October, 1885.
121 Seán Na Sagart or John of the Priests was born John Mullowney in Derrew near the village of Ballyhean about 4 miles from Tully, around 1690. By the time he was killed in the Partry Mountains in 1726 he had become the most notorious priest hunter of Penal Times in Ireland. Mullowney, a horse thief, agreed to become a priest hunter for the authorities in exchange for his life after he was sentenced to death by a Grand Jury.
122 Letter to the Editor of the CT from a *"Spectator"*, dated 14 October 1885 and published on 17 October 1885.
123 CT, 24 October, 1885.
124 CT, 19 September, 1885.
125 CT, 17 October, 1885.
126 The Criminal Justice Administration Act 1851 (14 & 15 Vict., c. 55).
127 CT, 17 October, 1885.
128 Slater's Directory of Ireland, 1881.
129 Cuffe evidence in an assault case taken against him by Catherine Dunne, CT, 2 October, 1886.
130 National Archives, 1901 Census Records for Ardnaree South, County Mayo.
131 CT, 11 September, 1886.
132 CT, 9 January, 1886.
133 CT, 9 January, 1886.
134 CT, 9 January, 1886.
135 CT, 9 January, 1886.
136 CT, 9 January, 1886.
137 Cancellation Books: County Mayo, Barony of Carra, Parish of Drum and Townland of Elmhall.
138 CT, 9 January, 1886.
139 CT, 9 January, 1886.
140 In the case of William Cuffe v. Catherine Dunne (September 1886), Cuffe gave evidence that he arrived in Tully about 10 months earlier.

141 The Balla branch met on 14 March. The Resolution was published in the 20 March 1886 Edition of the CT.
142 The Resolution was published in the 20 March 1886 Edition of the CT. Those present at the Bohola meeting included Rev. John O'Grady, PP., Chairman; P. Brennan; T. Killian; J. Mc Andrew; M. Danin; M. Lyons; T. Mc Nicolas; J. Walsh; P. O' Hora; P. Leonard; D. Jordan; U. Staunton; T. Walsh; J. Hunter; M. Lavin; J. Kilgallon; J. Mc Nicolas; W. Kilgallon; and John O'Connor, Secretary.
143 CT, 20 March, 1886.
144 O'Connor's letter and the letter from Mc Nicholas are published in the 3 April 1886 Edition of the CT.
145 Lyttleton's letter is published in the 20 March, 1886 Edition of the CT.
146 James Francis Xavier O'Brien (1828 – 1905), was an Irish nationalist, Fenian revolutionary and IPP MP. He represented the Constituency of South Mayo from 1885 to 1895.
147 James F.X. O'Brien's letter dated 24 February, 1886 is published in the 20 March, 1886 Edition of the CT.
148 The letter is published in the 20 March, 1886 Edition of the CT.
149 CT, 12 June, 1886. See also CT, 29 May, 1885.
150 Cancellation Books: Barony of Carra; Parish of Drum; and Townland of Tully.
151 CT, 23 June, 1886.
152 The Castlebar Prison Record records that John Garvey (Long) was 58 years old, 5ft 9" tall, 8s. 12lb, with grey hair, grey eyes and a fresh complexion.
153 CT, 21 August, 1886.
154 CT, 28 August, 1886.
155 Henn was born in 1848 at Paradise Hill, County Clare.
156 Letter from the *"O'Beirne"* to the Editor; CT, 18 September, 1886.
157 CT, 11 September, 1886.
158 CT, 11 September, 1886.
159 See Curtis, (2011), for an excellent review of the use of the Battering Ram in Irish evictions.

160 CT, 11 September, 1886,
161 FJ, 8 September, 1886.
162 In addition to extensive coverage in the CT, other newspapers that reported on the case included the FJ, 1 October 1886; and The Birmingham Daily Post, 10 October, 1886.
163 CT, 2 October 1886.
164 CT, 2 October, 1886.
165 CT, 2 October, 1886.
166 FJ, 10 September, 1886.
167 Moore (1887), 201.
168 Moore, (1887), 76-77.
169 Cancellation Books; Barony of Carra; Parish of Drum; and Townland of Tully Beg.
170 CT, 9 October, 1886 (From United Ireland).
171 Billy Cuffe's house, Tully, previously the home of the Macken family.
172 FJ, 10 September, 1886.
173 House of Commons Debates, 17 September 1886, Volume 309 cc 789-828.
174 CT, 18 September, 1886.
175 CT, 18 September, 1886. Rev. John Healy CC & L. Kearns were present at the meeting.
176 CT, 18 September, 1886.
177 Cancellation Books; Barony of Carra; Parish of Drum; and Townland of Tully.
178 Cancellation Books; Barony of Carra; Parish of Drum; and Townland of Tully.
179 For further details see: http://www.museumsofmayo.com/belcarra.htm
180 CT, 9 October, 1886.
181 CT, 27 November, 1886.
182 According to Castlebar Prison Records, Thomas Ward was 5ft 8" tall, 9 st. 12lb with grey hair, grey eyes and a sallow complexion. Based on the recorded age of 59 he was probably born around 1827.
183 CT, 4 December, 1886.

184 John Deasy (1856 – 1896) was elected to the House of Commons as an IPP MP for Cork City in 1884. At the 1885 General Election he took a seat in the new West Mayo Constituency. Re-elected in 1886, and again after joining the Anti-Parnellite Irish National Federation in 1891, he was returned as an Anti-Parnellite in 1892. His political career ended with a scandal in 1893.
185 Thomas Mayne (1832–1915) was a member of the IPP. Elected as an MP for County Tipperary in 1883 he held the seat until the constituency was divided at the 1885 general election. He was then elected for the new mid division of Tipperary, and held that seat until he resigned in 1890.
186 John Dillon (1851 – 1927) was an Irish land reform agitator, a Home Rule activist, a nationalist politician, an MP for more than 35 years, and the last leader of the IPP.
187 CT, 11 December, 1886.
188 CT, 1 January, 1887.
189 John E. Redmond MP., Chicago Convention 1886.
190 Devised by Timothy Healy (1855-1931), Irish nationalist politician and MP., the Plan of Campaign was used by tenants during the Land War as a strategy to secure rent reductions. When a landlord refused to agree to a reduced rent, the tenants paid no rent. The rents were then collected by campaigners and deposited in the name of a National League Committee of Trustees. The money was then used to assist evicted tenants.
191 Ireland under the Ordinary Law. A Record of Agrarian Crimes and Offences Reported in the Dublin Daily Press For the Six Months Running From 1 October, 1886 to 31 March, 1887, The Irish Loyal and Patriotic Union.
192 FJ, 4 January, 1887.
193 CT, 30 April, 1887 and CT, 7 May, 1887.
194 CT, 15 January, 1887.
195 CT, 15 January, 1887.
196 CT, 29 January, 1887.
197 CT, 19 March, 1887.

198 Oakum or tarred fibre was used in shipbuilding for packing the joints of timbers in wooden ships and the deck planking of iron or steel ships. In the 19th Century it was recycled from used tarry ropes. The task involved unravelling the ropes into individual fibres'. This task of *"picking"* and preparation was a common penal task in 19th Century British workhouses and prisons.
199 CT, 26 March, 1887.
200 The Castlebar Prison Records show that she and her child were committed by Tomas Wilson Walshe on 19 March.
201 Rev. John Healy, CC, Belcarra.
202 James Daly.
203 The CT reported that the following *"Professional Gentlemen"* were present at the hearing: Charles O'Malley, B.L; A.B. Kelly; C.P., Joseph Mannion; R.P Burke; John Garvey; H.J. Jordan; M.V. Coolican; and C.A. Lyttle.
204 CT, 8 October, 1887.
205 CT, 10 December, 1887.
206 CT, 14 April, 1888.
207 CT, 3 March, 1888.
208 CT, 24 March 1888.
209 CT, 23 September, 1893.
210 The case was heard before H. de V. Pery, RM and D.A. Browne.
211 CT, 9 June, 1888.
212 CT, 28 July, 1888.
213 CT, 11 August, 1888.
214 W. Brennan, M. Moran, R. Feeney, Dr. Jordan and James Daly were present.
215 CT, 18 October, 1888.
216 CT, 3 November, 1888.
217 *"Pringle at the Crowbar"* was a heading given to a letter published in the CT on 25 May, 1889. The letter to the Editor was signed *"Frenchill"*.
218 Letter to the Editor of the CT published in the CT on 25 May, 1889.
219 CT, 23 February, 1889.

220 CT, 6 April, 1889.
221 CT, 6 April, 1889.
222 CT, 6 April, 1889.
223 CT, 13 April, 1889.
224 CT, 13 April, 1889.
225 CT, 13 April, 1889.
226 CT, 25 May, 1889. This is likely to be a reference to Dr. Middleton O'Malley Knott, medical officer to the police, troops and Castlebar Prison.
227 John Williams Edward Dunstervill was born in County Fermanagh around 1851.
228 Letter to the Editor of the CT headed *"The She Tyrant"* and signed *"Frenchill"* published by the CT on 21 December 1889.
229 Letter to the Editor of the CT entitled *"Pringle at the Crowbar"* and signed *"Frenchill"* published by the CT on 25 May December 1889.
230 This description comes from evidence of Billy Cuffe in the case of Cunniff v. Gardiner (Mayo Assizes, 15 July, 1890), reported in the 19 July Edition of the CT.
231 The Belfast Newsletter, 3 April, 1890.
232 Letter to the Editor of the CT entitled *"The She Tyrant"* and signed *"Frenchill"* published by the CT on 21 December 1889. No further details are given as to the identity of the Widow Walsh.
233 Letter to the Editor of the CT entitled *"The She Tyrant"* and signed *"Frenchill"* published by the CT on 21 December 1889.
234 CT, 1 February, 1890.
235 CT, 1 March, 1890. On the arrival of Gardiner in 1883 there were 16 holdings in Tully. In 1890 the evicted holdings were those of Patrick Connor (house and land), Patrick and John Macken (house and land), John Garvey (house and land), Catherine Deacy (house and land), and Robert Cardy (house and land). John Connor (house and land) and Thomas Walsh (house and land), had been evicted but by 1888 their names were returned to the Cancellation

Books indicating that they had regained possession. John Garvey (James) (house and land), Thomas Garvey (house and land), Michael Lavelle (house and land) and Patrick Lavelle (land) had not been evicted. A house and lands held by the *"Reps of Maria Heffernan"* were also not evicted. This had been the tenement of John and Catherine Bourke. Patrick Connor of Gortaruaun (not to be confused with Patrick Connor of Tully), would also seem to have been evicted from land that had passed to him following the death of Owen Vahey. James Fallon's occupation of a building in the village (a Forge), had come to an end by 1888 without the intervention of Gardiner.

236 CT, 5 April 1890.
237 Cancellation Books; County Mayo, Barony of Carra, Parish of Breaghwy, Townland of Barney.
238 CT, 5 April 1890.
239 Reynolds Newspaper, (London England), 6 April, 1890.
240 CT, 5 April, 1890.
241 CT, 5 April, 1890.
242 The case is reported in the 19 July Edition of the CT.
243 CT, 17 May, 1890.
244 CT, 24 May, 1890.
245 Proceedings are summarised in the 14 June 1890 Edition of the CT. Members of the legal profession present included C. O'Malley BL; A.B. Kelly; M.J. Kelly; M.J. Jordan; and P.J Kelly. Gardiner was represented by her solicitor, John Garvey.
246 CT, 21 June, 1890.
247 CT, 27 June, 1891.
248 CT, 22 November, 1890.
249 Extract from a Letter to the Editor of the CT dated 25 February 1891 and published on 28 February 1891.
250 Belfast Newsletter, 3 April, 1890.
251 Letter to the Editor of the CT dated 25 February 1891 and published on 28 February 1891.
252 CT, 25 July, 1891.

253 See John Cunningham's excellent Chapter entitled *"A class quite distinct"* on the role of the Herd in King & McNamara, (2011).
254 CT, 27 June, 1891.
255 The FJ, 26 July, 1892.
256 CT, 30 July, 1892.
257 Possibly a reference to Mary Helen Mac Gregor, wife of Scottish folk hero Robert (Rob) Roy Mac Gregor (1671-1734).
258 The Dahomey Amazons were an all female military regiment of the Kingdom of Dahomney (modern day Benin).
259 CT 30 July, 1892.
260 John Morley, 1st Viscount Morley of Blackburn (1838-1923) was a Liberal Politician and Chief Secretary for Ireland in 1886 and again from 1892 to 1895. He introduced the Evicted Tenants Bill in the House of Commons. See The New York Times, 20 April 1894.
261 For a list of some of those present see Appendix II.
262 Daniel Crilly was an IPP and anti- Parnellite MP for the Constituency of North Mayo.
263 William O'Brien (1852-1928) was an Irish nationalist and agrarian agitator. In 1892 he was MP for Cork City.
264 The full text of the speeches of Rev. Colleran CC, Balla and Daniel Crilly MP., are published in the 3 December, 1892 Edition of the CT.
265 Extract from the speech of Rev. Colleran, CT, 3 December, 1892.
266 CT, 3 December, 1892.
267 Extract from the speech of Daniel Crilly MP., CT, 3 December, 1892.
268 CT, 17 December, 1892.
269 Henry Chaplin, 1st Viscount Chaplin (1840-1923), MP., and 1st President of the Board of Agriculture. James Lowther (1840-1904), Chief Secretary for Ireland, Conservative Party MP. An Agricultural Conference was held in London on 7 and 8 December 1892 under the Presidency of James Lowther MP.

270 FJ, 21 December, 1892. See Appendix V.
271 CT, 1 April, 1893.
272 CT, 1 April, 1893.
273 CT, 19 October, 1895.
274 This address to Lieutenant Colonel Elliot Lockhart, the Officers, Non-Commissioned Officers, and Privates of the Roxburgh and Selkirk Dragoons on the occasion of their departure from Castlebar appeared in the Caledonian Mercury on the 30 October 1800 just over 2 years after they were run out of Castlebar by General Humbert.
275 See S. Dunford " *In Humbert's Footsteps, 1798 & the Year of the French"*
276 Jordan (1994), 267.
277 Jordan (1994), 276.
278 SPO, CBS papers, Biography of James Daly. Cited by Jordan (1994), 276.
279 CT, 13 November, 1880.
280 CT, 30 May, 1896.
281 Extract from a speech delivered by Maude Gonne at the 1798 Centenary Celebrations at Castlebar reported in the FJ, 29 August, 1898.
282 FJ, 29 August, 1898. The report contains a detailed account of the proceedings on the day together with a long list of some of those in attendance. See Appendix III.
283 FJ, 29 August, 1898.
284 William Field (1843-1935), nationalist politician and MP., for Dublin.
285 William Rooney (1873-1901), Gaelic revivalist, poet, nationalist and journalist.
286 James Daly, Letter to the Editor of the CT dated 8 March, 1899. See CT, 11 March, 1899.
287 Feingold (1984), 95.
288 CT, 30 May, 1908.
289 CT, 18 March, 1899.
290 CT, 18 March, 1899.
291 CT, 4 March, 1899.
292 CT, 4 March, 1899.

293 CT, 25 February, 1899.
294 Charles Stuart Parnell, 1880.
295 See Appendix VI.
296 See Appendix IX for the 1901 Census Records.
297 John Garvey (James).
298 CT, 7 December, 1901.
299 CT, 7 December, 1901.
300 Dunamoona is a short distance from Belcarra.
301 CT, 21 December, 1901.
302 See Appendix VI.
303 Alan Bell (1857-1920), member of the RIC, RM and member of the British Secret Service. During the War of Independence Michael Collins had him taken off a tram on Sandymount Avenue, Dublin on 26 March 1920 and shot dead. See Hart, Peter, British Intelligence in Ireland 1920-21 the Final Reports, Cork University Press, 2002, 103.
304 According to the CT (14 December, 1901), the case attracted significant local interest. Those present included: Rev. William O'Connell PP, Carnacon; Rev. O'Malley CC., Robeen; John O'Donnell MP; Thomas Heraty JP., Chairman Ballinrobe District Council; Peter F. Regan, Ballinrobe; Patt Higgins MCC, Ballyhean and Michael P. Murphy, Mayo Abbey.
305 The meeting was chaired by T. J. Loftus. According to the Connaught Telegraph, (CT, 14 December 1901), those in attendance included: Messrs P. Timlin; T. Durkan; J. Gilmartin; Jas Gavin; John Hoban; P. J. McLynskey; P. A. Horkan; Peter Browne; J. J. Collins; T. H. Gillespie; P. Devanney; J. Burdish; J. Cannon; P. Doyle; J. Lally; M. Lavelle; J. O'Malley; R. McDonnell; T. Hoban; B. Begley; M. Butler; T. Gilmartin; M. Walsh; M. O'Brien; J. Tonra; T. Tonra; and Wm. Mc Namara.
306 CT, 14 December, 1901.
307 CT, 21 December, 1901.
308 CT, 21 December, 1901.
309 CT, 21 December, 1901.
310 CT, 21 December, 1901.

311 CT, 21 December, 1901.
312 CT, 21 December, 1901.
313 CT, 21 December, 1901.
314 CT, 21 December, 1901. The Castlebar Prison Records contain full personal descriptions of the five men. John Garvey (Long) was 75 years old, 5ft. 9" tall, 124 lb with grey hair, grey eyes and a fresh complexion. John Garvey (Laheen) was 34, 5ft 8.5" tall, 153 lb, with brown hair, grey eyes, a fresh complexion and a birth mark on his cheek. Conor O'Kelly was 28, 5ft 5.5", 142lb with brown hair, blue eyes, a fresh complexion and a number of distinguishing marks on his face and neck. Michael Horan was 36 years old, 5ft 3.5" tall, 201 lb with black hair, grey eyes and a fresh complexion. He had an ulcer on his left leg. Martin Staunton was 60, 5ft 7", 142lb, with grey hair, brown eyes and a fresh complexion.
315 CT, 21 December, 1901. For a list of persons in attendance at the court hearings reported in the CT, see Appendix VII.
316 CT, 21 December, 1901.
317 CT, 4 January, 1902.
318 The following were present at the meeting of the Guardians: Martin Cawley, DVC, Thomas Walsh, MCC, (Chairman) presiding; Martin Hopkins; H.M. Canning; J. Golden; Thomas Cleary; Martin Corley; A. Dempsey; M. Logan; M. Reilly; John Madden; Thady Hopkins; M. McHale; Richard Fitzpatrick; Pat Higgins MCC; Dr. Hopkins; and Dr. Callaghan.
319 Patrick Aloysius McHugh (1859-1909), Irish Parliamentary Party MP., for North Leitrim. Imprisoned on a number of occasions under the Coercion Acts, in 1902 he served a 3 month term for contempt of Court. See The New York Times, 10 September 10, 1902.
320 George Wyndham (1863-1913), Conservative Party, MP., and Chief Secretary for Ireland (1900-1905).
321 See extract from proceedings of the House of Commons at Appendix IV.

322 New York Times, 18 February, 1902.
323 For an account of the incident and subsequent proceedings see: CT, 31 October, 1903.
324 *House of Lords Debate, 12 July 1906, Volume 160 cc 1008-26.*
325 House of Lords Debate 12 July 1906, Volume 160 cc 1008-26.
326 CT, 6 December, 1879.
327 A list of some of the attendees was published in the 19 October Edition of the CT.
328 Quinn (2000), Vol. 1, 189.
329 www.landedestates.ie
330 CT, 29 March, 2011.
331 John Carney, a tenant of Pringle had his rent reduced by the Court in 1906. See CT, 31 March, 1906.
332 National Archives of Ireland, 1901 Census, Residents of a House No. 2 Lugaphuill, (Breaghwy, Mayo).
333 CT, 27 June, 1908.
334 CT, 3 December 1892.
335 FJ, 29 August, 1898.
336 Hansard, HC Deb 10 February 1902 vol 102 cc865-7.
337 This letter was published in the 21 December, 1892 Edition of the FJ.
338 This is a typographical error. The date should be 1st December.
339 CT, 2 December, 1901.
340 List published by CT, 19 October, 1907.
341 Source: Mayo County Library Microfilm 1901 Census of Ireland Reel ref 63/45.
342 The Cancellation Books seem to locate this house in Logaphuill. See 1911-1914.